Think First Certificate

Teacher's Book

Mark Foley,
Richard Acklam
and Jon Naunton

Addison Wesley Longman Limited
Edinburgh Gate
Harlow
Essex CM20 2JE
England
and Associated companies throughout the world

© Longman Group Limited 1989
This edition © Addison Wesley Longman Limited 1996
All rights reserved; no part of this publication may be reproduced, stored in a retrieval system, or transmitted in any form or by any means electronic, mechanical, photocopying, recording or otherwise, without the prior written permission of the Publishers.

First published 1996
Third impression 1996

Set in Sabon 9/12pt and
New Century Schoolbook 9/12pt
Designed by Eye II Eye, London

Printed in Italy
by Canale

ISBN 0 582 27630 6

Contents

Contents list for the Coursebook		piv
Introduction		pvi
Think First Certificate and the five exam papers		pviii
UNIT 1	– English Around the World	p1
UNIT 2	– Time Out	p12
UNIT 3	– Survival	p20
UNIT 4	– Storytelling	p27
UNIT 5	– A Sense of Adventure	p36
UNIT 6	– Changes	p43
UNIT 7	– The Natural World	p49
UNIT 8	– Judging by Appearances	p58
UNIT 9	– Teenage Cults	p64
UNIT 10	– Us and Animals	p72
UNIT 11	– Your Cultural Heritage	p80
UNIT 12	– Crime and Society	p88
UNIT 13	– Beyond Belief	p95
UNIT 14	– Destination USA	p101
UNIT 15	– Our Common Future	p109
PRACTICE EXAMS: Introduction, Answer Key and Tapescripts		p115

	SPEAKING		READING		LANGUAGE STUDY		VOCABULARY	
UNIT 1 p8 English Around the World	Breaking the ice Small talk Why study English World origins	p8 p9 p10 p16	People from around the world say why they use English (Part 1) Learning a language (Part 3)	p10 p16	Identifying basic constructions Adverbs of frequency	p12 p13	Identifying phrasal verbs Words to do with lanquage Verb and noun collocqtions	p12 p12 p20
UNIT 2 p22 Time Out	Role play – an evening out Sporting preferences All time greats Role play - an interview Keeping in touch	p23 p24 p26 p31 p32	All time greats (Part 3) Fiction to capture the imagination (Part 4)	p26 p28	It's time .../I'd rather ... Short replies Past simple or present perfect? Adverbs and word order	p22 p23 p30 p31	Do, play or go Word building Words to do with books Phasal verbs with take	p25 p27 p28 p33
UNIT 3 p34 Survival	Desert island Survival in the snow Discussing a photo Discussing texts A narrow escape	p34 p35 p40 p40 p42	Scaring ourselves to death (Part 1) Quick thinking (Part 3)	p36 p44	Countable and uncountable nouns Consequences Talking about ability Adding emphasis	p34 p38 p42 p45	Guessing words from context Phrasal verbs with give Live and die	p37 p39 p41 p43
UNIT 4 p46 Storytelling	Bedtime stories Modern versions of traditional tales Rags to riches, riches to rags Tall tales	p46 p48 p50 p56	Dick Whittington (Part 2) Pygmalion	p50 p58	Past tenses After + afterwards The grammar of phrasal verbs First sequencers	p47 p48 p54 p55	Fairy tales Phrasal verbs Time expressions	p47 p52 p52
UNIT 5 p60 A Sense of Adventure	Choosing a holiday Discussing a photo Role play – planning a weekend away Discussing texts Explorers and travellers	p60 p60 p67 p68 p68	A holiday with a difference (Part 2) Freya Stark The long and wounding road (Part 3)	p64 p68 p69	Obligation and necessity Ways of talking about the future	p62 p66	Holidays and travel Values	p61 p62
UNIT 6 p72 Changes			Maeve Binchy's childhood (Part 3) Manderley (Part 2)	p74 p78	Different forms of used to Causative have	p75 p77	Prepositional phrases Forming nouns Work	p76 p79 p80
UNIT 7 p82 The Natural World	Discussing a photo Big issues Giving opinions, agreeing & disagreeing	p82 p86 p91	Greenpeace advertisement (Part 2) The curse of the car (Part 3) Smokers' rights The Galapagos (Part 2)	p83 p87 p90 p92	The definite article The passive	p84 p88	The environment Cars	p82 p86
UNIT 8 p94 Judging by Appearances	Discussing people Lonely hearts What suits you Interpreting children's pictures	p94 p97 p101 p102	The secrets of the face (Part 2) What really suits you (Part 1)	p94 p100	Predictions and guesses – must be/can't be believed to be passive construction look	p95 p95 p102	Adjectives of personality Physical description and adjective order Word building	p96 p98 p103
UNIT 9 p104 Teenage Cults	Telling a story Discussing clothes fashions	p104 p105	Understanding teenage cults (Part 1) A letter to an agony aunt (Part 2) Socs (Part 1)	p106 p108 p114	Conjunctions Reported speech	p107 p110	Clothes Phrasal verbs	p105 p108
UNIT 10 p116 Us and Animals	A logic puzzle Which pet Animal quiz Attitudes to animals Discussing a photo	p116 p117 p120 p120 p122	Jane Goodall's study of chimpanzees (Part 2) Animal Farm (Part 1)	p118 p124	Contrasting ideas The comparison of adjectives too and enough	p119 p120 p121	take + noun preposition Preposition + noun + preposition Phrasal verbs	p123 p123 p123
UNIT 11 p126 Your Cultural Heritage	Monuments Festivals Tour guide Talking about the past Describing a painting	p126 p128 p132 p134 p136	Cleopatra's Needle Trinidad's Carnival (Part 1) Kids go through the Euroblender (Part 3)	p126 p128 p131	used to and would Prepositions following adjectives remind someone to do something Word order Adjective order	p130 p130 p132 p132 p135	remind, remember and forget Words meaning old made of/from/with Words connected to art	p132 p134 p134 p136
UNIT 12 p138 Crime and Society	You and your scruples questionnaire Crime Discussing photos Problem solving	p138 p139 p140 p140	A life of crime (Part 3)	p142	Conditional sentences Verbs followed by prepositions Ways of saying if Forms of wish	p143 p144 p145 p145	Phrasal verbs Different types of crime	p139 p139
UNIT 13 p148 Beyond Belief	Talking about the supernatural Imaginary friends Reincarnation Chilling tales	p148 p150 p152 p154	Doris Stokes – imaginary friends (Part 2) Creatures of the night (Part 4)	p150 p158	Relative clauses Inversion Abbreviating clauses	p148 p153 p157	Ways of looking Extreme adjectives	p151 p154
UNIT 14 p160 Destination USA	Talking about emigration Roleplay A sense of Liberty Discussing photos Florida fun The influence of English American heroes	p160 p161 p162 p166 p168 p170 p172	Emigration to the USA (Part 1) Florida fun (Part 4) Euro Disney American Dreams (Part 2)	p162 p168 p171 p172	Saying numbers The gerund and the infinitive Discourse markers	p163 p164 p171	Emigration British and American English	p160 p171
UNIT 15 p174 Our Common Future	Future questionnaire Predictions Making a living Unemployment	p174 p174 p178 p182	Brave New World (Part 2) CD ROMS (Part 4)	p178 p180	More complex ways of talking about the future	p177	Technology and Work Work	p175 p175

Reviser Guide p186 **Grammar Reference p202**

LISTENING		PRONUNCIATION		USE OF ENGLISH		WRITING			
English overheard	p8			Sentence transformation (Part 3)	p13,20	The compulsory letter (Part 1)	p19	UNIT 1	p8
In the exam	p9			Multiple choice (Part 1)	p14			English Around	
Linguapal	p18			Editing (Part 4)	p21			the World	
A night out (Part 4)	p22	Sentence stress	p31	Gap-filling (Part 2)	p25	Writing a report (Part 2)	p25	UNIT 2	p22
Sport (Part 4)	p24			Michael Jordan (Part 5)	p27	An informal letter – getting up-to-		Time Out	
Fiction (Part 3)	p29			Sentence transformations (Part 3)	p33	date (Part 2)	p32		
Collocations	p35	The questionnaire			p38	Editing (Part 4)	p45	UNIT 3	p34
Surviving in the snow (Part 2)	p40			Coming to get you (Part 5)	p41	Writing a report (Part 2)		Survival	
				Gap-filling (Part 2)	p43				
				Sentence transformations	p45				
An alternative Cinderella (Part 2)	p48	The pronunciation of regular verbs		Multiple Choice (Part 1)	p49	Expanding on a story	p49	UNIT 4	p46
Alexandre Aufreddi (Part 2)	p54	in the past	p48	Pygmalion (Part 5)	p58	Understanding style	p52	Storytelling	
A tall story (Part 1)	p56	Strong and weak forms of was		Editing (Part 4)	p59	The narrative composition (Part 2)	p56		
Pygmalion (Part 1)	p59	and were	p48			Picture composition	p57		
						Writing a report (Part 2)	p59		
Amanda and Martin (Part 2)	p60	Ways of saying "I"	p66	Editing (Part 4)	p61	Writing an article (Part 2)	p61	UNIT 5	p60
What a nightmare (Part 3)	p62			Gap-filling (Part 2)	p70	A letter of complaint (Part 1)	p63	A Sense of	
Julie talks about her holiday (Part 2)	p66					A semi formal letter (Part 2)	p67	Adventure	
Rosie talks about the important				Multiple choice (Part 1)	p73	A biography (Part 2)	p79	UNIT 6	p72
people in her life (Part 1)	p72			Word building (Part 5)	p76	Completing a description	p79	Changes	
A childhood in India (Part 2)	p77			Sentence transformation (Part 3)	p77	Compulsory letter (Part 1)	p81		
				Gap-filling (Part 2)	p79				
Greenpeace (Part 2)	p83	Say the *th* sound and *the*	p85	Sentence transformation (Part 3)	p88	The opinion question (Part 2)	p88	UNIT 7	p82
Air pollution (Part 2)	p85			Multiple choice (Part 1)	p92	Writing an article (Part 2)	p91	The Natural	
Cars and travel (Part 3)	p86			Gap-filling (Part 2)	p92	The compulsory letter (Part 1)	p93	World	
The by-pass (Part 3)	p90			Editing (Part 4)	p92				
Two friends discuss their weekend				Word building (Part 5)	p103	Writing a description of		UNIT 8	p94
dates (Part 1)	p97					someone's character (Part 2)	p96	Judging by	
The colour consultant (Part 2)	p101					Writing a physical description of		Appearances	
Pictures of the soul (Part 3)	p102					someone (Part 2)	p99		
Clothes (Part 3)	p105	Rising intonation	p105	Gap-filling (Part 2)	p108	Goths (Part 2)	p107	UNIT 9	p104
Goths (Part 3)	p107			Editing (Part 4)	p109	A letter of advice (Part 2)	p109	Teenage Cults	
A radio phone-in (Part 2)	p112			Word building (Part 5)	p109	The opinion question (Part 2)	p112		
				Sentence transformations (Part 3)	p111				
A logic puzzle (Part 2)	p116	Sounds in sentences	p123	Sentence transformations (Part 3)	p121	The opinion question (Part 2)	p122	UNIT 10	p116
Unrelated extracts (Part 1)	p117					A *for or against* composition		Us and	
A debate on animal rights (Part 2)	p122					(Part 2)	p123	Animals	
Animal Farm (Part 2)	p125					The set text (Part 2)	p125		
Festivals (Part 3)	p128			Word building (Part 5)	p127	Writing a description (Part 2)	p129	UNIT 11	p126
A day out in Cambridge (Part 2)	p132			Multiple Choice (Part 1)	p127	Writing an article (Part 2)	p131	Your Cultural	
In a folk museum (Part 2)	p133			Gap-filling (Part 2)	p133	Describing a building	p133	Heritage	
A family heirloom (Part 2)	p134					Describing articles	p135		
The Millais painting	p137					Describing a picture (Part 2)	p137		
Unrelated extracts (Part 1)	p144	Conditional sentences	p143	Multiple Choice (Part 1)	p141	The opinion question	p147	UNIT 12	p138
Crime and punishment (Part 4)	p146			Gap-filling (Part 2)	p141			Crime and	
				Word building (Part 5)	p146			Society	
				Sentence transformation	p146				
The Chaffin Will affair (Part 2)	p148	Rising intonation	p153	Gap-filling (Part 2)	p156	A letter of complaint (Part 1)	p153	UNIT 13	p148
Relative clauses	p149			Multiple Choice (Part 1)	p156	Making a story more interesting	p155	Beyond Belief	
Three friends discuss				Editing	p157				
reincarnation (Part 4)	p152								
Reincarnation (Part 3)	p159								
Stature of Liberty (Part 2)	p162	Saying numbers	p163	Word building (Part 5)	p161	Writing to a travel agent (Part 1)	p169	UNIT 14	p160
Different ways of saying numbers	p163			Multiple Choice (Part 1)	p166			Destination	
Mormons (Part 2)	p165			Gap-filling (Part 2)	p167			USA	
Baseball (Part 2)	p167								
Oldham family (Part 4)	p169								
Street gangs (Part 2)	p170								
Visions of the future (Part 3)	p176	Word building	p176	Gap-filling (Part 2)	p184	The opinion question – a final	p182	UNIT 15	p174
Renate Gross (Part 2)	p180			Sentence transformation (Part 3)	p184	look		Our Common	
Unrelated extracts (Part 1)	p183							Future	

Tapescripts p218   Language Focus Index p240

Introduction

Think First Certificate gives students a thorough preparation for the Cambridge First Certificate in English examination while at the same time providing them with a comprehensive general English programme in all four skills: listening, speaking, reading and writing.

As the title suggests, the emphasis of *Think First Certificate* is on students working things out for themselves and developing an independent attitude towards the learning process and passing the exam. The specific requirements of the five papers are introduced in a way which shows students clearly what is expected of them and which encourages them to devise their own strategies for doing the exam tasks.

The book presumes that students will have followed a general English programme to an upper-intermediate level and that they have a good basic vocabulary. Familiar grammar points are checked and revised in a way which allows the students to use their shared knowledge in class, and new grammar points are introduced in a way which makes students think consciously about language rules.

The 15 units of the book are topic based and, as you will see from the *Coursebook Contents* on pages iv-v, the structure and emphasis varies from unit to unit. For example, *Unit 4 Storytelling* concentrates not surprisingly on narrative writing and written style, whereas the emphasis in *Unit 14 Destination USA* is on Paper 4 (Listening).

This *Teacher's Book* provides unit-by-unit information on how to teach the *Coursebook*. Suggestions for homework are given as well as many ideas for practice and language development. All answers are keyed and the tapescripts are provided.

The Teacher's Book also contains an introduction, tapescripts and key to the *Think First Certificate Practice Exams*.

Think First Certificate and the five exam papers

The *First Certificate* examination tests all aspects of the candidates' English through five "papers". The papers have equal importance.

Paper 1 Reading   1 hour 15 minutes
Paper 2 Writing   1 hour 30 minutes
Paper 3 Use of English 1 hour 15 minutes
Paper 4 Listening   about 40 minutes
Paper 5 Speaking   about 15 minutes.

For examples of the questions refer to the pages given in *Think First Certificate Coursebook*.

Paper 1 READING

This tests candidates' reading and how well they can
- understand gist (general meaning).
- guess meaning and make intelligent assumptions
- find specific information
- identify the main points, style or purpose of a text.

The paper is divided into four parts.

Part 1 MATCHING
Candidates match headings to paragraphs. See pages 36-37.

Part 2 MULTIPLE CHOICE
Candidates choose the best answer to a question from four choices A,B,C or D. See pages 50-51.

Part 3 GAPPED TEXT
Candidates match sentences to gaps within a text. See page 27.

Part 4 MULTIPLE MATCHING
Candidates search for information in a number of short texts. See page 28.

Most of the reading texts in *Think First Certificate* are authentic and unabridged. Although they are usually longer than those found in the actual examination, they have been chosen for their interest, challenge and the richness of the 'roughly tuned input' they provide. See the *Coursebook Contents* list on pages iv-v for how the different exam tasks are dealt with in the units.

Paper 2 WRITING

Candidates answer two questions each between 120 and 180 words. There are five questions but Question 1 is compulsory, i.e. candidates <u>must</u> answer it.

Question 1 A letter based around a situation which is presented through one or more short texts. See page 67.

For all other questions you are given two or three lines of instructions.

Question 2 An article, report, a letter or application. See pages 25, 45, 91.

Question 3 a discursive (discussion), descriptive or narrative composition (i.e. a story). See pages 123, 129, 155.

Question 4 As question 2 or 3.

Question 5 A composition, article, report or letter based around a book. See pages 59, 125.

Think First Certificate assumes that students are able to write simple sentences and paragraphs but that their ability to write is weaker than their other language skills. Accordingly, written work receives much attention in the book. See the *Coursebook Contents* list on pages iv-v for details of how the five questions are dealt with in the book.

Paper 3 USE OF ENGLISH

This tests grammar and vocabulary. It is divided into five parts.

Part 1 MULTIPLE CHOICE CLOZE (GAP FILLING)
A text containing 15 gaps is followed by 15 multiple choice questions (i.e. choose A,B, C or D). This focuses on vocabulary. See page 15.

Part 2 OPEN CLOZE
A passage with 15 gaps to be completed. This focuses on grammar and vocabulary. See page 25.

Part 3 KEY WORD TRANSFORMATIONS
Candidates are given a sentence which they have to re-write using a "key word" and a maximum of four other words. See page 13.

Part 4 ERROR CORRECTION. 15 Questions
Candidates decide which lines of a text are correct. Other lines contain an extra and unnecessary word which candidates have to identify. See page 61.

Part 5 WORD FORMATION. 10 Questions
Candidates are given a text with ten gaps. Each gap has the base form of a word which they change into an appropriate form to provide the missing word. See page 38.

Paper 4 LISTENING

This paper is divided into four parts.

Part 1 UNRELATED EXTRACTS
Candidates listen to eight short unrelated extracts and answer multiple choice questions. See page 8.

Part 2 NOTE-TAKING OR BLANK FILLING
Candidates listen to a text and complete a set of notes. See page 35.

Part 3 RELATED EXTRACTS
Five short extracts related to a topic accompanied by a matching exercise. See page 20.

Part 4 EXTENDED TEXT
A longer text, either a monologue or text involving interacting speakers. Candidates answer questions where there are two or three possible choices, e.g. True/False, three option multiple choice (A,B,C), which speaker said what. See page 54.

Think First Certificate has a wide variety of listening activities to prepare students thoroughly for the tasks they have to do in the exam. Unit 14 provides a practice Listening exam and the listening passages in that unit should be done under exam conditions, if possible. All the tapescripts are provided at the back of the *Coursebook*. Many of the Listenings are unscripted or improvised to give greater authenticity and more spontaneity to the material.

Paper 5 SPEAKING

For this part of the examination candidates are tested in pairs, in other words, two candidates take the examination together. * (Of course they are assessed individually!) There are two examiners: the interlocutor who conducts the test and asks questions and the assessor who also gives marks but does not join in the conversation. Candidates are marked on grammar and vocabulary, fluency and pronunciation. The assessor will take into account how well candidates interact e.g. take turns to speak, negotiate etc.

The test is divided into four parts

Part 1: PERSONAL INFORMATION
The interlocutor asks candidates a few personal questions to help them to relax.

Part 2: TALKING ABOUT PHOTOGRAPHS
Each candidate is given two photographs around the same theme to talk about and compare.
Each candidate has a different theme. For example candidate A's photographs could show two different kinds of concerts, pop and classical; candidate B's photographs show two different jobs.

Candidates take it in turn to speak but there will usually be an opportunity to comment on the other candidate's photographs.

Part 3: INTERACTIVE TASK
Together, candidates carry out a task based around pictures or other prompts e.g. a diagram, plan, pictures of objects, photographs. This could involve planning, prioritising, problem solving, speculating etc.

Part 4: EXTENSION
The interlocutor joins in and asks questions to develop the discussion from part 3.
Think First Certificate gives the students ample opportunity for *speaking* throughout the units as well as providing specific practice for Paper 5. See the COURSEBOOK CONTENTS list on pages iv-v under the heading Speaking for a full breakdown of how the paper is dealt with in the book. Also important are the Pronunciation activities which are usually linked to a *Listening*.

For a full example of the interview see page 195 in the Reviser Guide.

We hope that you and your students enjoy using *Think First Certificate* and that they are successful in the exam.

Mark Foley and Jon Naunton 1996

1 English Around the World

BREAKING THE ICE

p.8 FIRST THOUGHTS

1 The aim of this first section is to encourage students to get to know each other and gain a sense of themselves as a group. Use the illustration to elicit suggestions about how to 'break the ice' when you meet new people.
- talk about the place you're in, reasons for being there, general topics such as the weather (very popular in Britain!) and travel.
- find out if you have anything in common (friends/colleagues, leisure pursuits such as hobbies and sports, cultural interests, education, etc.)
- ask lots of questions and show interest in the answers.

Explain/elicit that *break the ice* is an idiom which means to overcome the initial reserve/formality ('the ice') when meeting strangers by starting conversations and getting to know them better.

2 This is a mingling activity. Students can be encouraged to move around the classroom interacting with as many of their co-students as possible. With a shy or weak group you might want to give them a few minutes to prepare the questions they are going to ask in advance, e.g.
- lives near you
Where do you live?/Do you live near X?
At the end of the activity each student should have at least one name written against each of the categories in the list. They can report back to open class with any interesting discoveries, e.g. a student who has a birthday today or someone who has an unusual hobby.

p.8 LISTENING

English overheard

Examination advice
This listening exercise is an example of the task type found in Part 1 of Paper 4 (*Listening*). The focus is on understanding gist, main points, function, location, roles and relationships, mood, attitude, intention, feeling, opinion. In the exam, pieces are heard twice and time is given at the end of the section for candidates to choose their answers.
Explain that it is important to read through the questions before listening (time is given for this in the exam) in order to focus in on the important information when listening. It is not necessary to understand everything on the tape. In fact the exam deliberately contains some words (in the reading and listening papers only) which students at this level are not expected to know – this is for the sake of authenticity and understanding these words is not necessary for successful completion of any of the tasks. After playing the tape students can confer to compare answers.

ANSWERS
1 B; **2** C; **3** A; **4** B; **5** B; **6** C

TAPESCRIPT

1
A: So remember. You never get a second chance to make a first impression. Look the person in the eye, smile and shake their hand. Say something like, 'It's a pleasure to meet you Mr Jones or Mrs Brown ...' Use the other person's name, it makes them feel good ... Perhaps pay them a compliment. For example: 'That's a lovely brooch you're wearing. Where did you get that beautiful bag?' You'll win their confidence, and in no time at all ...

2
B: So what did you think?
C: Of her? The last one?
B: Yeah ...
C: Well ... erm, she was really lively, wasn't she?
B: Yes ... her pronunciation wasn't that good though ...
C: But a clear communicator.
B: Absolutely, and good vocabulary.
C: She made a couple of grammar mistakes.
B: All the same, I think she performed well.
C: Yes. Definitely a pass.
B: Oh yes. Would you say she was a strong pass?
C: I'm not really sure. I know, shall we come back to her in a minute?
B: Yes, why not?

3
D: So, if I could have your details.
To change? From this course to the one in September. Oh dear, I am sorry. No, no, that shouldn't be a problem. Let me check ...
Um ... Well, we should be able to squeeze you in. No, no the fees will be the same. Don't worry, just concentrate on getting better.

4
E: It's Mrs Greenaway, isn't it?
F: That's right. Goodness me, it's Carmen!
E: That's right.
F: I hardly recognised you. You've changed ... Carmen Fernandez.
E: You've got a good memory.
F: How lovely to see you.
E: Ha, ha.
F: So what ... How long have you been working here, then?
E: Since I left the college.
F: That's seven ...
E: Eight years actually.
F: And what has kept you here?
E: Well, I married an Englishman and had a child.
F: Well done ha ha ... And your English, it's perfect!
E: Well, it's thanks to you.
F: You're too kind.
E: And are you still working there?

5
G: Anyway, I really must be going. I've got an essay to write.
H: It's been lovely talking to you.
G: Yes ...
H: And you're sure you're settling in?
G: Yes, Mum.
H: And there's nothing you want?
G: No, no. Everything's fine.
H: I'll give you a ring next week.
G: After six ...
H: After six and you know ...
G: Right then. Speak to you next week ... Bye ... Bye. Phew ... Sorry about that. Give me a minute ... I'm coming ... I'll just get my racquet. Oh no!

6
Now you can take incoming calls but you can't make calls from here, I'm afraid. Now about the kitchen. It's fine if you want to have a snack or something like that, a sandwich or something, eggs, you know, and of course you can make hot drinks. Help yourself to tea or coffee. It's just here in this cupboard ... but nothing too elaborate. Sorry but, you know, sometimes people think they can take over the whole kitchen. Three-course meals and that. There was this boy last year from ...

p.9 SPEAKING

In paper 5 of the First Certificate (*Speaking*) the usual format is two candidates and two examiners. One examiner acts as the assessor and does not join in the conversation. The other examiner (the interlocutor) manages the interaction. There are four sections to the exam. In the first two the candidates mainly speak to the examiner and in the final two they mainly speak to each other. The first section is designed to help the candidates relax and feel at ease, it also shows the examiners whether the students are able to provide basic information about themselves and take part in a simple 'social' conversation.
The dialogue on tape provides a typical example of this phase of the exam.

1 Introduce the task, ask students to read through the points. They should listen and make rough notes.

ANSWERS

- She comes from near Florence, in Italy.
- She is a student at high school.
- She'd like to study archeology.
- She spends her free time studying, meeting friends and playing basketball.
- English is important for her because she thinks it's an important qualification and useful because Florence is full of foreigners.

2 Focus students' attention on the gap-filling task and play the tape again.

TAPESCRIPT AND ANSWERS

EXAMINER: OK Jean-Luc. I'll come back to you in a minute. Now it's Adriana, isn't it?
ADRIANA: That's right.
EXAMINER: So, **(1) er, where are you from, Adriana?**
ADRIANA: From Italy.
EXAMINER: I see. **(2) Whereabouts in Italy?**
ADRIANA: From near Florence.
EXAMINER: Mm, lovely and, **(3) er, what do you do?**
ADRIANA: I'm a student. I'm finishing high school.
EXAMINER: Huh, huh. And **(4) what do you want to do after high school?**
ADRIANA: Well, I'd like to study archaeology.
EXAMINER: Really? **(5) Why archaeology?**
ADRIANA: Well, we live quite near some, erm, ancient ruins and ... I have always been fascinated by them.
EXAMINER: I see ... And erm ... tell me, **(6) what do you do in your spare time?**
ADRIANA: Studying and meeting friends. Oh, and playing basketball.
EXAMINER: **(7) Do you play in competitions or just for fun?**
ADRIANA: Just for fun. Nothing serious.
EXAMINER: Oh really. **(8) And, erm, how long have you been learning English?**
ADRIANA: For four years now.
EXAMINER: Right ... And, **(9) erm, why do you like Italy?**
ADRIANA: Well, it's a Mediterranean climate so it's hot and sunny most of the year.
EXAMINER: Lucky you, and erm **(10) why are you taking the First Certificate?**
ADRIANA: It's an important qualification to have and also because in summer my city is full of foreigners. So, it's important to know English.
EXAMINER: Huh, huh. Right, right.

3 Managing conversations
To show he understands:
I see.
Oh really.
Right

To show he is interested:
Really?
Lucky you

To show he is going to move to another topic:
And ... er ... tell me ...
And er ... how long have you ...
And ... er ... why do you like Italy?

4 Get students to work in pairs. This will be more effective if students work with someone they don't usually sit next to and/or don't know very well. Monitor and check for effective questioning techniques and listener tactics.

p.9 SPEAKING

Check that students understand the phrase 'small talk'. This activity will be more effective if students stand up and are able to move around the classroom. Ideally, they should not be next to people they already know. You can join in as one of the 'guests' at the party, encouraging students to move around so they 'meet' as many people as possible. If the members of your class already know each other well it might be more effective to make the activity into a role play. You could say that it is a cocktail party in Hollywood and you are all famous movie stars. Students can use their imagination to create their roles and personal information.

THERE'S NO STOPPING IT!

p.10 FIRST THOUGHTS

Students work alone to put the reasons into order of importance then compare answers with a partner. The information which emerges will be of interest when planning the rest of the course and can tell you a lot about the interests and motivations of your students, so you might want to ask them to report back to you. One way to do this is to put the reasons on the board and ask for a show of hands, i.e ask *How many of you put 'to get a good job' as reason number one?* Keep a record of the results for future reference.
Elicit these in open class.

p.10 READING

1/2/3 This exercise introduces students to a task type to be found in Parts 1 and 4 of Paper 1 (*Reading*). As the exam takes 1 hour and there are four sections students will have about 15 minutes to complete this section. The task tests general understanding of the main points of the text and ability to distinguish the key point of a paragraph. To emphasise the purpose of headings, ask the class how they decide which articles to read when they look at a newspaper. Read through the introduction and examples with the class, allowing time to find evidence and clarify any questions. Once students are clear about the task ask them to complete the remaining matches. Check that they read through the remaining headings before they start. It will be useful if they underline the evidence they find. They should work individually at first then compare their answers in pairs or small groups. Monitor and check that they are able to find the evidence and justify their decisions.
Elicit the answers and their interpretations and evidence.

ANSWERS
1 B; 2 A; 3 D; 4 C; 5 E; 6 G

Notes
D *It was all so different*
Interpretation: This heading is probably for a paragraph about someone who found living in an English speaking environment very different from their previous life.
Evidence: Cathy Wong says that she felt homesick when she arrived in England and it took her a long time to get used to living on her own. So her life was obviously very different. = paragraph 3
E *ashamed of my mother*
Interpretation: This seems to say that the person in this paragraph was embarrassed by their mother for some reason.
Evidence: Rob Giuliani says that his mother didn't speak very good English and her mistakes were embarrassing. = paragraph 5
F *You'll need it at conferences*
Interpretation: This is a heading for a paragraph about somebody who uses English for conferences, in other words for business.
Evidence: None of the paragraphs refer to this so this is probably the extra, or 'dummy', heading.
G *Songs are best!*
Interpretation: This seems to be about someone who thinks songs are the best thing about English, or perhaps thinks songs are a good way to learn English.
Evidence: Ana Gonzales says that she loves listening to English pop music and she thinks it is a great way to learn vocabulary. = paragraph 6
H *English around the World = paragraph 0*

p.11 WRITING

Before you set the writing task it will be useful to discuss some of the issues raised in the reading text. Begin with some of these questions:
- What do you think is the best way to learn a language?
- How important is a good accent?
- Given that there are lots of different 'types' of English, what type do you want to speak and why?
- In future, do you think English will become more widely used? If so, what will happen to other languages?

These questions could well lead into students talking about themselves around the six points, in order to prepare them for having to write this up. If done as homework, don't correct mistakes of form, just comment on content, and perhaps make suggestions where students refer to problems they are having. If you are worried about letting mistakes go by, note common errors to come back to at a later date. However, above all, this should be a chance for students to really concentrate on communicating their concerns and experiences of learning English.

p.12 VOCABULARY

Language

Give students a short time to look through the exercise individually and then put them in groups of three to check their answers together. As the groups finish, check that their answers are correct and ask them to go back and decide on the exact pronunciation, including word stress, of the target vocabulary. The final stage is to elicit the answers with good pronunciation of the target vocabulary.

> **ANSWERS**
>
> **1** accent; **2** jargon; **3** slang; **4** pick up; **5** dialects; **6** languages; **7** mother tongue; **8** bilingual

Vocabulary storage

It is very important from the earliest stages that students have an organised system for recording new vocabulary. Clearly, different students will have different systems but you should create awareness of the various possibilities and particularly the range of information necessary to ensure a full and accurate record, e.g. word + pronunciation + definition + example sentence + appropriate collocations. Here is an example.

> fascinated /ˈfæsɪneɪtɪd/ = very interested
> 'He was fascinated by the story.'   pp.95-100

Phrasal verbs

Note: In our view, it is not helpful to make a distinction between phrasal and prepositional verbs or to treat as phrasal verbs those which have a literal meaning. Consequently, a narrow definition of what is a phrasal verb is followed in this course.

1 Put the two model sentences on the blackboard and let students try and analyse the differences. Then ask them to read the explanation in the book to see how it compares with their ideas.
Take exercises 2, 3 and 4 one by one. Give students time to attempt them on their own, then confer and then check answers in open class.

> **2 ANSWERS**
>
> **1** No; **2** No; **3** Yes; **4** Yes; **5** Yes; **6** No; **7** No; **8** Yes

> **3 ANSWERS**
>
> **1** put up with; **2** pick up; **3** have run out of; **4** get by

> **4 ANSWERS**
>
> **1** get by; **2** picked up; **3** ran out of; **4** put up with

p.12 LANGUAGE STUDY

Identifying basic constructions

Firstly, be prepared for students to have other terminology, e.g. *progressive = continuous*, *preterite = past simple*, *pluperfect = past perfect*, but, at the same time, for the sake of simplicity say that the terminology on page 12 of the Coursebook will be used in the book and, consequently, also in the class. Secondly, as you go through the answers to this exercise there will almost certainly be questions regarding the appropriate usage of the various forms. Don't get drawn in to trying to give on-the-spot analyses, but reassure students that the different areas will be gone into in depth during the course. Nevertheless, out of interest, it may be worth getting students to indicate via a show of hands which of the various areas they feel most uneasy about.

> **ANSWERS**
>
> **A** 15; **B** 10; **C** 7; **D** 14; **E** 1; **F** 3; **G** 4; **H** 11; **I** 6; **J** 9; **K** 5; **L** 12; **M** 2; **N** 8; **O** 13

Adverbs of frequency

> **1 ANSWERS**
>
> <never, rarely/seldom, occasionally, sometimes, often, always>

> **2 ANSWERS**
>
> **1** Wrong – *She seldom uses ...*
> **2** Right – but it is more common to say *We occasionally read ...*
> **3** Right
> **4** Wrong – *She always comes to class late.*
> **5** Wrong – *He is sometimes late.*
> **6** Wrong – *He never checks ...*
> **7** Wrong – *He often gives ...*
> **8** Right
> **9** Wrong – *We usually study ...*
> **10** Wrong – *They always go ...*
> **11** Wrong – *Do you often speak ...*
> **12** Right
> **13** Wrong – *We should always ...*
> **14** Right

> **3 ANSWERS**
>
> **1/2** The safest place to put these adverbs is **after** the verb *to be* but **before** all other verbs.
> **3** The adverb is put after **modals** like *can*, *will* and *should*.

After exercise 3, see if students have any other adverbs of frequency they want to add to the list. Students may bring up expressions of definite frequency, e.g.

once
twice | a day / week / month / year
three times

4 Either students do this in pairs and then report back in open class or divide the class into groups with each group taking one question and conducting a mini-class survey covering all the students. (To organise a class survey, get students to stand up and move around the classroom, asking as many other students as possible their question/s.) Make sure students are aware of the question form *How often do you ... ?* At the end get students to report back along the lines of:
15 people in the class rarely speak English outside the class, but only two people never speak English outside.

p.13 USE OF ENGLISH

1/2 This exercise introduces the task type found in Part 3 of Paper 3 *(Use of English)*. The task tests knowledge of grammar and vocabulary, particularly understanding of grammatical relationships between words and the ability to make transformations. This type of task can seem daunting at first but it becomes easier with practice and you can reassure the students that all the areas of grammar required will be dealt with in this course. (Most common are verb patterns, dependent prepositions, prepositional phrases, phrasal verb patterns, near synonyms, and collocations. A summary of useful areas is given in the *Study Advice* section on Coursebook page 15.)

Read through the introduction, emphasizing that the key word must not be changed in any way, the meaning must be the same, but between two and five new or changed words can be added (a contraction counts as two words). As this is the first example of this type of activity in the course, students should work together to complete the sentences. This will increase the likelihood of correct answers.

Do not check the answers but move on to exercise 2 where students will be able to check their own answers by finding the sentences in the paragraphs on Coursebook page 10 and 11.

ANSWERS
1 ... discourage people from using ... (paragraph 0)
2 ... hardly spoken by ... (paragraph 0)
3 ... able to make myself ... (paragraph 1)
4 ... approve of foreigners using ... (paragraph 1)
5 ... get used to living ... (paragraph 3)
6 ... 'd rather not ... (paragraph 4)
7 ... it impossible to understand ... (paragraph 5)
8 ... is supposed to be ... (paragraph 6)
9 ... doesn't speak slowly enough ... (paragraph 1)
10 ... is useful to know ... (paragraph 1)

CHOOSE YOUR WORDS CAREFULLY

p.14 FIRST THOUGHTS

Introduce the topic of working abroad in order to learn a language. Elicit personal experiences if possible and relate any anecdotes of your own.

p.14 USE OF ENGLISH

1 This exercise introduces the task type to be found in Part 1 of Paper 3 *(Use of English)*. This section of the paper is a cloze text with 15 gaps. Each gap has to be filled from a choice of four options. Candidates have about 15 minutes to complete the task.
Use the examples to explain the format of the task and the process required when working out the correct answer.
It helps to outline these three stages:
- meaning (from the context, what do you think the missing word means?)
- grammar rules (look at the surrounding words, what comes before and after the gap?)
- elimination (look at the four options one by one, cross out any which are not possible because of meaning or grammar)

Ask the class if they have any advice or special methods which they use for this type of exercise – they often come up with interesting and useful suggestions.
Go through the 8 examples with the class, checking that students understand the explanations given. The areas which are tested are dealt with in the study advice section below.

2 Read through the examination advice with the class. Before beginning the task ask students to explain the joke in the cartoon (*bloody* is both a swear word and an adjective. The woman confused it with *blood* – the name of a type of orange). If your students have monolingual dictionaries encourage them to use them for this type of task. (Note that bilingual dictionaries will be of little or no use in this context.)
As this is the first exercise of this type in the course, students may find it helpful to work together in pairs, comparing their answers in small groups and justifying their decisions in the case of disagreement.
Ask students to report back with their answers. Encourage them to explain why and how they reached their decisions. Check that they are considering both meaning and grammar and are paying attention to the context of each missing word. It can be helpful to ask them to explain why the three incorrect options are not possible rather than why they chose the correct one (this 'elimination' technique can be very useful in the exam). Their explanations can be a useful diagnostic tool in finding out which areas they will need to concentrate on in preparation for the exam.

ANSWERS

1 B; 2 B; 3 C; 4 D; 5 A; 6 B; 7 D; 8 B; 9 B; 10 B; 11 D; 12 B; 13 C; 14 A

Study Advice
Go through the five categories with the class and ask students to add to them from the texts they have just studied. Check that students have found suitable examples (see below) and ask them to find further examples from their dictionaries. This can be set as a homework task. Ask students to read through the extract from *Right Word Wrong Word* and point out the value of context sentences in explaining the exact meaning of words. Ask them to prepare similar sentences for the four words in 5 below (melt/fade/vanish/dissolve).

1 verb patterns
to allow someone **to do** something
to let someone **do** something
to stop someone **from doing** something

2 adjectives commonly followed by prepositions
interested **in**   bored **with/by**

3 preposition + noun + preposition
on account of

4 phrasal verbs and their common meanings
to settle down   to live something down

5 words of similar meaning and their important differences
melt/dissolve/vanish/fade

ROOTS

p.16 FIRST THOUGHTS

Use this matching task as a lead-in to the topic of learning languages and links between words in different languages. You can also link this topic back to some of the issues raised in the paragraphs on page 11 *There's no stopping it!* If you have a monolingual class you could build up a list of borrowed words on the board. With a mixed class it is probably easier to limit this to a short class discussion.

ANSWERS

bistro – *Hungarian*
anorak – *Eskimo*
safari – *Swahili*
tycoon – *Japanese*
cannibal – *Spanish*
algebra – *Arabic*
swastika – *Sanskrit*
kiosk – *Turkish*
pagoda – *Portuguese*
ketchup – *Malay*

p.16 READING

1 At this stage ask the students to cover the rest of the page and concentrate on reading the first half of the text to answer the gist question.

ANSWER

Louise found it easier than she expected because there were so many similarities between English and Greek words.

2 This, with exercise 3, introduces the task type found in Part 3 of Paper 1 *(Reading)*. Candidates have about 15 minutes to complete this section which is mainly designed to test understanding of coherence in text, as well as general comprehension. Explain that the best way to tackle this task is to read the text first for general understanding and then to read the sentences. This is the same technique advised for Part 1 *(Matching headings)* on Coursebook page 8 and Teacher's Book page 3.
Read through the explanations given in the book with the class and deal with any questions they may have. Ask students to underline the parts of the sentences before and after the gaps which provide the 'clues' described in the explanation.

Study Advice
Read through this with the class. Highlight on the board these three phrases: *logical connections*
forward and backward references
different vocabulary to say the same thing.
Ask the students to look out for examples of each technique when they complete the next task. You can then refer back to this section and highlight the examples. See exercise 3 below.

3 Students now have a go at completing this task. Having seen the example above they shouldn't find it too difficult but, as before, allow them to check their ideas in pairs or small groups before going through the answers.

ANSWERS

1 D; 2 G; 3 B; 4 F; 5 A; 6 H.
Sentence E is the extra answer.

Once everyone has agreed on the answers ask them to go back and underline the parts of the text which gave them 'clues'. In order to clarify the techniques listed in the *Study Advice* section in this book you should ask the students to find examples of some of the features listed. Give them sufficient time to do this and then elicit and write the following on the board:
- Cause + result
  I never managed to read more than a few pages + it really put me off (sentence C)
- Explanation + example
  she was surprised at how good she was + almost all her

guesses were correct (sentence B)
some words were easier than others + *things that the people picked up ... were the easiest* (sentence F)
- Statement + contrasting idea
Louise ... needed to be more accurate than that ... + *Fortunately, the same words kept coming up ... she got a few more clues ...* (sentence H)
- Reference words
some Greek books ... Not Homer ... + *these were romantic novels* (sentence D; *these* refers to *books*)
- Pronouns
she'd be unlikely to say he was stupid.. + she might say something along those lines when she quarrelled with him ... (sentence A: *him ... he*)
- Same or different vocabulary
Louise needed to be more accurate to understand ... + *she got a few clues to what they really meant* (sentence H; *understand = what something means*)
Louise used a marker pen to highlight ... + *... she found that she highlighted about 20 words* (sentence G; repetition of *highlight*)

MAKING CONTACT

p.18 FIRST THOUGHTS

1/2 Use the questions as a lead-in to the topic of pen-friends and English as a means of international communication.

p.18 LISTENING

1 This activity introduces the task type found in Part 2 of Paper 4 *(Listening)*. In the exam the task may be note-taking, blank-filling or sentence completion. In each case one word or a short phrase is all that is required. Remind students of the exam technique of reading through the prompts **before** listening (time is allowed for this in the exam) and making a preliminary guess at the answer – this helps to 'focus the ears' when listening.
After the first listening students should compare answers with a partner before listening again to check.

ANSWERS

1 one of their advertisements
2 fill in a form
3 choose the right people
4 43
5 family pets
6 problems
7a bathroom
7b servants
8 anxious
9 engineering
10a a home where the father was a butcher
10b someone with a terrible allergy to horses

TAPESCRIPT AND ANSWERS

INTERVIEWER: So how does it work?
ANDREW: Well, basically a school or an individual responds to one of erm our advertisements and we send them a form and ask them to write a letter all about themselves and why they want to do an exchange.
INTERVIEWER: I see. And what's the point of the letter?
ANDREW: Well, one thing, it helps us to choose the right people. We reject quite a few people on the basis of the letter. You know, ones who have obviously got the wrong kind of attitude. Some just can't be bothered to write a letter at all.
INTERVIEWER: I see. What kind of thing do you deal with on the form?
ANDREW: We try to get as much detail as we can about the background and interests of the applicant. There are forty-three questions which cover everything from religious persuasion to family pets. As far as possible we want to match up people in terms of age and interests but also in terms of family background. We ask participants to give a description of their homes, what their parents do for a living and so on. A parent has to sign the form saying that they have checked it and that everything is accurate. Afterwards we make our decision on the basis of the form and the letter.
INTERVIEWER: Why do you want so much background about family circumstances?
ANDREW: Well we don't want people to go and stay in exactly the same kind of family, but on the other hand we don't want there to be enormous social differences or inequalities. As far as I am concerned it just causes problems.
INTERVIEWER: Why? What can go wrong?
ANDREW: Well, it can lead to all kinds of problems and embarrassment. For example, if someone from a less well-off family goes to stay with someone who is comparatively very rich then it can cause anxiety and jealousy for obvious reasons. Someone from a rich family might take it for granted that they would have their own bathroom or that there would be servants.

Children who have perhaps stayed with a very well-off family get incredibly anxious about what the other person will think when they come into their house.

INTERVIEWER: Doesn't this mean that you are just helping to reinforce social differences between people?

ANDREW: I know what you mean. When I started the agency I thought I would be able to take advantage of the situation for a bit of social engineering but I quickly realised that it just didn't work. For a young person to go abroad – perhaps for the first time – to a strange family is already stressful enough. We don't want to add to anyone's problems.

INTERVIEWER: And have you ever got it wrong?

ANDREW: Well, we have difficulty in making an exact match but I've made a couple of mistakes too. On one occasion I sent someone who was a strict vegetarian to a home where the father was a butcher.

INTERVIEWER: Oh no!

ANDREW: And another time someone with a terrible allergy to horses was sent to a family where everyone was keen on riding. However, I should say that in the second case they erm hadn't said anything about allergies in the box provided.

INTERVIEWER: Well, it sounds as though you really try to take everything into consideration.

ANDREW: We try to do our best.

2 Vocabulary in context.

ANSWERS

1 D; **2** E; **3** C; **4** F; **5** A; **6** B

p.19 WRITING

The compulsory letter

This section introduces the task type to be found in the Part 1 section of Paper 2 *(Writing)*. This paper contains two parts. The first part has one writing task which is compulsory (question 1). The second part has a choice of 4 tasks from which the candidate chooses one. The paper lasts an hour and a half so candidates can spend about 45 minutes on each question.

1/2 Question 1 is always a letter-writing task and is given a context or situation by means of short introductory texts and/or visuals. Students are asked to write between 120 and 180 words. Addresses should not be included.

Print out to your students that it is very important to read through the information carefully before beginning to plan their letter. The instructions should be followed exactly if they want to maximise their chances of good marks.

Begin by asking them to compare the two letters, focusing on the five areas listed in the Coursebook.

ANSWERS

– A is a more appropriate style.
– B answers the question more fully.
– B covers the points in the notes.
– A is better organised.
– A looks better.

3 Possible answer (optional extras in brackets)

Dear Mr and Mrs Williams
I am writing in response to your advertisement in Polyglot Magazine, as I would be interested in receiving further information (about your service).
I am eighteen years old and studying (for my 'A' levels in) French, German and Spanish. I am hoping to go on to university next year. I would like an exchange with a Spanish boy or girl, preferably one who is keen on sailing, like me.
This August we are renting a house near the sea in Wales, and it would be preferable/nice if he or she could be with us for that month. Is there a minimum time for an exchange, or do we decide?
We will be spending the summer with my mother, who is a professional musician, and my father, who manages a garage. I do not have any brothers or sisters.
I look forward to receiving further information, including details of the cost of the service.

Yours sincerely,
Raymond West

4 Ask the students to work in pairs to make notes about what they should include in their letter to Linguapal. They should make careful note of the instructions in the rubric and the handwritten notes. When the pairs have made their notes they should report back to class so that everyone can jot down any useful ideas.
The final letter-writing task can be set as homework. Remind the students to use the other letters as a model, but to make changes to fit in with the comments they have made and the additional ideas they came up with in their pairs.

Notes on marking written homework

In order for students to be adequately prepared for the exam and, in particular, Paper 2, they need to be given regular written homework, both controlled, e.g. cloze texts, sentence transformation exercises and other grammatical exercises, and less controlled, e.g. various types of composition.
In order to develop the self-critical awareness of students towards their own work, various techniques can be employed in relation to the freer written work. Where compositions are set and students are being marked on all aspects of their English, a marking code should be adopted which will direct students towards the type of mistake they have been making. The following example shows how you

> I have 19 years old. I live at the middle of Paris. I am ∧ student at the Sorbonne and I study english at a language school in the evenings. I studied english since 6 years. I enjoy to play squash, tenis and rugby but I have always to make my homework in the evenings wich mean I don't have a lot of free time.

- ww = wrong word
- wo = word order
- sp = spelling
- p = punctuation
- t = tense
- gr = grammar
- ∧ = word missing
- ? = meaning not clear
- // = new paragraph
- TA = try this section again

might mark part of the letter written to Linguapal for the task outlined above.

It is important, however, to use such a code only in cases where you believe students will be able to self-correct. During the course, you may want to progressively give less and less direct indication of where mistakes are and of what type, as clearly in the exam itself students will have no such help. An interim stage can be to put a number at the beginning of each line indicating how many mistakes have been made. Clearly the introduction of editing tasks in Paper 3 will make students more aware of (and capable of) self-correction.

To reduce the time spent on correcting homework in class, it can be useful to prepare a list of ten or so sentences from students' work that incorporate typical mistakes for students to work on together. This can be instructive for all and cut down the amount each individual has to correct in their own work. If there has been some preparatory work in class on a particular area, e.g. narrative tenses, and students are subsequently set a narrative composition for homework, it is important that, in marking the homework, you particularly focus on the target language area – either to praise the successful application of target language in context or to give directions for correction. So that the marking of students' written work does not become too negative a process, when a particularly good piece of written work is produced, photocopy it and give copies to all the students in the class in order that they can analyse what has made this so good. After students have become accustomed to critically analysing their own work, you may want to ask students to spend time considering each other's work in small groups before they hand it in to be marked. In these groups they can try and detect mistakes and think of better ways of expressing what is intended. As the exam approaches, it is important that students are told/shown the criteria by which their compositions are going to be marked. Having explained the system, start marking their work with explicit reference to the relevant criteria.

18–20 Excellent
Natural English with minimal errors and complete realization of the task set.

16–17 Very good
Good vocabulary and structure, above the simple sentence level. Errors non-basic.

12–15 Good
Simple but accurate realization of task. Sufficient naturalness, not many errors.

8–11 Pass
Reasonably correct though awkward OR natural treatment of subject with some serious errors.

5–7 Weak
Vocabulary and grammar inadequate for the task set.

0–4 Very poor
Incoherent. Errors showing lack of basic knowledge of English.

Right from the beginning of the course students should keep their own *Personal Mistakes Record Sheet*. They should make a note on this of all mistakes they make which they have a tendency to repeat, divided into appropriate categories, e.g.

SPELLING
wich ✗   which ✓

GRAMMAR
since 10 years ✗   for 10 years ✓

PUNCTUATION
august ✗   August ✓

This record sheet should be used as a checklist prior to the handing in of written work and also should be mentally gone through before students give in their compositions in the final exam.

p.20 LISTENING

This activity introduces the type task found in Part 3 of Paper 4 *(Listening)*. Students should read through the list of

options before they listen. After the first listening let students confer. Remind them that they will hear each listening text twice in the exam, and play it again. If there is still disagreement about the correct answer, play the specific part which contains the answer. If necessary, elicit word by word until the answer is clear to all. In later units, just let the students listen twice before comparing answers or giving the answers, so they get used to the exam format. Remind students that one of the answers A–F is not needed.
Speaker 1 D; speaker 2 A; speaker 3 F; speaker 4 B; speaker 5 E;
Sentence C is the extra answer.

TAPESCRIPT

SPEAKER 1: My biggest fear was that I wouldn't be able to make myself understood. And in fact when I turned up at the family I couldn't understand a word. This was because in the home they spoke a dialect, you know, from their region. Anyway, when I was around they always made sure they spoke erm ordinary Spanish, you know, Castilian. I was really homesick at first but after a week I didn't want to come back. And I had a really great time.

SPEAKER 2: Well, I got erm very upset because I was standing in a shop waiting my turn, when people kept on jumping the queue. I started to get a bit angry but then my friend told me that in her country queuing, you know, like we do over here, was less important. And I must say that this is a bit of an English obsession.

SPEAKER 3: Well, let me see, I think the worst thing was on the first night. They had prepared this wonderful meal and we had erm artichoke as a starter. You know, the vegetable. Well, I tried to eat everything, instead of just the tips of the leaves. I was so embarrassed, you see I'd never eaten one before. I felt like I'd made a real fool of myself.

SPEAKER 4: For me, the erm biggest shock was the toilets. I went to this village miles from anywhere and the toilet wasn't like ours, it didn't have a seat. In fact you had to squat down to use it. I just didn't know what to do at first, and the first time I erm tried I dropped a set of keys down it.

SPEAKER 5: That's easy. The thing that got me was the way, you know, everybody kissed. I just couldn't believe it. I come from a family where nobody ever touches anyone or hardly ever, and I found it difficult to feel comfortable with all the kissing and handshaking and stuff. I was quite used to it by the end though.

p.20 VOCABULARY

Collocations

This exercise includes the type of word links which students will need to know for Parts 1 and 3 of Paper 3 *(Use of English).*

1 ANSWERS

- do something for a living; do one's best
- take advantage of someone/something; take something for granted; (take a decision = US English)
- give a description
- make a decision; make oneself understood; make a fool of oneself; make sure; make a mistake; make the most (of something)
- find difficulty in doing something
- have a good time; have difficulty in doing something
- jump the queue

2 POSSIBLE ANSWERS

2 Do you have difficulty in understanding the listening exercises?
3 Have you ever been in a situation where you couldn't make yourself understood?
4 What does your mother do for a living?
5 Do members of your family take having a television for granted?

p.20 USE OF ENGLISH

1 This is the same exercise type as the one on Coursebook page 13.

ANSWERS

1 ... take advantage of ...
2 ... sister do for a living ...
3 ... gave a description of ...
4 ... have a good time ...
5 ... you to do your best ...
6 ... are making a fool of ...
7 ... had difficulty (in) turning ...
8 ... took his mother for granted.
9 ... jump the queue ...
10 ... to make myself understood ...

2 This exercise introduces the task type found in Part 4 of Paper 3 *(Use of English).* This task tests the ability to spot errors, in other words, knowledge of grammatical and lexical systems. This type of task may be unfamiliar to many students and will therefore need careful explanation and plenty of practice. It has the advantage of raising students' awareness of 'editing' skills in general and this can have a very positive effect on the accuracy of their written work. Read through the introduction with the class and ask them to read through the text for general understanding.
Ask the students to cover the explanations and, in pairs, look carefully at each word in bold. Can they explain why it is wrong? They should make a few brief notes about each error and then compare their ideas with the explanations given in the book.

Some students may spot that several of the errors come under the same categories as some of those we highlighted in the introduction to Part 1 of Paper 3 (*Choose your words carefully* page 14). This list and the explanations given in this section make up a useful guide to many of the areas of accuracy which are regularly tested in the exam. As with the previous tasks, students' performance can be a good diagnostic tool for use in planning areas of particular study for your class.

3 Ask students to complete the editing task on the second text. Remind them to read it through first for general understanding and then work through it line by line. As with the first text, they should try to explain why the unnecessary words are wrong. Students can get together to compare their answers and explanations in pairs or small groups.
When they have finished go through the errors one by one, eliciting the explanations and writing on the board any which cause any difficulty.

ANSWERS
line ...
1 **does** – 'I would like to know ...' is one of the phrases which introduces an embedded question. These follow the syntax of statements and do not have question auxiliaries or question marks at the end.
2 ✓
3 **years** – We can say *seventeen years old* or *seventeen* but **not** *seventeen years*.
4 **together** – *live with* contains the meaning of *together* so this word is unnecessary.
5 **got** – *got used to* is followed by *-ing*, not by the infinitive. *used to* is followed by the infinitive *(live)*.
6 **have** – On the next line we can see *six years ago*, which is a specific time in the past so we don't use the present perfect tense, we use the past simple.
7 **for** – We use *for* with a period of time (duration or length) not a specific time. *Ago* shows she is referring to a specific point of time.
8 **a** – *progress* is an uncountable noun so it does not have an indefinite article in front of it.
9 **an** – same explanation as number 8.
10 **she** – *My mother* is the subject of the sentence so *she* is unnecessary.
11 **the** – *this/that would be best* is a standard phrase.
12 **myself** – *relax* is not a reflexive verb.
13 **to** – *I like to go shopping*, there is no *to* before an *-ing* form.
14 **of** – *of* cannot be used after *most* unless the following noun has a determiner (e.g. *our*, *these*, *that*, *the*) in front of it. So we say *most of these people* or *most people* but not *most of people*.
15 **else** – *else* is repeating the idea of *One other*.

2 Time Out

DECISION TIME

p.22 FIRST THOUGHTS

Use the questions as a lead-in to the topic of students' favourite leisure activities. You might like to elicit the names of a few more activities which are of specific relevance to your class to add to the box. Students should make short notes about their opinions of the listed activities and compare opinions in pairs. Check that they understand the expressions in exercise 2 before they start comparing (if they're not sure ask them to put them into a scale from VERY POSITIVE to VERY NEGATIVE). Don't spend too long on the discussion as students will have a chance to discuss their opinions later in the unit.

p.22 LISTENING

This exercise introduces the task type found in Part 4 of Paper 4 (*Listening*). In the exam candidates may be asked to identify/match speakers (as in the following exercise) or to answer true/false or yes/no questions. Make sure that the students read through the rubric and questions carefully before playing the tape. After the first listening they can confer in small groups. Play the tape again (the conversation will be heard twice in the exam) for students to check and fill in any boxes they were unsure about after the first listening.

> **ANSWERS**
>
> **1** J; **2** R; **3** E; **4** J; **5** J; **6** R; **7** E

TAPESCRIPT

JOHN: I'm really fed up, I mean, we've been stuck here all day. Why don't we go out?
ELEANOR: You're right John, what shall we do then?
RICHARD: But there's something good on telly ...
JOHN: Come on, Richard! Something good on telly.
ELEANOR: Telly, telly, it's all you think about.
JOHN: You'll end up with square eyes.
RICHARD: All right ... What do you want to do then?
JOHN: Well we, could go to that new café ... what's it called ...
ELEANOR: Video Café.
JOHN: Yeah, that's right, Video Café.
RICHARD: It's boring. We might as well watch telly.
ELEANOR: It'll be packed too ... Full of smoke. I'd rather we did something else.
RICHARD: So would I.
JOHN: There's that Burger, em, Tex-Mex place ... what's it called ... Ranchero.
ELEANOR: Yuk, you know I can't stand burgers.

JOHN: How about ... there's ... I know it's a film ... there's a really good film with Sylvester Stallone on. I've heard it's really good ... *Cliffhanger*. Why don't we er ...
RICHARD: I've already seen it.
ELEANOR: I have too.
RICHARD: I don't like these action films much.
ELEANOR: I don't either.
JOHN: All right then Richard. How about ... ? Look I'm getting fed up with this ... I suggest something to you and you ... you just knock it down.
RICHARD + ELEANOR: Ah! You poor old thing!
RICHARD: Hold it ... I know, we could always go to the rink. There's an ice hockey match on.
ELEANOR: Ice hockey ... I've never been to an ice hockey match.
JOHN: Neither have I ... a bit brutal isn't it?
ELEANOR: Yeah. Um, let's go.
RICHARD: Well, there you are you see. A new experience ... What do you think?
ELEANOR: OK, but I'll hold you responsible if I don't like it.
JOHN: Me too.
RICHARD: Brilliant. And I didn't even want to go out. Anyway ... What's the time? It starts at eight ...
ELEANOR: It's half seven now.
JOHN: It's time we left, we're going to have to get our skates on if we're going to get there on time.
RICHARD: Get our skates on ... Ha ha ... That's almost funny, John.
ELEANOR: Anyone seen my car keys?
JOHN + RICHARD: Oh no ... Not again!

p.22 SPEAKING

Managing conversations

Play the tape and ask the students to read the tapescript at the same time. They should underline the expressions. Check the answers and put any unfamiliar phrases on the board, eliciting further examples to clarify meaning, e.g. *Why don't we go out/go for a meal/watch a video/play tennis?* etc.

> **ANSWERS**
>
> **Ask for suggestions:**
> What shall we do then?
> What do you want to do then?
>
> **Make suggestions:**
> Why don't we go out?
> We could go to that new café
> How about ... there's a really good film ... *Cliffhanger*.
> Why don't we ...
> I know, we could always go to the rink.
>
> **Express preferences:**
> It's boring. We might as well watch telly.
> I'd rather we did something else.
> I don't like these action films much.

p.22 LANGUAGE STUDY

It's time .../I'd rather ...

1 Which tenses are used? The point here is that although the past simple is used (... *we did ...,* ... *we left ...*) we are talking about now/the future.

> **ANSWERS**
>
> **1A** It's time to leave for the airport. (*correct*)
> **B** It's time for us to go to the airport. (*correct*)
> **C** It's time that we go to the airport. (*wrong*)
> **D** It's time we went to the airport. (*correct*)
> **2A** I'd rather go to the theatre. (*correct*)
> **B** I'd rather that we go to the theatre. (*wrong*)
> **C** I'd rather we went to the theatre. (*correct*)

The rule the students should be able to work out for themselves is that, if *It's time ...* or *I'd rather ...* are followed directly by a noun or pronoun, then the verb which follows goes into the past simple.

2 Give one or two of the situations to each pair of students. Let them work out the target sentence, and then, having checked that with you, get them to extend the situation backwards and forwards in time to create a short, but more contextualised, dialogue. Students could act out their dialogues in front of each other.

> **ANSWERS**
>
> 1 It's time for me to have a holiday./It's time I had a holiday.
> 2 I'd rather go to a disco./I'd rather we went to a disco.
> 3 It's time for you to go to bed. It's time you went to bed.
> 4 I'd rather take a taxi. I'd rather we took a taxi.
> 5 It's time we bought tickets. I'd rather buy the tickets now./I'd rather we bought the tickets now.
> 6 I'd rather walk/take a taxi. I'd rather Simon/I drove.
> 7 I'd rather have Thai food./I'd rather we had Thai food.
> 8 It's time we finished this exercise!

p.23 SHORT REPLIES

To be tried individually, then checked in pairs.
Having sorted out the rules in small groups (exercise 2), go round the class making quick-fire statements to which students must give appropriate short replies, e.g. *I can't stand football.*

> **1 ANSWERS**
>
> **A** 4; **B** 7; **C** 8; **D** 1; **E** 2; **F** 3; **G** 5; **H** 6

2 We use *so* and *too* when the structure of the stimulus, i.e. the first sentence, is **positive**. *So* comes at the beginning of the reply, and the subject and auxiliary verb which follow are inverted, e.g.
STIMULUS: I like Jane.
So I do. (*wrong*)
So I like. (*wrong*)
So do I. (*correct*)

Too is used after the subject followed by the auxiliary verb, e.g.
STIMULUS: I like Jane.
I   do   too
subject   aux.   + too

Neither comes at the beginning of an answer which is agreeing with a negative statement and *either* comes at the end, e.g.
STIMULUS: I can't stand cabbage.
Neither can I.
I can't either.

When students are moving around the class to find another student with similar opinions on the activities, make sure that they use statements rather than questions to initially describe their feelings about the various forms of entertainment, e.g. *I really love heavy metal music,* to which another student will be able to respond with an appropriate short reply.

p.23 SPEAKING

An evening out

1 To focus attention briefly on the *useful language* before starting the activity, put the following sentences on the blackboard with gaps which students together must try and complete appropriately, without reference to their books. Point out that the context is *An evening out*.

- What ____ ____ like ____ do?
- Why ____ we ____ to the disco?
- ____ have a hamburger instead.
- How ____ eating out?
- Do ____ fancy ____ to the cinema?

When students have attempted to complete the gaps, then let them refer to their books.
Put students into groups of three or four for the discussion. Before beginning, make sure the students understand exactly what they have to do and then let them get on with the activity with as little interference as possible. Make a note of mistakes around the target language of expressing preference and agreeing so that you can follow up the activity with a brief 'correction spot'.
In order to stimulate discussion you may want to give out the short role cards given here. You can photocopy these cards.

> **A**
> You hate all modern music, particularly when it is played so loud that you can't hear what anyone is saying – which it normally is!
>
> ------
>
> **B**
> You have recently become very concerned about the nature of the food that you and other people eat. You are shocked by the amount of 'rubbish' that we all consume on a daily basis – it is very important for you that you eat <u>healthily!</u>
>
> ------
>
> **C**
> You have had a hard week at work and you really just want to do something as relaxing as possible. In general you don't like sport and are not an energetic person by any means, but this is especially true tonight!
>
> ------
>
> **D**
> Although you do have £20 to spend, you are actually trying very hard to save as much money as you can to buy a ring for your boy/girlfriend. However, for the moment, this is a secret. Try and spend as little as possible when you go out tonight.
>
> ------
>
> © Copyright Longman Group UK Ltd. 1989

To conclude this activity, one way of getting feedback might be for each group to describe the 'programme' they have finally decided for themselves and at the same time try and persuade you, the teacher, to come with their group by selling the positive features of the programme they have worked out.

2 This exercise simulates the task type to be found in Part 3 of Paper 5 (*Speaking*). In the exam, candidates will have picture prompts to generate a discussion. The discussion will be based on a task such as planning, problem-solving, decision-making, prioritising, etc.
Divide the class into pairs for this exercise. Monitor and check that students are addressing themselves to the specific tasks and making use of a range of language.

THE SPORTING LIFE

p.24 FIRST THOUGHTS

1/2 Use the pictures and questions to lead in to the topic of sports. In order to prepare the vocabulary for the unit ask the students to brainstorm the names of as many sports as they can and list these on the board. Use this opportunity to highlight the difference between a 'spectator sport' and a 'participation sport', and between team sports and individual sports.

p.24 LISTENING

1 ANSWERS

A ice hockey; B archery; C chess

TAPESCRIPT

A I guess you could say that this is our national sport – we certainly have got the right kind of weather for it. It has the reputation of being a pretty rough and tough game. Anyhow, as its name suggests we play it on ice, on skates and the object of the game is to score by hitting the puck into the net. You have to be really well dressed up and padded and protected for this 'cos it's easy otherwise to get badly hurt.

B This sport has a long and traditional history in my country. It is a mixture of meditation and concentration, and accuracy. It's important to breathe properly. Obviously you need a bow and arrow and to aim at the target.

C I don't know whether you can really call this a sport but it is something that people from my country have been very good at. We have had lots of grand masters and international grand masters. It is an ancient game, I think it originally came from Persia, now Iran. It is about strategy and it requires a very good memory of other games and intense concentration. You play it on a board with sixty-four squares and the object of the game is to capture the enemy's king. Each player has sixteen pieces which move around the board in a certain way.

2 In a monolingual class this is best done in small groups. Remind students of their answers to the lead-in questions (*First Thoughts* above). If you have a mixed nationality class students can work individually and the activity can be made more challenging by asking them not to mention the name of the sport in their descriptions. Once they have finished you can take in the descriptions, shuffle them and give them back to different students, asking them to guess which sport is being described.

p.25 VOCABULARY

Do, play or go?

This and the following vocabulary exercises are best done by students working in small groups in order to pool their knowledge. Encourage the students to use dictionaries if they are available.

ANSWERS

1 do
athletics; gymnastics
play
baseball; chess; volleyball; tennis; football; ice hockey; cricket; American football
go
windsurfing; sailing; motor racing; horse riding; swimming; jogging

2 court: tennis; volleyball
track: athletics; motor racing
rink: ice hockey
pool: swimming
field: cricket; baseball
pitch: football; American football; cricket
board: chess
ring: horse riding

3A board: chess
gloves: baseball
net: volleyball; tennis; football
racquet: tennis
stick: ice hockey
piece: chess
horse: horse riding
puck: ice hockey
bat: cricket, baseball

B a goal: football; American football
a set: tennis; volleyball
a game: baseball; chess; volleyball; tennis; football; ice hockey; cricket; American football
a draw: football; American football; ice hockey; cricket
a round: baseball
a half: ice hockey; football; American football

4 You can't *train, tackle, run, foul, score* or *cheat* a ball.

5 a referee: football; American football
a fan/a spectator: any spectator sport
an umpire: cricket; tennis
a linesman: football; tennis
a cheerleader/a quarterback: American football
a hooligan: football
a forward: football; American football
a goalkeeper: football; ice hockey

6A correct
B *She beat her opponent.*
C correct
D correct

You win a game, a competition or a prize.
You beat another team or another person.
e.g. Real Madrid **won** the European Cup.
Real Madrid **beat** Zaragoza.

p.25 USE OF ENGLISH

This exercise introduces the task type found in Part 2 of Paper 3 (*Use of English*). In the exam there are 15 gaps, each of which must be filled with one word only. No multiple choice options are given. This is a challenging task and it is important that students are trained to read the whole text first for general understanding and then to study the context of each gap for clues.

1 Ask students to read the text and answer the three comprehension questions first.

ANSWERS

1 All the teams played against each other to decide who would go through to the last sixteen. Then there were knock-outs between the winning teams to find who would go through to the semi-finals.
2 At first she treated it as fun but she became more serious as they got closer to the semi-finals.
3 At first the other team was winning but they lost the last point they needed, so Eva's team were able to get the points they needed to win.

2 Read through the examination advice. Ask the students to try filling the gaps without looking at the prompts in the box. They should underline any parts of the surrounding sentence which they think give clues to the missing word. Go through the first couple of gaps with the class as follows:
It was a beautiful sunny day and (1) ___ of families and friends turned (2) ___ .
gap 1 is followed by *of*. Which expressions which are followed by *of* would be suitable in this context? (*lots of*)
gap 2 is preceeded by *turned* so we can guess that it is a phrasal verb. Which particle would be suitable in this context? (*up*).
After students have tried doing the gap-fill without looking at the prompt words they can compare answers in pairs. Finally, allow them to look at the words in the box. By a process of elimination they should be able to check their own answers.

ANSWERS

1 lots; **2** up; **3** down; **4** against; **5** would; **6** more; **7** had; **8** the; **9** last/more; **10** so; **11** afterwards; **12** back; **13** felt; **14** all; **15** too

p.25 WRITING

A report is one of the writing tasks which may be given in Part 2 of Paper 2 (*Writing*), this is the part where candidates choose one composition task from a choice of four. As with Part 1 (see page 8) they should write between 120 and 180 words and they will have about 45 minutes to spend on the task. Students are not expected to produce a business-type report. The context will be given in the rubric and is usually of a general nature such as an article for an international magazine or local newspaper.

After introducing the task, ask students to match the structure guidelines given in the Coursebook with the relevant sections of Eva's description of the Brazilian volleyball game. They should then use the guidelines to make notes and plan their report. Do not let them start writing the actual report until they have shown you their notes and plan (this is an important part of training them in the techniques required for successful task-based writing). Refer back to the notes for Unit 1 on planning and marking of compositions (pages 8–9).

ALL TIME GREATS

p.26 FIRST THOUGHTS

1/2/3 Use the questions as a lead-in to the topic of dangerous sports and Formula One motor racing in particular. If students are unfamiliar with Formula One you may need to give some **background information**.

Formula One Grand Prix racing began in 1906. There are many famous motor racing circuits e.g. Brands Hatch and Silverstone in the UK, Hockenheim and Nürburgring in Germany, Monza in Italy and Indianapolis in the USA. Some races are held on normal streets, the most famous being Monte Carlo, Monaco. There has been a world championship for drivers since 1950, and for constructors since 1958. The first six drivers and cars in each race are awarded points and the total at the end of a season (usually 16 races) decides the winners. Apart from the world championship, other famous races are the Le Mans 24 hours, which dates from 1923, and the Indianapolis 500. The cars are specially built for the races, and famous makers include Bugatti, BRM, Mercedes, Alfa Romeo, Ferrari, Lotus, Brabham, Williams, and McLaren.

Ask students if they know anything about Ayrton Senna and elicit some background information. (Ayrton Senna was Brazilian, born in 1960. He was the leading Formula One driver in the late 1980s and early 1990s. He was killed in a crash during a Grand Prix race in Imola, Italy in 1994).

p.26 READING

This activity gives further practice in the task found in Part 3 of Paper 1 (*Reading*) and introduced in Unit 1 (page 16). Refer back to the notes on page 6 for ideas on exploiting this task type.

> **ANSWERS**
>
> 1 C; 2 G; 3 A; 4 F; 5 H; 6 D
> B is the extra sentence.

p.27 USE OF ENGLISH

This exercise will help students prepare for Part 5 of Paper 3 (*Use of English*).
Encourage students to use dictionaries for the exercise.

> **ANSWERS**
>
> **0** decision; **1** tragedy; **2** player; **3** championship;
> **4** collection; **5** success; **6** competitor; **7** opportunity;
> **8** ability; **9** height; **10** wealth; **11** disappointment;
> **12** boredom

BOOKWORMS

p.28 FIRST THOUGHTS

This pre-reading discussion should allow you to hear just how much vocabulary associated with the topic of books and reading the students know. Begin by asking the class to brainstorm the titles of any books they know of/have read in English.

Write the titles on the board and use these to get the students started on the categorising task. Use the exercise to check they understand the meaning of the categories. You can get the students started on describing their favourite books by telling the class about your own likes and dislikes. Use the opportunity to recommend suitable books for the class to read. There are many simplified versions of novels and readers available from publishers which are specifically aimed at students of this level. Explain the importance of extensive reading for effective language learning. If library facilities are limited or unavailable in your school/area you can set up a class library by asking each student to buy one book and then circulating them on a rota.

Note: Candidates for the First Certificate have the opportunity of studying a set book for the exam. If you choose to offer this to your students they will be able to write about the set book in Question 5 of Paper 2 (*Writing*). Contact your local University of Cambridge Local Examination Syndicate office for a list of the current set books.

p.28 READING

This activity introduces the task type found in Part 4 of Paper 1 (*Reading*), which is known as a multiple matching task. Make it clear that there is not a one-to-one relationship between the questions and the options (i.e. the letters A–H), some options may be needed more than once.

Explain this carefully as many students will be more familiar with traditional matching tasks where each option can only be given once and thus an elimination approach can be adopted. This approach will not work with this type of task!

1 As with the other reading tasks, make sure that the students read through the texts first for general understanding before reading and answering the questions.

> **ANSWERS**
>
> **1** F; **2** H; **3** E; **4** D; **5** B; **6** C; **7** A; **8/9/10** B/G/F (in any order)

> **2 ANSWERS**
>
> *Where has the text come from?* A
> *Why would someone read this text?* A

3 Students can discuss these questions in small groups. Ask them to report back with their decisions and encourage the students to justify and explain their choices, where appropriate, using *keen on*, *can't stand* and so on. It can be fun to get the class to vote (by a show of hands) on their choice for each of the recipients/themselves.

p.29 LISTENING

1 Read through the questions before playing the tape.

> **ANSWERS**
>
> Speaker 1 B (*Fist of God*)
> Speaker 2 E (*The Body Farm*)
> Speaker 3 D (*no specific book suggested by the speaker*)
> Speaker 4 A (*Mrs de Winter*)
> Speaker 5 C (*Family and Friends*)

2 Students should read through the texts once more before listening again to the tape. Answers above in brackets.

TAPESCRIPT

SPEAKER 1: It was awful ... I mean it was all ... such an improbable story ... I loathed the hero ... you know, killing people all over the place ... running round the desert ... he wouldn't have lasted two minutes in real life ... I don't know what possessed me to read it ... or for that matter to get to the end ... suppose I thought it might get better but it didn't. Dreadful rubbish. I got rid of it, threw it away in disgust you know. You'd have to be a bit sick in the head I imagine to enjoy it ... A book for men – definitely.

SPEAKER 2: It was pretty good, I suppose ... Very clever plot ... And a bit too realistic in a way. The detail, you know some of the erm detail about cutting up bodies, 'cos she was a pathologist was rather disgusting really, but the book took me over. I can't say I lost any sleep over it but it was a bit ... um gruesome.

SPEAKER 3: It was absolutely riveting, I mean I couldn't put it down. Poor old Malcolm, he kept shouting down the stairs, 'When are you coming up?' and I just said 'Five more minutes, dear.' He was really fed up. Finally I got to bed at about two. Still it was worth it. He was asleep of course, snoring his head off ...

SPEAKER 4: It was good. I won't deny it, but all the while I was reading it there was a little voice sort of saying: 'You know it's not the real thing.' It was good, terribly clever and everything and she took off the style of the original quite well, all the same, but it didn't have the same feel, erm, you know, the flavour of the, of the first one by the, er, original writer, what's her name – du Maurier, that's right. I suppose I was silly to have, erm, expected, it.

SPEAKER 5: Well, I wouldn't exactly say it was the best book I've ever read. All the same I think she really does manage to express, um, what every, well you know, normal people's lives are like ... all of her characters ... even though they were in a family set up, they all seemed somehow so, erm, alone, if you know what I mean. Very astute ... well observed but a bit depressing. I'd only recommend it to someone who was feeling, erm, you know, not feeling down. You'd need to feel quite strong inside, not for the vulnerable; most people's family lives are bad enough as it is without reading about more ...

p.30 VOCABULARY

> **ANSWERS**
>
> **1** look ... up; **2** looking forward; **3** looking; **4** look after; **5** looking out for

p.30 LANGUAGE STUDY

Past simple or present perfect?

Amongst other things, the aim of this exercise is to act as a diagnostic test to see whether your students can sort out when to use the past simple and the present perfect, and how much remedial work will be necessary in this area.

1 Give students about a minute to do the first task.

> **ANSWER**
>
> He has had 7 occupations: (author, photographer, waiter, advertising man, railway clerk, art student, comic strip writer)

2 Let students take their time, working in groups, on this exercise. Rather than going through the answers immediately, we would suggest that, having worked through the three *When we use the present perfect* exercises, students could go back to the Len Deighton text in pairs/small groups and see if they want to change any of their original ideas. Where they are happy with their choice and it is present perfect, students should decide which of the categories of use it corresponds to.

ANSWERS

0 has led; **1** has been writing; **2** has also been *(note position of **also**)*; **3** was born; **4** took; **5** did; **6** was; **7** came; **8** went; **9** worked; **10** was; **11** became; **12** produced; **13** Following; **14** returned; **15** went; **16** has lived/been living; **17** was; **18** has written; **19** has he written *(note inversion after **not only**)*; **20** has also written

When we use the present perfect

1 Past simple or present perfect

We use the present perfect to talk about the indefinite past. *He has been a photographer* is an example of this use. When we use this tense, there is no reference to a point in time or a period of time in the past, and so the addition of *five years ago* makes it wrong. In this case, we would have to use the past simple, i.e. *He was a photographer five years ago*. In the second pair of sentences, we are talking about a period that began and finished in the past, and so we cannot use the present perfect which, generally, expresses some kind of connection to the present.

2 Different uses of the present perfect

ANSWERS

A 2; **B** 4; **C** 1; **D** 3

3 Present perfect simple or continuous

Students should now be able to go through the Len Deighton biography and be able to fully explain which uses of the present perfect are being employed, e.g. *2: has also been* – happened in the past but we do not know when, *16: has lived/has been living* – started in the past and is still going on now.

4 Adverbs and word order

After the correct orders have been sorted out, encourage students to think about what exactly they were getting wrong, if anything. Were there consistent mistakes? You may want to give some rules/guidelines to help. (See Sections 211 and 579 *Practical English Usage* 1980 M. Swan, OUP.) Weaker classes may need further work in this area.

ANSWERS

1. She has not spoken to him for ten years.
2. They have just had their house decorated.
3. I have never had such a wonderful meal before.
4. Have you seen that movie yet?
5. She has never been to a musical.
6. Are they still waiting or have they already left?
7. Has she ever eaten this kind of food before?
8. Has he not ever seen the film? (→ Hasn't he ...)

p.31 PRONUNCIATION

Sentence stress

1 Establish the idea of the telegram and the charge per word. Get students to reduce the target sentence to telegram proportions before looking in their books. Then let them check to see how closely their version resembles the book's. Students then attempt to match sentence to message and then try pronouncing the target sentence with correct sentence stress and expression, e.g. 1 with a **horrified** intonation pattern.

Having practised this a little, put students in pairs to try and construct mini-dialogues to demonstrate different contexts for the different types of sentence stress – the more humorous the better. This can also be done for the second sentence *You might have killed him*.

ANSWERS

1 C; **2** A; **3** B

2 TAPESCRIPT AND ANSWERS

A He's been living in France.
B He's been writing books for ages.
C What have you done to my car?
D How long have you been a dancer?
E How long have you been learning English?
F It's late. Where have you been?
G I've been trying to phone.

When students attempt to imitate the sentence stress patterns, you could put them in pairs with the second student trying to respond appropriately to the particular sentence stress pattern, e.g.

STUDENT A: He's been living in France.
STUDENT B: Funny. I was sure it was Belgium.

p.31 SPEAKING

Role play

Put the students together initially in small groups of As and

Bs: As to think through different questions they might ask; Bs to look through and understand the given information on page 33 and possibly invent more. Monitor carefully and be sure that the students are 100% clear about the situation before they start the interview.

Pair up As and Bs – if possible, get interviewers to come in from outside the classroom in character. This helps to establish the new situation in the minds of the students.

KEEPING IN TOUCH

p.32 FIRST THOUGHTS

Use the questions as a lead-in to the topic of letter writing. Remind students of some of the features looked at in Unit 1.

> **ANSWERS**
>
> (suggested continuations in brackets)
> a good news, formal (...that your job application has been successful)
> b formal (...the cost of a double room in July)
> c bad news, informal (...that you have been feeling unwell)
> d good news, formal and informal (...Have you decided on a name for the baby?)
> e formal (...your insurance claim of 13th September)

p.32 WRITING

An informal letter

1 Start by recalling the work on informal letters in Unit 1, e.g. lay-out, useful phrases. Then let students order the letter and sort it into appropriate paragraphs. Students check their ideas in pairs. Encourage them to justify their answers by reference to discourse markers.

> **ANSWER**
>
> The correct order is 6, 3, 4, 7, 12, 8, 11, 5, 9, 10, 2, 1

2 Understanding the organisation of the letter

> **ANSWERS**
>
> 1 You'll be sad to hear ...
> 2 Incidentally, by the way, anyway.
> 3 I am really sorry ...
> 4 What's more ...
> 5 Would you like to ...
> 6 Guess what!

3 Changing the subject

This refers back to 2 in exercise 2 above. Ask students to assess whether there are any differences in the function of each expression. Then let them read the explanation.

4 One approach is to divide students into pairs, then allocate half the pairs situation 1 and the other half situation 2. Set a time limit to write their letters and at the end of this time you should act as 'postman' and 'deliver' all the letters to the pairs who were writing for the other situation. Then in the same pairs students read and answer the letters they have received. Finally, deliver the second batch of letters for students to read. During the activity you should monitor, helping students with any problems and checking that the target words and expressions highlighted in exercise 2 are being correctly used. The third situation could be set for homework.

p.33 VOCABULARY

Phrasal verbs with *take*

1
> **ANSWERS**
>
> A 6; B 4; C 5; D 1; E 3; F 2

2
> **ANSWERS**
>
> 1 off; 2 on; 3 to; 4 over; 5 after; 6 up

Extension
After the two written exercises, you can ask students to respond to the following questions in small groups:
- Can you take any famous people off? (Demonstrate it!)
- Who do you take after in your family? In what ways?
- If you could take over the running of this school/country, how would you change things?
- Have you taken on anything new recently? If so, what and why?

p.33 USE OF ENGLISH

This is further practice of the exam skill introduced on page 5 (Paper 3 *Use of English*, Part 3). Remind students that they must not change the given word and they must use a maximum of 5 words altogether.

> **ANSWERS**
>
> 1 It's the first time I have seen her at this disco.
> 2 I'd rather we stayed at home this evening.
> 3 Extra staff are taken on in the summer.
> 4 Graham has been beaten (by Waters) in the final.
> 5 Why don't you take up sailing?
> 6 Susan is in charge of student registrations.
> 7 It's years since she last appeared live.
> 8 Don't get rid of that dictionary.
> 9 I am fed up with this terrible weather.
> 10 I could do with a drink/something to drink.

3 Survival

COLD CAN KILL

p.34 FIRST THOUGHTS

To cover the vocabulary needed, write the ten words on the board. Students match words to objects in the picture.

> **ANSWERS**
>
> axe, radio transceiver, bottle of painkillers, penknife, box of matches, rope, rifle and bullets, compass, survival manual

One way to organise this selection activity is to ask each student to write down their three objects individually. Then put the students into groups of about four and tell them they have to make a group decision. Each student then has the opportunity to justify his/her choices. Explain that their decision must be unanimous. Finally, each group should report back to class and a final class decision can be made.

p.34 LANGUAGE STUDY

Countable and uncountable nouns

1 ANSWERS

> Caitlin is a woman and Squib is her dog. She is a volunteer mountain rescuer. They are special because they make a team which goes out in all weathers to rescue people and accepts no publicity.

Ask your students to look carefully at the context of each item, paying particular attention to countable and uncountable nouns as this is often the clue which will help them choose the correct item.
If you wish to revise the main differences elicit and/or write on the board the following general rules:
Countable nouns have a singular and plural form and can be used with an indefinite article.
Uncountable nouns have no plural form and cannot be used with an indefinite article.
Clarify the explanation by eliciting further examples from the students when they have finished exercise 2.

> **ANSWERS**
>
> 1 none; 2 several; 3 all; 4 a few; 5 much; 6 little; 7 number; 8 many; 9 many; 10 few; 11 Both; 12 all; 13 little; 14 anyone; 15 a little; 16 a few; 17 any; 18 hardly; 19 Everyone; 20 amount

2 ANSWERS

> 1 few friends (a negative meaning, fewer than normal, perhaps only one or two)
> a few friends (a positive meaning, a small number of friends)
> 2 little hope (a negative meaning, almost no hope at all)
> a little hope (a positive meaning, a small amount of hope)
> 3 each person (each person individually, not in a group)
> every person (each person, either in a group or individually)

Note: *(a) few, each* and *every* are only used with countable nouns, *(a) little* is only used with uncountable nouns.

3 ANSWERS

> **Followed by countable and uncountable nouns:**
> all
> **Followed by countable nouns:**
> every
> a large number of
> **Followed by uncountable nouns:**
> a great deal of
> a great amount of

p.35 LISTENING

1 Focus students' attention on the photo and ask them to guess the situation and what probably happened. Ask students if they have ever been in a similar situation. If so, what happened exactly? Then put students in pairs to discuss their survival plans and then select one or two to give their ideas in open class.

2 For the first listening students should simply listen for general understanding. Ask them if they think they would have survived or not in this type of situation.

TAPESCRIPT

PRESENTER: Now, I'd like to move on to the next item. The weather certainly seems to have taken a turn for the worse and it looks like we're in for some heavy snowfalls in the next few days. Now, of course, every year there are cases of motorists who break down and get caught out in really bad weather. Tragically, some die and this is even more tragic when we consider that most of these deaths could be avoided. Now we have in the studio this evening Julie Mitchell from the Canadian Automobile Club and she's going to tell us how to stay alive if we get caught out in the snow and our car breaks down. Hi, Julie.

JULIE: Hi.

PRESENTER: So what should we do?

JULIE: Well, the first thing that you should remember is that your car is your most important piece of survival equipment you have if you get caught in a drift. So don't leave it unless you can actually see the place you want to get to. People have died when they needn't have because they have gotten impatient, left their cars and got lost in the snow.

PRESENTER: So, rule number one is stay in your car unless you can see where you're going.

JULIE: Your destination.

PRESENTER: Right. Anything else we should remember?

JULIE: Oh, certainly! First of all, use your common sense. If you have to drive and know you're going to hit bad weather, make sure you have blankets, a sleeping bag and a shovel in case you have to dig yourself out, and ideally food and hot drinks.

PRESENTER: Is there anything we can do to help ourselves if we're stuck, apart from keep warm, that is?

JULIE: Oh, sure. You've got to keep warm but you've also got to keep the car well ventilated – there have been cases of drivers suffocating in their cars. So have the window on the side away from the wind open a little, say half an inch or so.

PRESENTER: OK. What about using the car heater to keep warm?

JULIE: Oh, I'm glad you asked me about this because this can be fatal unless you take extreme care. The risk of death from exhaust fumes is high. The cold takes hours to kill you but exhaust fumes can kill you in a matter of minutes. Before you run your engine, make sure the exhaust is competely free from snow. Otherwise, the fumes will escape into the car. Anyway, only run the engine for ten minutes every hour and every time make sure the exhaust is free.

PRESENTER: Any final tip?

JULIE: Yes, if you know you're setting off in bad weather, ring up your destination just in case something happens on the way. That way, if you're late, your friends will know something is wrong and will be able to tell the police to go out and look for you.

PRESENTER: Thanks Julie for coming in and I hope our listeners out there....

3 Play the tape again for students to answer the sentence-completion task.

ANSWERS

1 your car
2 stay in your car unless you can see where you are going.
3 a sleeping bag
4 a shovel
5 food and hot drinks
6 half an inch or so
7 side away from the wind
8 a matter of minutes.
9 10 minutes
10 ring up your destination.

4 Students should underline the expressions in the tapescript. Put the answers on the board and highlight the use of the imperative, expressions such as *should*, *you've got to* and *make sure*, and the first conditional.

ANSWERS

– the first thing that you should remember is ...
– So don't leave it ...
– stay in your car
– First of all, use your common sense.
– If you have to drive ... make sure you have blankets
– You've got to keep warm
– make sure the exhaust is competely free from snow
– only run the engine for ten minutes ...
– So have the window ... open ...
– If you know you're setting off in bad weather, ring up your destination ...

p.35 SPEAKING

Divide students into A/B pairs. Monitor and check for use of suitable advising language.

SCARING OURSELVES TO DEATH

p.36 FIRST THOUGHTS

Use the questions as an introduction to the topic.

p.36 READING

1 Use the questions as a lead-in to the topic of the text. Write on the board any useful vocabulary which emerges but do not concentrate on this as this will be dealt with in exercise 3. The text does contain some challenging vocabulary but it is important to point out and demonstrate to the students that this should not stop them finding the correct answers to the headline-matching task.

2 Remind the students of the usual advice for tackling this task. That is, to read the text through for general understanding before reading the headlines and attempting the matching task. When they have completed the matching they should compare answers in small groups, justifying their choices by pointing to evidence in the text.

ANSWERS

1 F; **2** H; **3** A; **4** C; **5** G; **6** B
E is the extra headline.

3 Vocabulary in context

Encourage students to look at the contexts to help with finding the matching words. When they have completed the task deal with any additional vocabulary difficulties in the texts. Allow students to work in pairs or small groups in order to pool their knowledge.

ANSWERS

0 mugged / stroll / lurid
1 obliterated / wiped out / perished
3 grip
4 spikes / plea
6 lurks / stealthily

4 ANSWERS

0 A; **1** B; **2** B; **3** A; **4** C; **5** A; **6** B
Note: Number 2 – in order of danger they are motorcycle, cycling, walking, car, tube/underground.

p.38 LANGUAGE STUDY

Consequences

1 Ask students to study the context of the words in bold in the text. When they have completed the task highlight some of the grammatical features of the expressions (in brackets below):

ANSWERS

because of + reason (+ *noun phrase*)
due to + reason (+ *noun phrase*)
so + result/precaution (+ *verb phrase*)
because + reason (+ *verb phrase*)
That's why + result/precaution (*must go at the start of a sentence*)
in case + possible consequence/result (+ *verb phrase*)
owing to + reason (+ *noun phrase*)
Consequently + result (*must go at the start of a sentence*)

Note: A 'precaution' is taken to avoid a negative situation/consequence. A precautionary action usually **precedes** in

case and *so (that)* (as seen in section 2, answers to numbers 1, 3, 4, 6).

2 ANSWERS

1 You should insure your house in case you have a fire.
2 The film star wore dark glasses because he didn't want anyone to recognize him.
3 She packed the glasses carefully so that they wouldn't get broken in the post.
4 He always took a map with him in case he got lost.
5 The thief didn't want to leave any fingerprints. That's why he wore gloves.
6 The notices in the hotel are in seven languages so that foreign guests (will) feel welcome.
7 The show was cancelled due to (her) illness.
8 There had been a heavy snowfall. Consequently, the trains were late.
9 The judge didn't send him to prison because of his youth.
10 We got more money owing to the improved exchange rate.

3 Explain to students that any advice they give should contain a reason. You can start them off by describing from your own experience in a strange town (e.g. getting lost, not being able to find a hotel, etc.) Students can make notes or give the advice to a partner in pairs. Elicit some examples, e.g.
You had better take traveller's cheques so that if they get stolen you'll be able to get some more.
If your students come from different locations this can be made into a role play.

p.38 USE OF ENGLISH

1 Ask students to describe their experiences with shared rooms.

2 Students read the text quickly and answer the gist question.

ANSWER

The writer was happy because she thought a gorilla might come in through the window. Sue was happy because she thought a lion might come up the stairs. So both of them thought the other sister would be attacked first while she escaped!

3 This task type (Part 5 of Paper 3 *Use of English*) was introduced in Unit 2, Coursebook page 27.

> **ANSWERS**
> 1 terrified; 2 unfortunate; 3 irrational; 4 difference;
> 5 selfish; 6 sympathise; 7 guiltily; 8 belief;
> 9 childhood; 10 harmless

p.39 VOCABULARY

Phrasal verbs using *give*

1 The aim of this exercise is to introduce students to the multiplicity of meanings that some phrasal verbs have. It will also help them familiarise themselves with how different meanings appear in dictionary entries. With the first of the two examples of *give up* it is being used with meaning 1 of the dictionary definitions. The second has meaning 2.

> **2 ANSWERS**
> 1 give out – 1
> 2 gave away – 1
> 3 gave off
> 4 gave up – 5
> 5 give up – 2
> 6 give in – 1
> 7 gave away – 3
> 8 give up – 1
> 9 gives back

3 Introduce the task by telling students about something you have *given up* (e.g. taking sugar in tea, smoking), *not given back* (e.g. a book from the library), *given away* (e.g. an item of clothing). In pairs they should describe similar events to their partners. When they have finished ask one or two students to report back to class.

DEVIL'S ALTERNATIVES

p.40 FIRST THOUGHTS

1 Use the description task to check and, if necessary, pre-teach vocabulary including the following.
First picture:
poisonous snake, cobra, black mamba, venom, antidote
Second picture:
bungee jump, elastic cord, to jump off
Encourage the students to use the phrase *I'd rather ...* when expressing their preference.

2 In small groups students choose *a* or *b* from each of the four options. Organise a class vote (by a show of hands) to find the majority choice amongst your students. As a fun extension activity ask students to think up two or three more 'devil's alternatives' to try out on their classmates.

p.40 LISTENING

1 Put this chart on the board without the *a/b* answers and ask the students to copy it and use it to note their answers.

> **ANSWERS**
>
> | OPTIONS | LUCINDA | DAMIEN |
> |---|---|---|
> | 1 | b | a |
> | 2 | a | b |

TAPESCRIPT

DAMIEN: Honestly ... Have you seen this?
LUCINDA: Yeah ...
DAMIEN: What'll they come up with next?
LUCINDA: There are some pretty sick people around.
DAMIEN: Right ... Fun though. All the same, what would you do?
LUCINDA: What! Come off it ... I wouldn't even ...
DAMIEN: Come on. You know. Suppose you had to?
LUCINDA: Well ... Clean the toilets ... definitely.
DAMIEN: Now that's interesting. I'd never have guessed it.
LUCINDA: What do you mean?
DAMIEN: Well, I've always thought you were, you know, confident ...
LUCINDA: With some things maybe, but I'd rather die than stand up in front of that many people.
DAMIEN: Me, I'd do it.
LUCINDA: Oh yeah ...
DAMIEN: Sure ... I mean ... it's over in ten minutes.
LUCINDA: Anyway ... What about this other one?
DAMIEN: What's a bungee jump?
LUCINDA: You don't know?
DAMIEN: That's why I'm asking.
LUCINDA: Well, it's a sort of ... you know ... it's when you tie a cord, kind of cord around your legs and then you jump off a bridge or something like that. It's kind of, you know, elastic.
DAMIEN: Gosh! What, like in Samoa, was it, when they used to do it? Um ... as a ... you know a ... a sort of coming-of-age ... initiation ceremony.
LUCINDA: This is the modern version ... you keep bouncing up and down ... it's much safer.
DAMIEN: Should hope so too.
LUCINDA: Modern technology.
DAMIEN: Well. You know, they seem just as bad as each other ...
LUCINDA: I'm not sure ... Snakes, brr... that's my absolute nightmare, I couldn't do that if you paid me, a million pounds.
DAMIEN: Just imagine them sliding and slithering all over ...
LUCINDA: Oh do shut up! No, the bungee jump, even though I'm terrified of heights.
DAMIEN: That's funny, I'm the complete opposite, I mean, I'd go for the snakes ...

2 Managing conversations

1 Divide the class into A/B pairs. Play the tape again and ask all the As to listen for *I mean* and all the Bs to listen for *you know*.

> **ANSWERS**
>
> I mean x 2
> you know x 6

2 Read through the explanation with the class. Explain the usefulness of this tactic in Paper 5 *(Speaking)*. Ask them when they might use the expressions (when they've forgotten or don't know an English word). Reassure students that the use of these 'fillers' is not 'bad English', they are used by native speakers very frequently.

3 Get the students started and provide a model by describing one or two objects yourself, e.g.
It's a kind of square, plastic thing ... you know ... when you want to put a program on your computer. It's a sort of method of storing information ... you know, it's metal, quite small ... (computer floppy disk)
It's a sort of truck, but it's much smaller ... I mean, it's bigger than a car, I suppose it's a kind of car ... you sort of use it to carry things, you know, plumbers and florists have them. (a van)

p.41 USE OF ENGLISH

Refer to the photo of the snake cage and the associated vocabulary. Ask the students to predict the reasons why the man was there. List any predictions on the board.
Ask the students to read through the text quickly to find out if their predictions were correct. (He did it to break the world record for living in a cage with poisonous snakes.) Introduce the cloze task, reminding the students that in the exam they will not have the box with jumbled words to help them.

> **ANSWERS**
>
> **1** had; **2** It; **3** fewer; **4** and; **5** whose; **6** able; **7** any; **8** them; **9** case; **10** already; **11** no; **12** instead; **13** was; **14** that; **15** a

p.41 VOCABULARY

Before attempting these three exercises, let students brainstorm all the different words coming from the root words *live/die*, and also any associated phrasal verbs and expressions. Put all correct ideas on the board and then let them attempt exercises 1–3.

> **1 ANSWERS**
>
> **1** alive; **2** life; **3** live; **4** lively; **5** life (time); **6** lives

> **2 ANSWERS**
>
> **1** dying; **2** deadly; **3** death; **4** dead; **5** deathly

> **3 ANSWERS**
>
> **1** dying for; **2** live on; **3** dying out; **4** live down; **5** life, death

A NARROW ESCAPE

p.42 FIRST THOUGHTS

In groups of four ask students to share any 'narrow escape' they may have had, **if they are happy to talk about it**, but there is no obligation.

p.42 LISTENING

This activity can be used as exam practice. Give the students a couple of minutes to read through the multiple-choice options before playing the tape. After the first playing allow them a minute to note their preliminary answers then play the tape again.

> **ANSWERS**
>
> **1** A; **2** C; **3** B; **4** B; **5** B; **6** A; **7** C; **8** C

TAPESCRIPT

1

NARRATOR: When the plane crashed all the lights went out. Everybody panicked, except Jemima Blond. Her years of training meant she could control her fear. She remembered her sergeant major's words, 'Crawl along the floor where the air is cleanest.' The terrorists stood up and fought for the exit, their screams turning to coughing and silence, while Blond was able to get out of the smoke-filled cabin. She got to the door, her lungs bursting, and with a mighty kick, managed to force it open. As she fell to the runway, the plane exploded above her.

2

NEWSREADER: The search is continuing for members of the capsized fishing boat. The Royal Navy has taken charge of the rescue operation and Sea King helicopters are combing the area. Lifeboat services from Sidmouth have already succeeded in rescuing nine of the crew but hope is fading fast for the remaining two. We will now go over to the village of Sidmouth for a live report from the centre of rescue operations.

3

MAN: Come on! Damn you Billy. Don't give up now, boy. The sheriff and his posse ain't that far behind. When Momma was dying I gave her my word that I'd take care of you and I ain't gonna break that promise.

There ain't no water here, but you'll be able to have all you can drink when we get somewhere safe. Come on, when you was a kid you could walk for miles. You can do it. We'll be at the hideout soon. On your feet, don't make me lose my temper.

4
WOMAN A: Yes ... yes ... anyway, this car, it just came from the middle of nowhere. It just smashed straight into my door, on the passenger's side.
WOMAN B: You poor things ...
WOMAN A: Jeremy didn't have time to react or avoid him ...
WOMAN B: And is he OK?
WOMAN A: He was shaken, that's all.
WOMAN B: And what about the other driver?
WOMAN A: He was angry but the police said it was definitely his fault. They gave him a formal warning that they are going to prosecute.

5
TEACHER: What do you mean, you weren't able to do it? Didn't we go through it last time? Look, we can find out the value of X in the first equation, like this, can't we? Stop looking out of the window and pay attention. That means we can put that value into the second equation to discover the value of Y. Simple! If you carry on like this, then I just don't know if you're going to make it ...

6
FATHER: Before you go off, I want a word with you. Whales, whales, whales ... that's all you think about.
SON: Dad ...
FATHER: You don't have to go to the other side of the world to find a good cause you know.
SON: Come on Dad ... What about the animals?
FATHER: I think you should spare a thought for some of the old people in this town and how they survive. If you really want to make a difference why don't you go and give old Mr Johnson a hand with the housework? I know that helping an old person isn't as romantic as saving the whales, but ...
SON: All right, all right, I don't want to have an argument about this.

7
DOCTOR: That's it. Now, roll the dummy onto its side. OK. Now what you have to do is check that the airway is clear. One of the problems is that people can sometimes choke 'cos they've swallowed their tongues, or false teeth and things ... so always make sure that you check that there aren't any obstructions. That's it ... don't worry, you can't hurt it ...

8
TV HOST: So now it gives me enormous pleasure to introduce my next guest whose recent book 'Without a Paddle' tells us about how an ordinary teacher survived when she just drifted for 43 days in an open boat, when most of us would have just given up. She had to come to terms with the fact that she might die there, thousands of miles from anywhere. So let's put our hands together and have a round of applause for the courageous and resourceful Kay Bradshaw.

p.42 LANGUAGE STUDY

Ability

1 Students work in pairs or small groups to find all the different expressions of ability and complete the *Language Study* activities.

> **ANSWERS**
>
> **Listening passage 1:**
> She *could* control ...
> Blond *was able to* get out ...
> ... *managed* to force it open
> **Listening passage 2:**
> They have *succeeded in* rescuing ...
> **Listening passage 3:**
> ... *you'll be able to* have ...
> ... you *could* walk for miles.
> You *can* do it.

2 We say Blond *was able to* get out because this describes the ability to do something on a particular occasion. *Could* describes a more general ability.

3 ANSWERS

manage is followed by the infinitive, e.g.
We managed to do it.
succeed is followed by *in* + verb + *-ing*, e.g.
We succeeded in doing it.

2 ANSWERS

1 A or B; **2** A or B; **3** B; **4** A; **5** A or B; **6** B; **7** B

p.43 VOCABULARY

Collocations

1 ANSWERS

a make; **b** take; **c** keep; **d** break; **e** lose; **f** give;
g pay; **h** have; **i** make; **j** have; **k** make; **l** come

ANSWERS

a 6; **b** 5; **c** 12; **d** 7; **e** 8; **f** 11; **g** 10;
h 2; **i** 4; **j** 9; **k** 1; **l** 3

2 Answers

1 Please pay attention to what I am about to say.
2 The boys were given a warning about playing by the lake.
3 Jenny had an argument with her mother about the wedding dress.
4 He succeeded in coming to terms with his wife's death.
5 I am going to lose my temper in a minute.
6 Unless you make more effort you'll fail.
7 It doesn't make any difference what they say.
8 She took charge of the business when her father retired.
9 I wasn't able to have a word with her.
10 We should never break a promise.

QUICK THINKING

p.44 FIRST THOUGHTS

Use the questions and the photograph as a lead-in to the topic of emergency rescue services. Elicit any personal experiences from the class. Ask the students to describe the photographs and check the following key vocabulary: *road accident, wreck/wreckage, victim, rescuer, resuscitation, lifesaver, dilemma*

p.44 READING

Ask the students to quickly read the text to find the sections which match the incidents in the pictures.

Introduce the gap-matching activity. This task type comes from Part 3 of Paper 1 *(Reading)* and was introduced in Unit 1, Coursebook page 16. As they have already read the text for general comprehension they can get straight on with the matching activity. As previously, get the students to compare answers in small groups and justify their choices by reference to the clues in the context.

Answers

1 C; 2 E; 3 D; 4 I; 5 F; 6 G; 7 B
A is the extra sentence.

p.45 LANGUAGE STUDY

Read through the explanation with the class. Point out the difference between the two emphatic constructions.
To emphasise a noun:
It is/was X who ... (for a person)
It is/was Y that ... (for a thing)
To emphasise a verb phrase:

What ... is/was that ...
Go through the first transformation sentence with the class:
He was rescued from the mountain by Caitlin.
We want to emphasise Caitlin so we say
It was Caitlin who rescued him from the mountain.
Point out that the subject *(He)* is now the object so it changes to *him*.
Students complete the remaining sentences.

Answers

1 It was Caitlin who rescued him.
2 What moved me was her act of courage.
3 It was her telephone call that raised the alarm.
4 What makes me angry is people who ignore weather warnings.
5 What took us all by surprise was his rescue.
6 It was (only) by chance that we found the missing sailor. OR It was the missing sailor who(m)/that we found by chance.

p.45 USE OF ENGLISH

1 Use the illustrations to elicit/check vocabulary: *dive, sky-diving, sky diver, parachute/chute, tackle, knock out.*
In pairs students cover the text and describe/predict what happened from the illustrations. After they have reported back their ideas allow them to check by reading the passage.

2 Answers

1 one; 2 it; 3 to; 4 to; 5 himself; 6 ✓; 7 him; 8 was; 9 of; 10 to; 11 the; 12 at; 13 ✓; 14 ✓; 15 of

p.45 WRITING

This can be set as homework. In preparation, ask each student to choose one of the incidents from the text or the illustrations. Put students into groups with classmates who made the same choice and give them a few minutes to brainstorm ideas for their report. If there is time they could make a joint plan for the composition.

4 Storytelling

BEDTIME STORIES

p.46 FIRST THOUGHTS

Get students to describe the illustration and then see how many of the stories are familiar to them. In small groups each student should try and recall one favourite story they remember being told as a child. In multilingual classes it can be interesting to see in what ways the same stories differ from country to country. The illustration shows, from left to right, Puss in Boots, Sleeping Beauty, Snow White and Tom Thumb.

p.46 LANGUAGE STUDY

Past tenses

1/2 Find out if anyone knows the story of Little Red Riding Hood and then ask them to summarise it for the class, with the other students adding anything that gets missed out or forgotten, or giving alternative versions. Then ask students to read the opening part of the story to see if there are any differences between the class version and the version in the book. When they have done this, students should find examples of the target tenses and in small groups try and analyse **why** each is used when it is. Then they should look through **2** to compare their ideas with the explanations given in the book. Allow time for discussion of any points which are not immediately clear.

3 In the same groups let students work together, applying the rules given in the Coursebook.

> **ANSWERS**
>
> **1** had been having; **2** had come; **3** didn't want; **4** was feeling; **5** smiled; **6** asked; **7** was going; **8** had never seen; **9** told; **10** lived; **11** had finished; **12** had already eaten; **13** was making up/had made up/made up; **14** heard; **15** hurried; **16** knew; **17** had been looking; **18** had disappeared; **19** thought; **20** made/was slowly making; **21** had had; **22** rushed/was rushing; **23** was; **24** had forgotten; **25** pretended; **26** opened

4 Monitor while this is being done, helping with vocabulary but, above all, checking the use of narrative tenses. At the end, let each group read out their ending to compare. (Tell students they do not have to keep to the original version but can create their own ending if they wish.)

Just to remind you how the story goes: Granny lets the wolf inside, the wolf eats her up and then gets into bed disguising itself as the old lady. Little Red Riding Hood arrives to find 'Granny' lying in bed. 'Granny' says she's unwell and asks the girl to get into bed with her. In the English version their dialogue goes:

'Granny, what big ears you've got.'
'All the better to hear you with, my child.'
'Granny, what big eyes you've got.'
'All the better to see you with.'
'Granny, what big teeth you've got.'
'All the better to gobble you up!'

Here the English version of the story ends, but for those of a sensitive disposition you could add that two hunters/woodcutters see the wolf later that day and slay it. When they open the creature up, they find the girl and her grandmother inside none the worse for wear!

p.47 VOCABULARY

1 Students can link the words and expressions according to various criteria. For example:

- words which appear in the same fairy story
  (e.g. a beanstalk, a giant; a genie, a flying carpet, to grant a wish)
- words which describe opposites
  (e.g. cast a spell, break a spell; hero, villain.)
- words which describe people
  (e.g. hero and heroine, evil queen, a handsome prince)
- words which are often linked in a sentence
  (e.g. the witch turned the handsome prince into a frog)

2 In groups, students tell each other a traditional story from their own country using the vocabulary in **1**. Monitor, making sure the correct tenses are used.

VERSIONS

p.48 FIRST THOUGHTS

Get the students to choose a fairy story and work on it in groups. How would they change it to make it more modern? Encourage the students to think of alternatives to the 'magic' ingredients listed in the Coursebook. Bright students will probably point out that many of today's films and novels have plots based on traditional fantasy tales. They may be aware of the widely held view that these stories encapsulate many of the dilemmas and issues which face all human beings – one of the reasons why they exist in so many cultures.

As an introduction to the listening passage ask students in pairs to try and recall the story of Cinderella. If anyone does not know the story, put them in a group with someone who does and who can explain it to them.

p.48 LISTENING

An alternative Cinderella

This activity introduces the task type found in Part 2 of Paper 4 *(Listening)*. In the exam the task may be note-taking, blank-filling or sentence-completion. In each case one word or a short phrase is all that is required. Remind students of the exam technique of reading through the prompts before listening (time is allowed for this in the exam), making a preliminary guess at the answer – this helps to 'focus the ears' when listening.
After the first listening students should compare answers with a partner before listening again to check.

> **ANSWERS**
>
> **1** a clothes shop; **2** finance the setting-up of a hamburger restaurant; **3** find a wife and settle down; **4** FG; **5** charm course; **6** dress up, go to the ball and be photographed; **7** he was almost bankrupt and he wanted to find a millionaire's daughter for his son; **8** re-organising his kitchens, opening the palace to the public, etc.; **9** a financial adviser; **10** getting him to cut down on his drinking and involving him in social work.

TAPESCRIPT

NARRATOR: Once upon a time there were three sisters who lived with their widowed father. The two eldest ran a beauty parlour and a clothes shop. They were both interested in finding a rich husband. The youngest daughter, whose name was Cinderella, looked after the house. Her father had refused to set her up in business as he wanted someone to look after him. Cinderella did not mind too much as she was doing a correspondence course in accountancy and marketing.

One day Cinderella decided to enter a competition in a woman's magazine because it offered some good cash prizes. If she won one of them, it would help her finance the setting up of her own hamburger restaurant. Around that time the newspapers were full of stories about a big party that was going to be held at the palace. It was said that the prince, a real playboy, wanted to find a wife and settle down. From the moment they heard about the ball, the two eldest sisters spent days and days trying to make themselves look beautiful. As for Cinderella, she wondered what all the fuss was about and didn't have the slightest interest in going to the ball.

One morning, while she was doing some work for her accountancy course, there was a knock at the door. She opened it and saw an extraordinary woman standing there with a ridiculous-looking tiara on her head. The woman, who called herself Fairy Godmother or FG for short, told Cinderella that she'd won first prize in the magazine competition she'd entered. The prize was a 'charm course' worth hundreds of pounds as well as books and records. Cinderella wasn't really that keen on doing the course but she realised she could probably make a small profit if she sold the prizes. However, in return for the prizes she would have to dress up in lots of fine clothes and be driven to the palace where she'd spend the night at the ball and be photographed for the woman's magazine. The big day arrived and a shiny Rolls Royce came to pick her up. The man from the car hire firm said he was only on duty until midnight. Moments later a woman arrived bringing a fur coat and a diamond necklace which would be Cinderella's just for the evening. When she turned up at the palace, she noticed that one of the servants was stealing food from the buffet tables. The palace itself was cold and draughty and the king himself was a man with a sad smile. Cinderella felt sorry for the man and told him why the food was disappearing so fast. The king then told her about his financial problems. He was almost bankrupt and he had organised the party in the hope that he might find a millionaire's daughter for his son. Cinderella suggested lots of ways of making money: reorganising the kitchens, opening the palace to the public and so on.

By this time it had turned midnight. The car hire firm drove away and the woman came to collect her fur coat and necklace. The king showed Cinderella around the palace and they eventually came back to the ballroom where the party was still going on. The prince, who by this time was hopelessly drunk, took one look at Cinderella and asked her to dance. She kicked off her glass slippers, which were killing her, and joined him on the dance floor. Soon afterwards, she left the palace and hitch-hiked home.

The following day the newspapers were full of the big story about the prince who had fallen for a beautiful and mysterious woman who had disappeared. Her glass slippers, which she had left behind, were the only clues that would lead him to her. When Cinderella read the news, she was absolutely furious. Nevertheless, she saw quite a bit of the prince because she started work at the palace as financial advisor. In no time at all the palace was making a profit again. Naturally, Cinderella refused to marry the prince but she did help him cut down on his drinking and involved him in useful social work in the community.

p.48 PRONUNCIATION

Past tenses

1 Regular verbs in the past

First let students predict in which columns the verbs belong and then listen to the cassette.

ANSWERS

/d/	/t/	/ɪd/
stayed	asked	waited
carried	promised	invited
contained		decided
frightened		

2 *was* and *were*

1/2 Go over parts **1** and **2** in open class. The stressed words would probably be: *lovely, spring, morning, sun, shining, birds, singing. Was/were* are unstressed.

3 Let them predict the pronunciation of *was/were* before listening. Then listen to check.

TAPESCRIPT AND ANSWERS

MAN: Where were you last night?
(weak)
WOMAN: I was at the office.
(weak)
MAN: Were you?
(strong)
WOMAN: Yes, I was. I was working late.
(strong/weak)
MAN: You were with Paul!
(weak)
WOMAN: No, I wasn't.
(strong)
MAN: Yes, you were.
(strong)

4 Get students to act out the dialogue – once or twice with scripts and then without, encouraging them each to sound as outraged as possible!

p.48 LANGUAGE STUDY

After and *afterwards*

Read through the examples and explanation with the class. Use a time line on the board to clarify the sequence if necessary, e.g.
He rescued the princess after killing the dragon,

Using the events from the Cinderella story, elicit further examples from the class, e.g.
She danced with the prince, and after that she hitch-hiked home.

p.49 WRITING

A narrative is often included as one of the four choices in Part 2 of Paper 2 *(Writing)*. Students will be given an explanatory rubric and should write between 120 and 180 words. The first or last sentence of the compostion is often given to the candidates rather than a title.

1 Focus students' attention on the illustration and give them two to three minutes to discuss it in pairs. Then elicit one sentence of description from each pair, helping them with vocabulary as the need arises. Particularly encourage students to predict who the man is, what he is doing and why. Students then read the story to check their ideas and decide on an appropriate title. If they have any problems with vocabulary, make sure they attempt to deduce the meaning of words from context before consulting dictionaries or you.

2 Brainstorm in open class ways of making the story more interesting. Put on the blackboard vocabulary elicited from the class which may be useful. In addition, these words and phrases will help them:
just then, one day, that afternoon, many years ago, when, while, as, so, before.
Having given time for students in groups to expand the story, put up each version on the walls of the classroom and let students move around and read them.

> **An expanded version of Brave Gelert**
> This story is set, many years ago, in Wales, in the Middle Ages. At this time, towards the south of the kingdom, there was a prince whose name was Llewellyn. The prince was a tall, powerfully-built young man with long black hair and an equally black moustache. He was well known in the area for his generosity but he also had a reputation for behaving rather impetuously at times. The prince lived in a long fertile green valley which had large forests on both sides extending for many miles in each direction. He lived there with the daughter of a local chief whom he had had the good fortune to marry two years before. She had recently had a beautiful baby boy who was now the pride and joy of the young prince. Of scarcely less importance to the prince was his dog, Gelert, a great shaggy Irish wolfhound. The prince had found him wounded and starving in a nearby forest five years before, and since then the dog had been his constant companion.
> One day, shortly after sunrise, the prince decided to go hunting, leaving Gelert to look after the baby. However, while he was away, one of the many ferocious packs of wolves who roamed the land in search of food and were the terror of the area, came out of a nearby wood and ran towards the small wooden cottage where the baby was sleeping. Gelert, however, saw them coming and managed to hide the baby. Having done this, he ran outside and fought the wolves, killing two of them but being wounded in the process. Finally the wolves ran off and Gelert, exhausted from the fight, lay down to sleep. When Llewellyn returned, in the late afternoon, the first thing he saw was the sleeping dog covered in blood.

> On entering the cottage he also saw that his son's cot was empty and so in a fit of rage he took his sword and, with a mighty stroke, cut the dog in half while he slept. Just then, he heard the cry of a baby and discovered the hidden child. As he was picking up the infant he happened to notice the two dead wolves lying outside the cottage and then he understood what had really happened.
> Full of sadness and remorse for what he had done, he carried Gelert through the howling wind and pouring rain to the highest hill in the region and buried him, placing a pile of stones on the spot to mark the position of the grave.
> The spot has survived the test of time and you can still see the pile of stones to this day.
>
> © Copyright Longman Group UK Ltd. 1989

p.49 USE OF ENGLISH

1 Students read the story quickly for general understanding. Elicit suggestions for a title, e.g. *The Manufactured Myth*.

2 As examination practice, students should work individually. However, once they have completed the multiple choice task they should compare answers in groups – justifying their decisions by reference to the text.

ANSWERS

1 D; **2** B; **3** A; **4** C; **5** D; **6** C; **7** D; **8** B; **9** A; **10** D; **11** A; **12** A; **13** C; **14** C; **15** B

Extension
As a homework exercise students could write about famous modern myths (the Loch Ness monster, the Yeti, the Big Foot, etc.), or even invent a myth of their own.

RAGS TO RICHES, RICHES TO RAGS

p.50 FIRST THOUGHTS

If students can't think of any examples ask them to brainstorm the ways in which people can get rich, e.g. discover treasure, marry someone rich, make money from trade; this should spark off some ideas.

p.50 READING

Students read the story quickly in order to sort out the picture sequence. Also ask them to report back on whether their predictions about the story were correct. Then answer the questions.

ANSWER

C, G, I, F, J, H, E, A, D, B
(Students may decide on a slightly different order and should be encouraged to do so if they can justify this from the text.)

ANSWERS

1 C; **2** B; **3** A; **4** C; **5** C; **6** C; **7** D

p.52 WRITING

Understanding style

1 ANSWERS

his – the captain's
he – the captain
there – the palace
where – the dining room
they – the king and the guests
their – the king's and the guests'
royal host – the king
guest who – the captain
him – the king
good man – the king
sailor – the captain
Dick's pet – the cat
one – a cat
creature – the cat
The writer avoids repeating himself by using pronouns, relative pronouns, replacement nouns and possessive adjectives.

2 Students begin by underlining all the instances of the four words in the text. Ask them to refer back to exercise 1 for ideas on substitute words, e.g.
princess: she, her (students can give her a name), *beautiful girl*
pond: there, pool of water, that place
frog: the creature, the animal, him, he
witch: enemy, her
Students work individually to rewrite the story. When they finish read out versions from different students and discuss in open class any instances where pronoun substitution leads to confusion or lack of clarity.

A rewritten version of *The Princess and the Frog* story

Once upon a time there was a beautiful young princess who happened to be out walking through some woods. Suddenly she saw a frog in a pond. A little distance away she also noticed a large and magnificent castle. At that moment the small green creature spoke to the young woman. She was quite astonished, not being accustomed to hearing animals speak!

Anyway, every day she went to the same small pool of water to talk to her new-found friend. Gradually, after many months of this, Esmeralda, for that was her name, discovered that she had fallen in love with the frog. One day, during one of their regular chats, the frog ventured to ask his beautiful companion for a kiss. Hiding her disgust at the thought, she bent down to do as he asked. At that moment he was suddenly transformed into the most handsome prince Esmeralda had ever had the good fortune to come across. It turned out that a witch had cast a spell on him and taken his castle, where she now lived.

Having been released from the spell, the prince went up to the castle and killed his hideous enemy. He then went back to find Esmeralda whom he married shortly after. Needless to say, they lived happily ever after!

© Copyright Longman Group UK Ltd. 1989

p.52 VOCABULARY

Time expressions

ANSWERS

1 while; 2 during; 3 at the end; 4 for; 5 previously; 6 eventually; 7 Whenever; 8 In the meantime; 9 until; 10 afterwards; 11 in the end; 12 before

Phrasal verbs

1 ANSWERS

A 7; B 6; C 4; D 8; E 11; F 9; G 3; H 10; I 1; J 5 (This generally suggests a good relationship with someone.) K 12; L 2

2 ANSWERS

1 find out; 2 came across; 3 told ... off; 4 took ... in; 5 get on with; 6 putting ... off; 7 fell for; 8 put up with; 9 turned down; 10 looked after; 11 turned up; 12 set off

3 This could be done as homework.

p.53 LANGUAGE STUDY

1 Transitive and intransitive verbs

Clearly learners can't consciously think about the grammar of phrasal verbs every time they wish to use one or meet one in a text. Indeed, phrasal verbs can be acquired without any kind of formal conscious understanding of how they function. However, it can be useful to know something of the rules governing the use of both standard and phrasal verbs when it comes to the First Certificate examination and, in particular, in order to understand why some answers are right and others wrong in Part 1 of Paper 1.

1/2 Put the following on the board:
Anne likes.
Anne likes John.
The sun rose.
The sun rose the sky.
He understood.
He understood her.

Ask students to decide which of these sentences are possible and which are not and why. Then ask them to read the explanation in numbers 1 and 2, and do the task in number 3.

3 ANSWERS

rise I; raise T; thank T; understand I, T; go I; see I, T; open I, T; laugh I; arrive I
(Note that some verbs can be used either transitively or intransitively.)

2 Exploring the grammar of phrasal verbs

ANSWERS

1/2
A
a correct; b wrong; c correct
Turn up meaning *arrive* is intransitive. In other words it cannot take an object. *Late for everything* is a complement which finishes off the sentence, but it is not an object.
B
a wrong; b correct; c correct; d wrong; e correct
The rule one can work out from this is that *tell off* is transitive. What's more, sentences c and e show that it is separable. In other words, an object can be placed between the verb and its particle. The difficulty here is that if a pronoun is used, it must be placed between the verb and particle and not at the end.
Tell off is transitive and separable.

C

a wrong; b correct; c wrong; d correct; e wrong

Sentence a) is wrong so this tells us that *look after* is transitive; in other words, it must have an object. The other sentences show us that the noun or pronoun has to follow the phrasal verb and that the verb and its particle cannot be split. *Look after* is transitive but inseparable.

D

a wrong; b wrong; c correct; d correct

Three-part phrasal verbs are always transitive and inseparable.

If some students find this activity rather difficult, make sure that they get the basic message: **the most important thing you have to discover when you meet a new phrasal verb is whether it is possible to separate the verb and the particle.** One useful tip for remembering this is to always use a pronoun object when recording new phrasal verbs, e.g. *turn sth up   tell sb off   look after sb   get on with sth*

3 On examining the entry for *turn up*, students will notice that not only does it have a number of different meanings, but that its grammar may vary too. Ask students to write one more example sentence for each of the meanings. These should also exemplify the grammar rules, so make sure that students use an object whenever possible, splitting the verb and particle if this is possible.

p.54 LISTENING

Students read through the eleven statements before listening. Explain the three choices of *true*, *false* and *not stated*.

ANSWERS

1 F; 2 NS; 3 T; 4 F; 5 F; 6 T; 7 T; 8 F; 9 NS; 10 NS; 11 F

TAPESCRIPT

In the 1190s in the port of La Rochelle on the west coast of France, there lived a merchant called Alexandre Aufredi and his wife Pernelle. Although Aufredi was a successful man, he was dissatisfied. There were two main reasons for this: firstly he was proud and stubborn and next he wanted to become the most important merchant in his town. He dreamed of the fortune that could be made by trading over the ocean. Against the advice of his more cautious friends he decided on a risky venture. First of all he had four strong ships built and loaded them with goods that could be exchanged or bartered. Then he chose his most trusted steward to accompany the fleet which sailed away with much ceremony. He kept some money so he and his wife could live comfortably until the ships returned. At first, Aufredi continued to be well-regarded, but as time went on he was forced to borrow money.

Two, three, four years went by and still the ships had not returned. In the meantime, Aufredi's money had run out. Finally, a rumour started that the ships had been lost and all his creditors rushed to get their money back. The good man was forced to sell his house and Pernelle sold her rings and jewels one by one until, finally, they were forced to beg.

After seven years a small fleet of boats carrying gold and precious wood sailed into the port. At last Aufredi's fleet had returned! Many people had even forgotten about Aufredi's existence but he was eventually discovered begging in a church doorway. The steward – for this was the mystery stranger – could hardly believe that the silver-haired beggar dressed in rags had once been his proud master. Yet Alexandre and Pernelle's suffering had not been for nothing for in the end Aufredi was suddenly, by far, the wealthiest man in La Rochelle.

The news that Aufredi and his wife were now incredibly rich quickly spread like wildfire. However, the couple resisted the well-wishes of their old friends. Instead, they gave most of their fortune to the poor of the city. At the end of his life, Aufredi set up a foundation whose charitable work continued into the twentieth century.

p.55 LANGUAGE STUDY

1 Students underline the expressions in the tapescript. Elicit and write them on the board.
- put events in order:
  firstly   next   first of all   then   first in the meantime   finally   after seven years   at last in the end   now   at the end (of his life)
- Use a form/expression based on *first/last*:
  firstly   first of all   first   at last

2 Students should look at the context of some of the words in the tapescript in addition to the examples in the Coursebook to help them answer the questions.

ANSWERS

a At first: first impressions
b firstly: reasons
c First of all: instructions

3 ANSWERS

a In the end: suggests something happened after a lot of other actions
b at the end: describes the finish of an event
c Finally: introduces a last point
d at last: suggests something happened after a long time

> **4 ANSWERS**
>
> 1 *First of all* hold the racquet and ball together. *Then* throw the ball, bringing the racquet behind your head. *Afterwards*, throw your body forward. *After* hitting the ball, follow through. *Finally*, prepare yourself for the return.
> 2 Last month I went to my first football match. *At first* I thought I wasn't going to like it. However, *after* ten minutes I started to enjoy it. The other team scored *first* but *afterwards* we scored twice. Unfortunately *after* we had scored our best player was injured and *in the end* we lost.

5 The purpose of these tasks is to practise using the expressions, so check that students include two or three in each part. They can also use the other sequencing words extracted from the tapescript in exercise 1. If students need help put these prompts on the board:
- reasons/TV: *firstly, secondly, finally*
- instructions: *first, then, next, after that, afterwards, at the end*
- describe a journey: *at first, afterwards, in the end*
- revised impressions: *at first, but, then, in the end*

TALL TALES

p.56 FIRST THOUGHTS

Elicit further unlikely (but plausible) excuses, e.g. *"I left it on the bus,"* *"My sister took my file/book by mistake."*

p.56 LISTENING

A tall story

1 In pairs or small groups students think of ways of linking the three items. Encourage them to be as imaginative as possible. After sharing their stories and reporting back to you, put on the board brief details of the most amusing scenarios. Play the tape; students compare the story with their predictions, explaining any differences.

2 Students read through the questions before listening again. They may be able to answer some of the questions immediately.

> **ANSWERS**
>
> 1B (... *not another one of your stories.*)
> 2C (... *the cat asleep in the driveway.*)
> 3A (... *she can't put it in the dustbin 'cause the kids might see. You see, she thinks her friend will have some clever idea about what to do with the cat.*)
> 4A (... *into the department store where she's meeting her friend.*)
> 5B (*she hears this scream ... this middle-aged woman ... she'd fainted*)

TAPESCRIPT

CAROL: I heard this wonderful story the other day which I must tell you.
ARTHUR: Oh my god, not another one of your stories.
CAROL: You're going to hear it anyway, so ...
ARTHUR: Go on then, I'm all ears.
CAROL: Well, you see there's this woman and she's driving off to meet a friend in town one day. She's in a bit of a hurry and she doesn't notice the cat asleep in the driveway. Anyway, you can guess what happens next.
ARTHUR: I think I can, yes.
CAROL: She's backing out of the driveway when she hears this little cry as she goes over something.
ARTHUR: The cat.
CAROL: Right first time.
ARTHUR: Go on.
CAROL: Anyway, so she gets out of the car and sees the cat lying there stone dead. And she doesn't know what to do. She's already late for her meeting with her friend and she's thinking 'Where am I going to put Java?'
ARTHUR: What's Java?
CAROL: Oh, Java's the name of the cat. Well, she can't leave it there and she can't put it in the dustbin 'cos the kids might see. Anyway, to cut a long story short, she looks in the car and sees this plastic bag from a rather smart department store.
ARTHUR: I don't believe a word of this.
CAROL: No, it's all true. Cross my heart. So she puts the cat in the bag and drives off to meet her friend. Well, when she's parked the car, she decides to take the bag with her into the department store where she's meeting her friend. You see, she thinks her friend will have some clever idea about what to do with the cat.
ARTHUR: You've got to be kidding!
CAROL: No, no. She goes into the shop, oh, and spots a rather nice-looking handbag on the counter and puts down the plastic bag for a sec to have a quick look at it. Can you guess what happens next?
ARTHUR: No. I hate to think.
CAROL: She puts the handbag down and looks for the plastic bag. It's gone, of course. And just then, she hears this scream and commotion out in the street. She goes to the door and sees this middle-aged woman lying in the street – she'd fainted – with the plastic bag with poor old Java in it beside her on the

pavement. You see, she was a shoplifter and when she'd got outside, she hadn't been able to resist having a peep at what was inside the bag.
ARTHUR: Ridiculous. Still, it makes a good story.

p.56 WRITING

The narrative composition

1 A narrative compostion is usually included as one of the four choices in Part 2 of Paper 2 *(Writing)*. Students will have about 45 minutes and are expected to produce between 120 and 180 words.

Get students to brainstorm what they think they should aim to do in writing a good narrative composition. Put the list on the board and then ask students to compare their ideas with the seven points of advice in the Coursebook.

2 ANSWERS

1 three: past simple, past perfect, past continuous
2 use of sequencing words: *when, as, after*; use of tense to show sequence, e.g. past simple and past perfect
3 use of adverbs and adjectives: *snowing hard, freezing cold, clean and respectable*
4 Yes, for example the use of phrasal verbs: *held up, pulled up, drove off, found out*; the use of expressions: *we could hardly believe our luck, needless to say.*

p.57 WRITING

Begin by getting students to describe the pictures. Use this to elicit useful vocabulary and write it on the board, e.g. *secondhand bookshop, alley, bundle, moped, mannequin.* In small groups, students sort out the pictures into two stories. There are eight pictures for each story. Check that they have chosen the right pictures before they begin sequencing them.

Students then work out the order of the pictures. Move students between groups to compare ideas and if they are struggling help them by giving the first and last picture of each story. When they are ready ask them to report back to the class with their stories. To make this more interesting you can elicit one sentence or 'paragraph' from each group in turn, building up the story picture by picture. Check for the use of sequencing words and correct tenses.

ANSWERS

| STORY A: | 8 | 5 | 13 | 3 | 11 | 2 | 16 | 6 |
| STORY B: | 14 | 1 | 12 | 4 | 9 | 10 | 7 | 15 |

This can be set as homework.

ACCENT AND CLASS

p.58 FIRST THOUGHTS

Begin by asking students if they can distinguish any accents in English. Students can usually spot the difference between American and British pronunciation, for instance. Demonstrate if necessary. Ask them if there are geographical accents in their language(s). Students often enjoy demonstrating these to their classmates. Encourage the class to discuss any social prejudices which exist in connection with accent (in some cultures this is more associated with vocabulary and grammar than with pronunciation).

Read through the questions and elicit responses. Demonstrate some cockney pronunciations/slang, e.g. *apples and pears = stairs, plates of meat = feet!*

p.58 USE OF ENGLISH

1 This section focuses attention on the meaning of the summary.

ANSWERS

1 Eliza Doolittle is a cockney flower seller who wants to get a job in a flower shop.
2 She thinks Professor Higgins will teach her to speak correct English.
3 Higgins is a phonetician who takes Eliza on for a bet.
4 Eliza develops into a woman of beauty, sensitivity and good manners who achieves a sense of her own self-worth.

2 Get students to consider the **type of word** and decide if it has **a positive or negative meaning** before they attempt the gap-filling task. They can compare their ideas in small groups; check these before setting the gap-filling task.

ANSWERS

1 *noun* transformation
2 *noun* pronunciation
3 *noun (negative)* arrogance
4 *nouns* friendship
5 *adjective (negative)* ashamed
6 *adjective (negative)* ungrammatical
7 *adverb (negative)* rudely
8 *adjective* irresistable
9 *adverb (positive)* successfully
10 *noun (positive)* beauty
11 *noun* treatment
12 *adjective (negative)* intolerable
13 *adverb (negative)* shamefully
14 *noun (positive)* freedom
15 *adjective* various
16 *adjective* musical
17 *adjective* interested
18 *adjective* classical

p.59 LISTENING

As preparation for the listening passage, get students to describe the picture in detail. They should identify the characters (Eliza, Higgins, etc.) and predict what they are going to hear. Students read through the multiple choice questions before listening. Play the tape twice if necessary.

ANSWERS

1 C; 2 C; 3 A; 4 B; 5 B

TAPESCRIPT

MRS PEARCE: A young woman asks to see you, sir.
HIGGINS: A young woman! What does she want?
MRS PEARCE: Well, sir, she says you'll be glad to see her when you know what she's come about. She's quite a common girl, sir. Very common indeed. I should have sent her away, only I thought perhaps you wanted her to talk into your machines. I hope I've not done wrong; but really you see such queer people sometimes – you'll excuse me, I'm sure, sir –
HIGGINS: Oh, that's all right, Mrs Pearce. Has she an interesting accent?
MRS PEARCE: Oh, something dreadful, sir, really. I don't know how you can take an interest in it.
HIGGINS: Let's have her up. Show her up, Mrs Pearce.
MRS PEARCE: Very well, sir. It's for you to say.
HIGGINS: This is rather a bit of luck. I'll show you how I make records. We'll set her talking; and I'll take it down in broad Romic; and then we'll get her on the phonograph so that you can turn her on as often as you like with the written transcript before you.
MRS PEARCE: This is the young woman, sir.
HIGGINS: Why, this is the girl I jotted down last night! She's no use. I've got all I want of the Lisson Grove lingo, and I'm not going to waste another cylinder on it. Be off with you, I don't want you.
THE FLOWER GIRL: Don't you be so saucy. You ain't heard what I come for yet. Did you tell him I come in a taxi?
MRS PEARCE: Nonsense, girl! What do you think a gentleman like Mr Higgins cares what you came in?
THE FLOWER GIRL: Oh, we are proud! He ain't above giving lessons, not him, I heard him say so. Well, I ain't come here to ask for any compliment; and if my money's not good enough, I can go elsewhere.
HIGGINS: Good enough for what?
THE FLOWER GIRL: Good enough for you. Now you know, don't you? I'm coming to have lessons I am. And to pay for 'em too; make no mistake.
HIGGINS: Well!!! What do you expect me to say to you?
THE FLOWER GIRL: Well, if you was a gentleman, you might ask me to sit down, I think. Don't I tell you I'm bringing you business?
HIGGINS: Pickering, shall we ask this baggage to sit down, or shall we throw her out of the window?
THE FLOWER GIRL: Ah-ah-oh-ow-ow-ow-oo! I won't be called a baggage when I've offered to pay like any lady.
PICKERING: But what is it you want?
THE FLOWER GIRL: I want to be a lady in a flower shop 'stead of sellin' at the corner of Tottenham Court Road. But they won't take me unless I can talk more genteel. He said he could teach me. Well, here I am ready to pay him – not asking any favour – and he treats me 'zif I was dirt.
MRS PEARCE: How can you be such a foolish, ignorant girl as to think you could afford to pay Mr Higgins?
THE FLOWER GIRL: Why shouldn't I? I know what lessons cost as well as you do, and I'm ready to pay.

p.59 USE OF ENGLISH

ANSWERS

1 a; 2 you; 3 the; 4 very; 5 a; 6 yet; 7 ✓;
8 had; 9 of; 10 been; 11 me; 12 am; 13 ✓;
14 feelings; 15 ✓

p.59 WRITING

This type of composition often comes up as one of the four choices in Part 2 of Paper 2 *(Writing)*. Before they start ask the class to cover the list in the Coursebook and work out a list of the contents of a review using the *Pygmalion* text as a model. Point out that in the review the past tense is used to describe the particular performance seen by the reviewer, whereas the present tense is used for more general comments on the play.

One way to prepare for the writing task is to divide students into groups which have seen the same play or film recently. Each group can then brainstorm answers to the suggested points in the Coursebook and together think about how to organise the review.

The writing of the review itself should be done individually and can be set as homework.

5 A Sense of Adventure

THE BEST OF TIMES?

p.60 FIRST THOUGHTS

Get students to describe each photograph and the type of holiday it illustrates. The photographs show the following:

> **ANSWERS**
>
> Package holiday
> Camping holiday
> Adventure holiday/Activity holiday
> Seaside holiday
> Sailing holiday

Get students to talk about their own experiences and use the opportunity to elicit useful 'holiday' vocabulary.

p.60 LISTENING

1 The students should listen and answer the gist question only. They are talking about picture 4 (seaside holiday).

2 Managing conversations
Play the tape again for students to write in the missing lines. Play the tape twice or stop at intervals if necessary. Check their answers (in bold type below) then ask them to discuss the two questions. In addition to noticing the phrases Amanda uses, the class will probably comment on her use of intonation to show enthusiasm and interest. Play the tape again and ask students to repeat Amanda's responses. Drill the phrases until the class is able to imitate the intonation patterns convincingly.

> **TAPESCRIPT AND ANSWERS**
>
> AMANDA: So **(1) which one is your favourite,** Martin?
> MARTIN: The one of the seaside holiday and the Punch and Judy show.
> AMANDA: **(2) Oh really, why's that?**
> MARTIN: Well, I suppose it reminds me of when I was a child.
> AMANDA: **(3) So what you're saying is** you used to have holidays like this.
> MARTIN: That's right, and me and my sisters used to play on the beach.
> AMANDA: **(4) And what kind of thing did you do?**
> MARTIN: You know, make sandcastles, that sort of thing and hunt for crabs.
> AMANDA: **(5) Hunt for crabs?**
> MARTIN: Yeah, there were lots of rock pools where they used to live.
> AMANDA: **(6) Oh, sounds brilliant.**
> MARTIN: Yes, it was.

- **How does she get Martin to do most of the talking?**
She asks lots of questions:
why's that?
what kind of thing did you do?
She re-phrases his answers and/or makes them into questions:
you used to have holidays like this.
Hunt for crabs?
- **How does she show that she is a good listener?**
She uses expressions to show interest:
Oh really ...
That sounds like fun!
She repeats or re-phrases what he says:
So what you're saying is you used to have holidays like this.
Hunt for crabs?

p.60 SPEAKING

1/2 Divide the class into pairs for this activity. If possible get students to work with a partner they don't usually sit next to. Check that there are no difficulties with the listed vocabulary before pairs begin their conversations. Monitor and check that students are able to use the listener tactics highlighted in the previous section. If there are problems, demonstrate by holding an example conversation with a student in front of the class.

p.61 VOCABULARY

> **ANSWERS**
>
> 1 brochure; 2 package tour; 3 safari; 4 souvenirs;
> 5 charter; 6 resort; 7 half board; 8 self-catering

Extension
Students consider these questions in groups.
- Do you like package tours or do you find them restrictive?
- Have you ever been on a safari? Would you like to go on one? Why/Why not?
- Do you generally bring back souvenirs from holidays? If so, what kind of things? What is your most interesting souvenir?
- Have you ever been on a self-catering holiday? If not, would you like to? Do you think it would be too much hard work?

p.61 USE OF ENGLISH

1 Students quickly read the passage to answer the gist question.

> **ANSWER**
>
> The children might, but their parents probably wouldn't.

2 Answers

1 but; 2 of; 3 from; 4 to; 5 much; 6 such; 7 enough; 8 ✓ Note: although 'ourselves' is not wrong, it is more usual to omit it; 9 was; 10 ✓; 11 he; 12 a; 13 of; 14 else; 15 about; 16 ✓

p.61 WRITING

Unless your students have been on holiday together they will not be able to do this activity in groups. It can be done either as examination practice or set as homework. If you want it to be exam practice you should allow 45 minutes and ask the students to write between 120 and 180 words. Before setting the task get the students to match the list of points with the relevant sections in the model. Highlight the use of tenses and adjectives in the model.

WHAT A NIGHTMARE!

p.62 FIRST THOUGHTS

The questions can be used as a basis for brainstorming positive and negative features. An effective way to help students organise their thoughts is to draw a chart on the board and ask the students to copy it, e.g.:

	POSITIVE	NEGATIVE
Organised tour		
Independent travel		

p.62 LISTENING

Get students to read through the summary sentences before they listen. After the first listening students can compare with a partner. Play the tape again for them to check. (In the exam the listening passages are heard twice). After checking the answers ask the students to explain the type of holiday described by each speaker and then compare the comments on tape with their ideas from the *First Thoughts* activity.

Note: If you prefer the class to begin with a gist listening task you could ask them to listen and find the names of three cities mentioned on the tape – the answers are *Bombay, London* and *Petra*.

ANSWERS

Speaker 1 F; Speaker 2 D; Speaker 3 A; Speaker 4 E; Speaker 5 B. C is the extra sentence.

TAPESCRIPT

SPEAKER 1: All in all it was fantastic. The only thing is that I was terribly ill in Bombay for a while. You know, stomach trouble. If you go, you mustn't drink anything straight from the tap. I'd been incredibly careful but I think it was the ice cubes in one of the drinks I had that must have done it. I was totally helpless for two days. It's a good job I was on an organised tour. Jackie, the guide, was amazing, she was just so helpful. She'd seen it all before she said.

SPEAKER 2: Oh, we had an absolutely wonderful time; the weather was fantastic, really mild. I needn't have taken half my clothes. It was nice going out of season 'cos there were hardly any other tourists there. We didn't need to book, we just turned up. We bought a couple of guide books before we went. This one was completely hopeless, you know, out of date and inaccurate. This one, Roper's guide, was invaluable. I don't know what we'd have done without it.

SPEAKER 3: Well, I took plenty of cash, US dollars, with me. At the airport there's this sign which says you have to declare all your foreign currency and change a lot at the official rate. It's one of those things you're supposed to do but nobody in their right mind takes any notice. I got twice as much as the official rate on the black market. Don't bother to take one of the official guides either, they're a complete waste of time and unhelpful, all they're interested in is getting hold of your hard currency. Don't change too much into local money either, it's completely worthless outside the country.

SPEAKER 4: What a difficult lot. I told them, I said you must be here in the lobby by seven o'clock. I was hopeful we could make a quick getaway. We were going to the Tower of London. That was the first stop. You know what it's like when you get there. They all want to see the priceless crown jewels. Sometimes people have to wait an hour to get in. Anyway, I also warned them about not leaving anything valuable lying around. You know what it's like with thieves and pickpockets about. Well, to cut a long story short, it was a disaster from start to finish.

SPEAKER 5: You need to go there to really appreciate it. The people are lovely, really friendly and hospitable. The couriers took really good care of us. You don't have to worry about anything. But for me the highlight of the trip was the visit to Petra. I must get the pictures developed. It was a long way to go but one of the most worthwhile things I've ever done. The temples and buildings are just cut into the rock, you know. Incredible. One thing is, if you go, you should take some warm clothing. You wouldn't think it, being in the desert and everything, but it gets bitterly cold at night. I was frozen but I managed to buy a jumper at a street market.

p.62 VOCABULARY

Get students to find and underline the words in the tapescript. Ask them to list them under two headings: *positive* and *negative*.

ANSWERS

Positive: helpful, invaluable, hopeful, priceless, valuable, worthwhile.
Negative: helpless, hopeless, waste of time, unhelpful, worthless.

p.62 LANGUAGE STUDY

Obligation and necessity

1/2 Students work on exercise 1 in small groups, then put them in pairs to work out the responses for exercise 2, which can be developed into mini role plays if required.

1 ANSWERS

1 D; 2 C; 3 E; 4 G; 5 H; 6 A; 7 F; 8 B

2 POSSIBLE ANSWERS

1 You really must see this exhibition of African art.
2 I have to welcome customers and ask them to check in. I also have to answer the phone and take bookings. I don't have to write letters or anything like that. That's the secretary's job.
3 You have to do the washing-up when you've eaten your meals. You're supposed to keep quiet after 10.00, but everyone keeps chatting! And guests have to be out by 11.30. You mustn't smoke in the hostel.
4 I really must pay that bill.
5 I was going to take a taxi but in the end I didn't have to/need to.

p.63 WRITING

A letter of complaint

Ask students to read and describe the advertisement. Based on the advertisement only, get them to predict:
- the sort of person it would appeal to (sociable, fun-loving, sporty, etc.).
- the facilities that would be provided (villa, beach, swimming pool, etc.)
- the activities offered (discos, parties, watersports, etc.)

Read through the introduction. Let students work on tasks 1 and 2 in pairs.

ANSWERS

1 He has five complaints:
- accommodation in a modern hotel, not a small villa
- accommodation in poor condition, e.g. cracks everywhere, walls were paper thin
- only two other young people in the hotel (both men)
- only nightlife was bingo
- rudeness of company representative

2 This is really a matter for discussing between you and the students but examples might be:
I am writing to complain about ...
According to ... was supposed to be ...
To make matters worse ...
On top of everything ...
... I expect ...
I trust you will give this matter your immediate attention.
I look forward to receiving a satisfactory reply by return of post.

3 Reference should be made to the inclusion of the address of the person you are writing to, the particular formulae for opening and closing the letter and the various expressions employed which are specific to more formal letters.
This is the type of task students may find in Part 1 of Paper 2 *(Writing)*, which is the compulsory question in the exam. Note that in the exam candidates are told **not** to include addresses. Remind students of the importance of reading the rubric and input information very carefully before attempting any planning or writing.
Begin by asking the students to describe the advertisement and the sort of person, facilities and activities expected – as they did for the Club 20–30 advertisement in exercise 1. The preparation for writing can be done in pairs or small groups. Students begin by expanding the notes by adding further details, examples, reasons etc. They should then think about organizing the letter in paragraphs, using the model in the coursebook as a guide and making an outline plan. If time permits, you can ask groups to exchange and compare their ideas/plans.
The final writing of the letter can be set as homework.

ONCE IN A LIFETIME

p.64 FIRST THOUGHTS

Having given time for pairs to discuss their ideal holidays and perhaps had one or two of the most interesting described in open class, ask if anyone has been to West Africa and elicit what students know about the area, e.g. countries, climate, kinds of crops, what the area is famous for, typical souvenirs.

p.64 READING

A holiday with a difference

On the first read-through students concentrate on mapping the route the tour took. They check together.

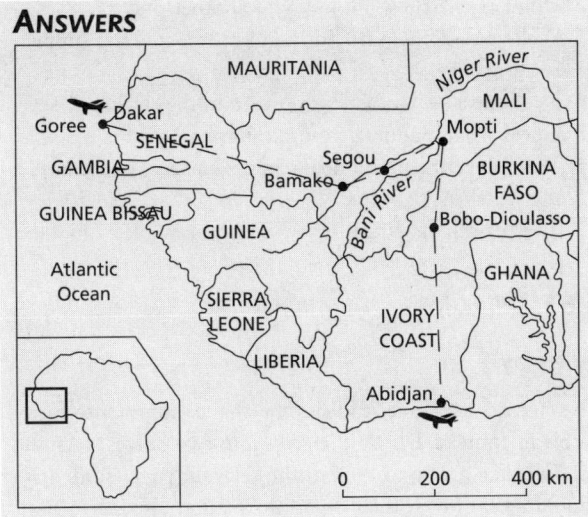

ANSWERS

Put students in small groups and nominate a 'secretary' for each group to note down what each group thinks are the correct answers, which part of the text indicates this and *why* the other choices are wrong. Students should underline those parts of the text which provide 'clues'. Having done this, they should consult the commentary on page 65 of the Coursebook and there should be time for open class discussion of any points that need clarification.

Conclusions
1 The multiple choice questions have a lot of tricks and traps. You must approach them with a great deal of respect.
2 This means that you have to study the questions carefully and read every word in them.
3 You can work out the correct answer by eliminating the possibilities that are wrong.
4 Do not make your choice without thinking very carefully. Answers that appear obvious are often traps.

Examination advice
Try following this pattern when dealing with multiple choice questions:
1 Quickly read the text to get a general idea of what it is about.
2 Carefully read the questions so you have a clear idea of why you are going to read the text.
3 Read the text extremely carefully, identifying those parts that carry answers to the questions.
4 Choose your answer by logically eliminating all the other choices. Don't rush.
5 If in doubt, guess from the most likely answers.

p.64 WRITING

Can be homework. One or two students may be prepared to make a presentation to the class of a region they know well and the various places of interest that can be visited.

FUTURE PLANS

p.66 FIRST THOUGHTS

1/2 Use the questions as a lead-in to the topic of planning holidays. Ask students to describe preparations they make for holidays and any interesting personal experiences.

p.66 LISTENING

1 Students in pairs attempt to name all the objects in the picture first. (You could turn this into a competition to see who could name the most objects.) The objects are: *a tent, waterproof clothing (trousers and jacket), rope, a safety helmet, a survival blanket, a map, walking boots, saucepans, a kettle, a camping gas stove, a spoon and fork, a tin-opener, a first-aid box, a compass* and *a sleeping bag*. Give students a little time to discuss and decide what they think is really necessary to take on a holiday like this. Then listen to the conversation.

TAPESCRIPT

FRIEND: What are you doing this summer for your holiday, Julie?
JULIE: I'm going off with some friends. We're going to the Lake District for about ten days or so.
FRIEND: Oh, are you camping?
JULIE: No, we'll be staying in youth hostels most of the time. We're going to do a lot of walking but we'll be able to get to a youth hostel by the end of each day.
FRIEND: Oh, tell me, what will you be taking with you, then?
JULIE: Well, a pair of really good walking boots for a start and quite a lot of clothing. You can never be sure what the weather's going to be like. It can be lovely one moment and grotty the next. When you're up high too, it can even snow on a summer's day!
FRIEND: Sounds a bit dangerous. Do you have to take any special equipment or anything with you?
JULIE: No, not really. Oh, we'll take those survival blankets which you can wrap yourself up in, you know, just in case, but apart from that nothing special.
FRIEND: Oh yeah, I know. One of those silver things you see them wearing at the ends of marathons.
JULIE: That's it. Oh, a map and compass, of course, sleeping bags for the youth hostel, waterproof jacket and trousers, oh and a camping gas stove and kettle so we can brew up. But no tent. I took one last year but I needn't have bothered. I didn't use it once.
FRIEND: So you've done this sort of thing before.

JULIE: Oh, yeah. This'll be my fourth visit to the Lakes. How about you? Have you got any plans?
FRIEND: Well, I'm not sure. I might be going to Greece or Turkey ...

> **ANSWERS**
>
> - a pair of walking boots
> - survival blankets
> - a map
> - a compass
> - sleeping bags
> - a waterproof jacket and trousers
> - a camping gas stove
> - a kettle

p.66 PRONUNCIATION

1 Play the models on tape and ask students to read the explanation in the Coursebook. Get the students to repeat the models and check that they can distinguish the clear /l/ in *hotel* and the syllabic /l̩/ in *hostel*.

2 When students have completed the chart get them to practise the words by repeating after the tape.

> **ANSWERS**
>
> | | HOTEL | HOSTEL |
> |---|---|---|
> | 1 holiday | ✓ | |
> | 2 tell | ✓ | |
> | 3 able | | ✓ |
> | 4 lake | ✓ | |
> | 5 kettle | | ✓ |
> | 6 This'll | | ✓ |
> | 7 Well | ✓ | |
> | 8 We'll | | ✓ |
> | 9 lot | ✓ | |

p.66 LANGUAGE STUDY

Ways of talking about the future

1 Students should work on this in small groups. When they have completed the matching they may find it helpful to draw up a chart of the forms and their uses with their own example sentences, e.g.
will
A future prediction, e.g. ....
Something in the future which will definitely happen, e.g. ....
A decision taken at the time of speaking, e.g. ....

> **ANSWERS**
>
> **A** 4; **B** 7; **C** 6; **D** 2; **E** 3; **F** 1; **G** 5

2 Students should work on this in pairs.

> **POSSIBLE ANSWERS**
>
> 1 Thanks for the invitation, but I'm so tired I'm going to stay at home.
> 2 Don't cry, darling. I'll buy you another one.
> 3 I'd love to come out with you but I'm cooking supper for everyone.
> 4 I will meet you at/pick you up from the station at seven.
> 5 Guess what. Samira's going to have a baby!
> 6 You'll love the monuments and the parks; you'll hate the weather.
> 7 You'll get lung cancer if you continue smoking like that.

p.67 SPEAKING

Role play

This activity will give students the chance to practise future forms in context. Divide the class into two halves – As and Bs. Tell each group to look at the relevant page (students should look only at their own information), giving them time to study their role information. It is probably a good idea to quickly check they have absorbed all the information by asking one or two comprehension questions, e.g. *What are you doing this weekend? How are you getting there?*
Then get each student to work with someone from the other group to make a pair. Monitor, and if you notice any consistent mistakes being made by a number of students, you may want to go over these at the end and then ask students to change partners (but keeping the same role) and try again. When they have finished select some or all to be acted out in front of the class. You may want to give feedback on language points after each role play, concentrating on accurate use of appropriate future forms.

p.67 WRITING

1 Before they begin correcting the letter get the students to brainstorm potential mistakes and put these on the board. This list may be helpful:
- Use of tenses (particularly future forms)
- Grammar of time clauses (clauses beginning *when*, *after*, *while*, etc.)
- Articles (especially with countable/uncountable nouns)
- Verbs followed by *-ing* or infinitive
- Appropriate formal expressions

Students should work in small groups to find the mistakes and write out the letter correctly.

> **POSSIBLE ANSWER**
>
> Dear Sir,
> Thank you for accepting me on your English course next month.
> I am writing to enquire about travel arrangements from

Gatwick airport to the school and between the school and my host family. I hope the accommodation is near the school and the family likes young people.
The flight takes three hours and arrives at Gatwick at two in the afternoon. How far is it from Brighton? Do you recommend taking a taxi or is it very expensive? Is there a bus I can take?
Can you tell me which class I will be in? I would like to make a lot of progress while I am studying with you because I am going to university next year and my English needs to be very good. How long does it take to pass the Proficiency examination?
Yours faithfully

2 This can be set as homework. If time permits, follow the usual procedure of getting students to plan the letter in small groups.

TRAVELLERS

p.68 FIRST THOUGHTS

1 Get the class to brainstorm the names, achievements and nationalities of famous explorers and travellers. Here are some ideas to get them started:
Eric the Red (Greenland/possibly America?, Viking)
Christopher Columbus (America, Italian)
Vasco da Gama (Sea route to India, Portuguese)
Captain Cook (Australia, British)
Marco Polo (China, Italian)
Thor Heyerdahl (rafts to Polynesia, Norwegian)
Jacques Cousteau (underwater exploration, French)

2 Students discuss the question in small groups.

p.68 READING

Students describe the photographs and make predictions about the two women's lives and achievements.

1 ANSWERS

1893	born in England
1905	injured in an accident
1921	decided to learn Arabic
1927	sailed to Beirut
1934	*Valley of the Assassins* published
1947	got married
1950s	visited/wrote books about Turkey
In her eighties	carried on travelling (went to Afghanistan and Nepal)
At age 85	travelled by raft down the Euphrates
At age 87	rode a mule through the Himalayas

2 Students underline the relevant phrases in the text.

ANSWERS

... in 1893
When she was 12 ...
while she was ...
... four years later.
In the 1950s ...
During her eighties ...

3 Phrasal verbs in context

ANSWERS

to recover from: get over
to postpone: put off
to continue: carry on

p.68 WRITING

Begin by checking through the notes for any vocabulary problems. Then get students in pairs to expand the notes into full sentences. Once this is done they should join the sentences into paragraphs, using the time expressions in the model (*when, during,* etc.) and noting the sequence used in the model (an introductory sentence followed by chronological details of the life). The writing can be set as homework.

POSSIBLE ANSWER

Christopher Columbus was born in Genova, Italy in 1451. He believed the world was round and you could go east by sailing west.
At the age of 25 Columbus was shipwrecked off the coast of Portugal while trying to find the short route to India for the spice trade. He developed his theories and ten years later approached the Spanish monarchs for support. On 3rd August 1492 he set sail in the *Santa Maria*. After six weeks at sea he landed on the coast of San Salvador. When he returned to Spain he was greatly honoured.
During the next eight years Columbus made two more journeys west, discovering Guadeloupe, Jamaica, Trinidad and the South American mainland. In 1499 there was a revolt against him and he was sent back to Spain as a prisoner. But he was pardoned and compensated.
In 1502 Columbus made his final voyage. When he returned home in 1504 he was ill. He died two years later in Valladolid, Spain.

p.69 READING

Students read through the text for general understanding before attempting to match the gaps. As a gist question you could ask the class to find out how many miles she travelled each day. (30)

When students have completed the matching exercise they should compare in small groups, justifying their choices by reference to clues in the context.
Follow up the reading with a discussion comparing the two women travellers. Ask them which one they think is the more 'genuine' explorer.

> **ANSWERS**
>
> 1 F; 2 B; 3 A; 4 E; 5 D; 6 G
> C is the extra sentence.
> Note that two of the links are grammatical ones only, as the subject matter does not help here.

p.70 USE OF ENGLISH

This section aims to give students a thorough introduction to this particular examination task by showing them the type of words which are often taken out and by providing some intensive practice on those words (in this case, conjunctions, adverbs and determiners).

1 Ask students to quickly read through the text to answer the following questions:
Where did they spend the night? (On benches.)
Why? (The cheap hotels were full up.)
Who do you think 'they' were? (Possibly students, as they had little money.)
Then, covering the list of the parts of speech, ask them to quickly try and decide, in pairs, what part of speech each of the words in bold is. Then check against the answers.

2 For this exercise you may wish to put students in teams and make it a race to see who can finish first.

> **1 ANSWERS**
>
> **A** Although; **B** As; **C** because; **D** if; **E** so; **F** Neither;
> **G** spite; **H** Either

2 As an introduction to this exercise and to help students where you think they may need it, you may want to write up the following definitions of the target words on the blackboard. Students suggest single words having these meanings before looking at the alternatives in the book:
(A) *sufficient*; (B) *in fact*; (C) *almost not*; (D) *surprisingly*;
(E) *no more than*; (F) *nearly*; (G) *rather*; (H) *other*;
(I) *more than is good*; (J) *completely*.

> **ANSWERS**
>
> **A** enough; **B** really; **C** hardly; **D** even; **E** only;
> **F** almost; **G** quite; **H** else; **I** too; **J** entirely

3 For variety, you may want to do this exercise in the following way: tell students that of the following answers half are correct and half are not. They have to identify the wrong ones and correct them:
A this; B all; C little; D few; E both; F which; G what; H those.

> **ANSWERS**
>
> **A** this; **B** all; **C** few; **D** little; **E** Both; **F** what;
> **G** Which; **H** those

3 Prior to the exercise, ask students to write down anything they know about Marco Polo. Elicit their ideas and note two or three on the board. Students read the passage the first time to check their ideas then read it a second time to decide between the various word choices.

> **ANSWERS**
>
> **1** both; **2** already; **3** that; **4** along; **5** Eventually;
> **6** where; **7** who; **8** Although; **9** provided; **10** must;
> **11** down; **12** the; **13** hardly; **14** them; **15** During

4 Students should refer back to the procedure in the first exercise – thinking about parts of speech – before attempting to fill the gaps. Get students to compare their answers in small groups, explaining and justifying their choices, before going through the answers with them.

> **ANSWERS**
>
> **1** whose; **2** Although; **3** have; **4** were; **5** with;
> **6** sorts/kinds/types; **7** into; **8** was;
> **9** After/Once/When; **10** there; **11** things; **12** would;
> **13** always/usually/often; **14** why; **15** on

6 Changes

BLOOD IS THICKER THAN WATER

p.72 FIRST THOUGHTS

1 Use the photographs as a lead-in to the topic of relationships. Get the students to describe the pictures and the events they illustrate. Elicit any cultural differences and students' opinions.

Picture 1: a traditional wedding
Picture 2: a funeral
Picture 3: a family lunch/dinner
Picture 4: a christening

2 Students discuss the question in small groups.

p.72 LISTENING

1 Students should predict the causes for the changes in the social circles in pairs. Encourage students to use appropriate structures for making deductions, e.g.
Her grandmother **must have** died.
She **might have** lost touch with Simon.

2 Students listen once to check their predictions/deductions.

TAPESCRIPT

INTERVIEWER: Rosie, you agreed to draw two social circles. Now, would it bother you at all to go into them?
ROSIE: Well, I suppose it could be a bit embarrassing but, well, I'll try and be as straightforward as I can.
INTERVIEWER: I guess the first question that anyone would ask is, what happened to Simon?
ROSIE: I was afraid you'd ask that. Well, to cut a long story short, I'd been going out with him since I was 16. When he was 18, he went away to university and, when he was away, I fell in love with Clive.
INTERVIEWER: Where had you met Clive?
ROSIE: Clive was Simon's best friend from school. I'd known him a long time.
INTERVIEWER: And he'd been going out with Lucy?
ROSIE: Yes, that's right. Well, they split up over something silly and the following weekend there was a party on, and Clive and I went together 'cos Simon was away. Well, it seemed the natural thing to do. Then quite simply we realised we loved each other.
INTERVIEWER: How did Lucy and Simon take this?
ROSIE: Well, Simon was really upset for a while but he soon found a new girlfriend at university. I think he got over it pretty quickly really. As for Lucy, well, she was furious because she said it had only been a lover's quarrel and that I'd pinched Clive off her.
INTERVIEWER: Well, in a way hadn't you?
ROSIE: Yeah, I know it sounds awful and I felt rotten at the time but I couldn't help myself. Later on I made it up with Lucy and we still see each other from time to time.
INTERVIEWER: And what about Simon and Clive?
ROSIE: Well, they fell out completely and haven't spoken to each other since.
INTERVIEWER: And what about your parents? There seems to have been something of a change there.
ROSIE: Well, my dad really liked Simon – he was going off to study to be a doctor and he's quite smart and was always polite – whereas Clive was unemployed at the time and wore an earring and things. Well, there were some terrible rows. Dad even refused to come to the wedding. We're just about talking to each other now but relationships are very tense still. Since Sophie was born, I've been getting on much better with my mum. I get on really well with Tom, my father-in-law, and I've grown much closer to my auntie Cathy.
INTERVIEWER: Why's that?
ROSIE: Well, I was brought up to think of her as the black sheep of the family. She'd been a bit wild when she was young and got kicked out of her home and I think she could understand what I'd been through.
INTERVIEWER: And your grandmother?
ROSIE: Oh, she passed away two years ago.

3 Ask students to read through the multiple choice questions before playing the tape again.

ANSWERS

1 C; **2** A; **3** C; **4** B; **5** B

4 When students have found all the expressions check they understand the meanings by asking them to make true sentences about themselves or their friends/families in small groups. They may like to draw their own social circles following the model in the Coursebook.

ANSWERS

to fall in love with someone; to split up; to pinch someone off someone else; to get over something; a lover's quarrel; to make it up; to fall out; to get on with someone; to grow closer to someone; to bring someone up; the black sheep of the family; to get kicked out; to pass away

p.73 VOCABULARY

1 Students should read the letters quickly to answer the gist questions before tackling the multiple choice task.

> **ANSWERS**
>
> 1 Katrina has had twins, Miranda is going to get a divorce.
> 2 Probably Katrina.
> 3 Katrina may be upset and disappointed.
> 4 Katrina may not be sympathetic to Miranda's marriage problems.

2 Students work in pairs, using dictionaries if they are available. When pairs have finished they can join up to make small groups to check the answers with each other.

> **ANSWERS**
>
> 1 C; 2 B; 3 D; 4 B; 5 C; 6 A; 7 D; 8 A; 9 D; 10 B;
> 11 A; 12 D; 13 A; 14 B; 15 A; 16 C; 17 A; 18 D;
> 19 A; 20 C; 21 C; 22 C; 23 C; 24 D

p.73 SPEAKING

Begin by asking students to tell you about their favourite soap operas. Get them to describe the basic ingredients of a soap opera: realistic or recognisable setting, set of stock characters – often from one family, street or school – conflicts between them (especially over romance and money), 'cliffhanger' at the end of each episode. Ask them to use the events described in this unit to invent a plot for one or two episodes of a soap opera. Students should work in small groups. Groups can compare their plots when they have finished.

LOOKING BACK

p.74 FIRST THOUGHTS

Use the question as a lead-in to the topic of childhood experiences. Ask students if they were ever jealous of their brothers and sisters (sibling rivalry) and elicit any personal experiences.

p.74 READING

1 You may want to pre-teach the following before students read the text quickly and answer the gist questions:
a pram, to look at the world through rose-coloured spectacles, to be insane, tactful, sticking plaster.

> **ANSWERS**
>
> 1 She feels positive about it. It seems to have been happy.
> 2 She had a good relationship with her parents.

2 Now that students have read through the text they should be ready to tackle the gap-matching task. They can compare answers in small groups.

> **ANSWERS**
>
> 1 I; 2 E; 3 A; 4 G; 5 F; 6 B; 7 D
> C is the extra sentence.

3 Working in the same groups, students can compare Maeve Binchy's childhood with their own. Monitor and draw out any experiences you feel the whole class would find interesting.

p.75 LANGUAGE STUDY

Different forms of *used to*

1/2 Students may be familiar with these forms and able to explain the differences between the three examples. If not, go through them and check that they are clear by referring to the expanded examples in the Coursebook.
1 *He used to play tennis* conveys the idea that it was a routine in the past but is no longer continued, i.e. he does not play tennis now.
2 *She was not used to living away from home* suggests that this was an activity/state that was unusual for her. She was not accustomed to this situation.
3 *She got used to living away from home* suggests that while, at first, she found it a strange and perhaps difficult situation, after a certain amount of time she adapted to the new way of life. (*Get* in this case means *become*.)

3 Pronunciation of *used to*
Highlight both the schwa in *to* and the soft *s* in *used*, the latter being the differentiating factor between: *He is used /s/ to getting up early* and *He used /z/ a hammer to break the window.*

4 ANSWERS

1 No, but it used to be (a part of Pakistan).
2 No, they're used to them/eating with them.
3 Not really, they're used to it/being criticised.
4 Not any more, but they used to.
5 They should be careful because they're not used to driving on the right.
6 Eventually you get used to them.
7 No, they're used to it/the cold.
8 No, they soon get used to it.

p.76 USE OF ENGLISH

1 Get the students to describe the picture and predict the story before they begin reading. Ask them to explain the purpose of the stocking (to collect money for the blind).

Then students read the text quickly and suggest a title, e.g. *The four-year-old thief* or *Stealing from the blind*.

2/3 Check that students have decided on a suitable part of speech before they complete task 3.

> **ANSWERS**
>
> 1 adjective – uncomfortable
> 2 adjective – charitable
> 3 adverb – mysteriously
> 4 noun – difficulty
> 5 noun – exception
> 6 noun – laughter
> 7 adjective – dangerous
> 8 noun – willingness
> 9 noun – contribution
> 10 noun – cartoonist

p.76 VOCABULARY

Prepositional phrases

With a strong class you might want to make this section more challenging by asking them to complete exercise 2 before they do the matching task in exercise 1. With a weak group it may be necessary to give further practice in the prepositional phrases after completion of the exercises, for example by asking the students to write an example sentence for each one.

> **1 ANSWERS**
>
> incidentally – by the way
> believing something to be true – under the impression
> using something to achieve an aim – by means of
> always – at all times
> responsible for – in charge of
> independently – on my own
> to represent someone else – on behalf of
> for the purpose of – in order to
> not visible – out of sight
> difficult to take – out of reach

> **2 ANSWERS**
>
> **1** at all times/all the time; **2** on behalf of; **3** by means of; **4** on your own; **5** in order to say; **6** she was out of sight; **7** by the way; **8** was under the impression (that); **9** was in charge of; **10** out of reach

3 Students can look at the phrases in pairs and confer. They should note down the most useful ones.

p.77 LISTENING

1 Begin by asking the students to brainstorm all the differences between Britain and India in 1920. In particular, ask students to think about climate, social position of Europeans, servants, schools.
You may want to pre-teach the following:
to not lift a finger, to be spoilt, boarding school, to make a mess of something, to shrink, to be waited on hand and foot, to buy clothes off the peg.

2 Play the tape once. Let students confer in pairs and then play the tape again for them to check.

> **ANSWERS**
>
> **1** F; **2** F; **3** T; **4** F; **5** T; **6** F; **7** T; **8** T; **9** F; **10** T; **11** T; **12** T

TAPESCRIPT

HARRIET: As you know, I was born in India. My father had a terribly important job – he was in charge of building projects for an entire region and supervised the construction of dams, roads, bridges and suchlike. I didn't see much of him as a child as he was often away. And when he was home, the house would be full of engineers with plans and papers.
The house I remember very clearly. You wouldn't call it a mansion but it was extremely large and painted white with a veranda and lovely grounds for me to play in. We had servants and all the years we were there my mother never had to lift a finger to do anything. I had a number of nannies and, being the only daughter, I was spoilt by everyone. My two elder brothers, poor lambs, were packed off to boarding school in England at the age of seven and I was brought up with a tremendous sense of my, and my family's, self-importance.
In the summer the women and children would go to the hills but the men worked on through the heat on the plains. And it was during the summer that my father fell ill and could not continue with his job. We had to return to England. That was in 1920 and I remember being very seasick on the journey home. In India everyone talked about going home but the reality for me was a terrible shock. When we landed, it was cold and grey and I was surprised at seeing so many white faces around me. I realised I wasn't special anymore. We travelled first class up to London but it was nothing compared to travelling first class in India. And I was so disappointed in our house. It seemed so cramped and dingy. I felt that I had really come down in the world. We only had one servant and she didn't live in. My mother tried to do the cooking – oh, she did her best but at first she made a terrible mess of everything.
But the worst thing about coming back was what happened to my father. From being responsible for major projects and hundreds of people, he suddenly

became just one of many working in the ministry. He never got used to it and somehow seemed to physically shrink in the last few years before he retired.

As for myself, oh, we had always had the best in India but in England we had to make do with ordinary things. In India I had my clothes made and I remember, I am ashamed to say, being terribly upset at having to buy clothes from a shop, off the peg as it were. I thought this was awfully common. And at first I expected to be waited on hand and foot but gradually I came round to the idea of doing some of the housework.

Looking back on it, it seems incredible how dramatically my life changed. Actually, I think the change did me good because my upbringing in India had made me into such a little snob and coming home to England taught me what ordinary life was really like.

3 You can make this into a competition. The first pair to write ten correct sentences using *used to* wins.

Some example answers

Harriet used to live in India/in a big house/in a hot climate.
Harriet used to have a lot of servants/several nannies.
Harriet's mother didn't use to do any housework/ cooking/cleaning.
Harriet's father used to be important/in charge of building projects.
It took Harriet a long time to get used to life in England.
She wasn't used to the weather when she first arrived.
She eventually got used to doing some housework.

p.77 LANGUAGE STUDY

Causative *have*

1 Put the two model sentences on the board and give students a little time to try and analyse exactly what the difference is between them. Then they should be directed to the explanation in the Coursebook to compare their ideas.

2 Students should attempt this on their own so that they and you can see any problems that individuals are having.

ANSWERS

1 We had our kitchen redecorated (by a local firm).
2 It's time I had my hair cut.
3 She had her tonsils taken out when she was six.
4 He had had his suit altered for the wedding.
5 The woman is having her temperature taken.
6 We are going to have our central heating fixed (by a plumber).

A SENSE OF PLACE

p.78 FIRST THOUGHTS

Ask the students if they can describe any buildings which are particularly atmospheric. Get them to describe any feelings they have experienced, for example feeling overawed in a large stadium or palace, frightened in an old castle or dungeon, nostalgic in an old house, excited and expectant in a theatre or cinema as the lights go down.

p.78 READING

Note: In past years some of Daphne du Maurier's novels have been Cambridge set books, if students enjoy the extract from *Rebecca* you could encourage them to read the whole novel and tell them about her other famous novels *Jamaica Inn* and *My Cousin Rachel*.

1 Get the students to describe the illustration and make predictions about the text. As a gist reading activity they can find out if their ideas were correct by reading quickly the first two paragraphs.

2 Students work individually. Give them plenty of time in order to enjoy the literary quality of the passage. Remind them that it is not necessary to understand everything in order to answer the questions.

ANSWERS

1 D; **2** B; **3** C; **4** D; **5** C; **6** A; **7** B

3 These questions are open-ended and are best discussed in small groups. Get groups to report back to open class with their ideas.

p.79 VOCABULARY

Forming nouns

1 Ask students to draw a chart with two columns: adjectives on the left, nouns on the right. They should do as many as they can and then use their dictionaries for the remainder.

> **ANSWERS**
>
> angry – anger
> poor – poverty
> bored – boredom
> tired – tiredness
> happy – happiness
> kind – kindness
> hungry – hunger
> wealthy – wealth
> free – freedom
> thirsty – thirst
> hot – heat
> cruel – cruelty
> calm – calm/calmness
> ambitious – ambition
> excited – excitement
> satisfied – satisfaction

2 Start the students off with one or two examples, then ask students to work in pairs, perhaps choosing five or six of the words to use in sentences. Pairs can then confer to build up examples of all the words.

Examples:
Happiness is more important than wealth.
Boredom isn't as bad as poverty.

Refer students to the lists on Coursebook pages 212-214.

p.79 WRITING

1 Students read the description for general understanding and answer the introductory question.

> **2 ANSWERS**
>
> **1** combination/mixture; **2** takes; **3** which; **4** the;
> **5** But/However; **6** around; **7** several/many;
> **8** all; **9** least; **10** whose; **11** to/towards; **12** how;
> **13** becomes; **14** gain/achieve/attain/enjoy;
> **15** from/despite/after

3 Get the class to analyse the structure of the description. Elicit or put on the board the following:
- introduction – name of book and author
- description of genre (type of novel, e.g. love story, mystery, etc.)
- setting (Manderley)
- main characters (Max, the narrator)
- outline of central plot (mystery of Rebecca's death)
- reasons for recommending it (1 cunning plot, 2 extraordinary characters + an example – Mrs Danvers, 3 atmospheric descriptions)
- conclusion – main reason for recommending (development of narrator)

The students should underline useful phrases, e.g.
One of my favourite books is ...
It is set in ...
The main characters are ...
It revolves around ...
I would recommend ... for the following reasons. First of all ...
The descriptions of ... are ...
Above all, I appreciate ...
Finally, ask students to list the powerful adjectives which help the summary to sound enthusiastic and exciting:
beautiful   cunning   extraordinary   evil   chilling   atmospheric   terrible

The writing itself can be set as homework.

A CHANGE OF JOB

p.80 FIRST THOUGHTS

Get the students to describe and name the jobs in the illustration. If any of your students are employed ask them to name and describe their jobs as well. They should discuss job considerations in small groups.

1: doctor
2: lorry driver
3: policeman
4: chef/cook
5: waitress
6: taxi driver
7: veterinary surgeon (vet)

p.80 VOCABULARY

Work

If students are unable to group some of the expressions correctly it will be clear which items need to be explained. The most difficult are probably:
to be sacked – colloquial for 'to be dismissed'.
to be cut out for – to have the right personality and skills for.
to be made redundant – to lose your job through no fault of your own e.g. because a factory closes.

> **ANSWERS**
>
> (some expressions fit in more than one category)
> **Getting a job:**
> reference, interview, having the right qualifications, to fill in a form, previous experience, skills
> **Doing a job:**
> to do overtime, to do/work a shift, to go on strike
> **Personal qualities:**
> conscientious, to be cut out for something, enthusiastic, reliable
> **Leaving:**
> to be sacked, to dismiss, to be made redundant
> **Not having a job:**
> retirement, training, to be unemployed, pension

p.80 WRITING

1 Ask students to read the advertisement and answer the question. It might help if they list the personal qualities, qualifications and experience needed by an applicant.
Check vocabulary:
afloat   liner   covering letter   C.V.

2 By this stage in the course the class should be aware of many of the differences between formal and informal letters. They start by reading each of the jumbled sentences and deciding whether it is formal or informal. Then it will be easier to sort out the correct sequence. If you feel your class needs the extra practice, you can ask them to copy out the two letters on separate pieces of paper.

> **ANSWERS**
>
> Letter to uncle Mike (informal): f o j m b r e n i
> Letter to Mr Edwards (formal): d q k a p l c g h

3 Students could copy the two columns on paper, or allow five or six lines under each heading.

> **ANSWER**
>
> **Formal**
> I will be available for interview at your convenience
> I would be able to commence almost immediately
> Consequently I shall be seeking a similar postion
> My current contract comes to an end next month
> **Informal**
> I could have a chat with you then, if that's OK
> I'd even be able to start straight away
> I'll be free and looking for work
> At the moment I'm finishing off a one-year contract

4 Compulsory letter

Ask the students to read through the advertisements and deal with any vocabulary questions. Get each student to choose one job to apply for. If possible, move the students around so that each student is in a small group with classmates who chose the same job. Together they can plan their letters. The letters can be written up as homework. The application for this job as chambermaid or porter should be formal. The one for the music shop should be informal.

7 The Natural World

COSTING THE EARTH

p.80 FIRST THOUGHTS

Once reaction to the photos has been elicited, see if they remind students of any recent events or if they know anything about associated environmental problems, e.g. the Greenhouse Effect.

p.82 VOCABULARY

Students should attempt this in pairs. Ask those who finish earlier than the others to mark the stress and think about the correct pronunciation of the target words. Ask students to read each answer out loud to check for correct pronunciation.

> **ANSWERS**
>
> **1** environment; **2** pollution; **3** extinct; **4** dumped; **5** acid; **6** reactor, contaminated, fallout; **7** Ecology; **8** waste

p.83 READING

As an introduction to the text, ask students to cover the text and discuss the meaning of the caption. *To make waves* means to cause problems or disturb established ways of thinking. Ask if the students know what Greenpeace is and if they know of any recent events in which Greenpeace has been involved. Possibly get them to brainstorm different ways in which the environment is currently in danger, if this has not already been done.

> **1 ANSWER**
>
> Its aim is to get people to join the pressure group Greenpeace.

> **2 ANSWERS**
>
> **1** A; **2** D; **3** C; **4** B; **5** C; **6** B; **7** A

p.83 LISTENING

1 Ask the students to read through the unfinished sentences before listening to the tape.

> **ANSWERS**
>
> **1** 4,600; **2** 46 year old; **3** nothing.; **4** one year ago; **5** 45; **6** ape-like men.; **7** 4 hours.; **8** agriculture; **9** industrial revolution; **10** rubbish tip

TAPESCRIPT

Planet Earth is 4,600 million years old.
If we condense this inconceivable timespan into an understandable concept, we can liken Earth to a person of 46 years of age.
Nothing is known about the first seven years of this person's life, and whilst only scattered information exists about the middle span, we know that only at the age of 42 did the earth begin to flower.
Dinosaurs and the great reptiles did not appear until one year ago, when the planet was 45. Mammals arrived only eight months ago; in the middle of last week, man-like apes evolved into ape-like men, and at the weekend the last ice-age enveloped the earth.
Modern man has been around for 4 hours. During the last hour Man discovered agriculture. The industrial revolution began a minute ago.
During those sixty seconds of biological time, Modern Man has made a rubbish tip of Paradise.
He has multiplied his numbers to plague proportions, caused the extinction of 500 species of animals, ransacked the planet for fuels and now stands like a brutish infant, gloating over this meteoric rise to ascendancy, on the brink of a war to end all wars and of effectively destroying this oasis of life in the solar system.

2 In small groups students discuss the effectiveness of the advertisement. Which did they prefer? Encourage them to analyse the advertisement by putting these questions on the board:
- *Did it catch your attention? How?*
- *Was it convincing? Why?*
- *Did it make you think? About what?*
- *Did it make you want to join Greenpeace or not?*

p.84 VOCABULARY

Word building

1 Students may use dictionaries for this exercise. Encourage them to use this type of word chart in their own vocabulary notes. This will be particularly useful for the activity in Part 5 of Paper 3 *(Use of English)*.

ANSWERS

ADJECTIVE	NOUN	VERB
wide	width	widen
strong	strength	strengthen
deep	depth	deepen
weak	weakness	weaken
short	shortness	shorten
high	height	heighten

2 ANSWERS

1 deepen; 2 widening; 3 strengthened/deepened;
4 weakness; 5 height

p.84 LANGUAGE STUDY

The definite article

Do number 1 in open class as an example and then put students in small groups to attempt both exercises 1 and 2.

1 ANSWERS

1 C; 2 B; 3 D; 4 I; 5 G; 6 E; 7 A; 8 F; 9 H

2 ANSWERS

1 D; 2 C; 3 B; 4 E; 5 A

3 Having sorted out any problems, let students work on this exercise individually before conferring in order to show you and them if they really have got the idea. In going over the answers, make sure students justify their responses with reference to the appropriate rules in exercises 1 and 2, e.g. no. 1: zero article {exercise 2: 1D}, definite article {exercise 1: 8F}

ANSWERS

1 ∅/the; 2 ∅/the; 3 the; 4 The /∅/∅/∅/; 5 ∅/the;
6 ∅/the; 7 ∅; 8 the/∅/The/the/the;
9 ∅/the/the/a; 10 a/the/the

4 ANSWERS

1 T̶h̶e̶ (M) most people in ^the United States have two cars.

2 Mary works in a̶n̶ (a) university.

3 Did you have t̶h̶e̶ (a) nice time at a̶ school today, Amanda?

4 ^The Rolling Stones are ^the most wonderful group I've ever heard.

5 What did you think of ^the book I lent you?

6 She is going to be ^a doctor.

7 They have two holiday homes, one in ^the mountains and one at ^the seaside.

8 ^All the people who live in this town work at ^the car factory.

9 Where's Mary? She is in ^the sitting room talking on ^the phone.

10 She's wearing jeans. In fact they're ^the jeans she wore last week.

p.85 PRONUNCIATION

Saying the *th* sound and *the*

1 Ways of pronouncing *th*

It is interesting to note Roach's comments on the teaching of these sounds in *English, Phonetics* and *Phonology*, (1983), Peter Roach, CUP:
'The dental fricatives have sometimes been described as if the tongue was actually placed between the teeth, and it is common for teachers to make their students do this when they are trying to teach them to make this sound. In fact, however, the tongue is placed inside the teeth ... with the tip touching the inside of the lower front teeth and the blade touching the inside of the upper teeth. The air escapes through the gaps between the tongue and the teeth.'
The sound /ð/ is a voiced version of /θ/. If students cannot recognise this get them to place their hands on their throats when they make the sound. They should feel vibration with /ð/ but no vibration with /θ/.

1 ANSWERS

/θ/	/ð/
throughout	the
earth	breathe
threatened	their
strengthen	this
thin	that
thank	with
	there
	those

2 TAPESCRIPT AND ANSWERS

Despite <u>th</u>e fact, too <u>th</u>at we can create environmentally-clean industries, harness <u>th</u>e power of <u>th</u>e sun, wind and waves for our energy needs and manage the finite resources of <u>th</u>e earth in a way <u>th</u>at will safeguard our future and protect all <u>th</u>e rich variety of life forms which share <u>th</u>is planet wi<u>th</u> us.

2 Ways of saying *the*

You may wish to elicit the different pronunciations by putting the examples (*the sun* / ðə /(schwa) and *the earth* /ði:j/) on the board so that students can analyse the differences before reading the explanation in the Coursebook. Having given them a minute to practise the pronunciation of the six examples in pairs, go round the class quickly checking students' accuracy.

ANSWERS

A schwa; B /i:j/; C schwa; D schwa; E /i:j/; F /i:j/

p.85 LISTENING

1 Students should describe any changes to the climate that they are aware of, especially in their own country(ies). Elicit the names of any air pollutants and put on the board the following:
sulphur dioxide   sulphur monoxide   carbon monoxide

2 Ask students to read through the true/false questions before playing the tape.

ANSWERS

1 true; **2** false *(sulphur **di**oxide)*; **3** true; **4** false *(causes sickness)*; **5** false *(the least dangerous)*; **6** false *(there is strong evidence that it has)*; **7** false *(will cause floods)*; **8** false *(the government has got to.)*

3 This activity can be done as a kind of jigsaw. Divide the class into groups of 3. Each member of the group listens for information on a different gas. After listening students combine their notes and then compare with another group.

ANSWERS

Sulphur dioxide:
– from power stations. Causes acid rain which kills off fish and plant life in lakes and destroys the forests.

Carbon monoxide:
– is mostly produced by cars. Can, even in small doses, cause sickness and a slowing of the reflexes
– it has an effect on the growth of children.

Carbon dioxide:
– in the longer term may be the most damaging
– build-up of carbon dioxide in the atmosphere is the main cause of the Greenhouse Effect. This will melt the polar ice caps and cause flooding of low-lying areas.
– is making the atmosphere warmer.

TAPESCRIPT

WHITEHEAD: The Campaign for Clean Air has just issued a report on air pollution and we have in the studio Frances Kelly of the CCA who's going to tell us something about the dangers we face from air pollutants.

KELLY: Hello.

WHITEHEAD: Let's start with sulphur dioxide which causes acid rain. I thought the government was doing something about that.

KELLY: Well, they are but slowly. Sulphur dioxide emissions from power stations are still going on and the resulting acid rain is still killing off fishes and plant life in lakes and destroying the forests. And we in Britain are among the worst culprits when it comes to this kind of pollution.

WHITEHEAD: What are the other pollutants?

KELLY: Carbon monoxide and carbon dioxide. Carbon monoxide, which is mostly produced by motor vehicles can, even in small doses, cause sickness and a slowing of the reflexes and there is strong evidence to show that it has an effect on the growth of children.

WHITEHEAD: And carbon dioxide?

KELLY: Well, in a way this is the least dangerous of the pollutants we've mentioned but in the longer term it may be the most damaging.

WHITEHEAD: Why?

KELLY: There is clear evidence that the build-up of carbon dioxide in the atmosphere is the main cause of the Greenhouse Effect. This will have dreadful results like the melting of the polar ice caps and subsequent flooding of low-lying areas.

WHITEHEAD: So what you're saying is that the increased amounts of carbon dioxide in the atmosphere is making it warmer.

KELLY: Yes, that's right and the results will be catastrophic.

WHITEHEAD: And what should we be doing about this?

KELLY: Frankly, the government has got to impose far stricter controls on these emissions and bring in tough legislation to deal with the problem.
WHITEHEAD: Frances Kelly, thank you very much.
KELLY: Thank you.
WHITEHEAD: After the news we hope to be talking to the Minister for the Environment, Patrick Hilliard ...

BIG ISSUES

p.86 FIRST THOUGHTS

Let the students discuss their choices then hold a class vote (by a show of hands) to find the issue which is of most concern. Ask the students to say something about **what** they would do if they had the power and use this to bring out any useful vocabulary connected with the topics.

p.86 SPEAKING

Ask students about their personal methods of transport. Do they use cars, buses, trains, bicycles, etc? Ask them to describe the pictures and talk about their own views.

Photographs show:
1. Clear, open motorway, people in cars pleased to be on the road, feeling free.
2. Racing driver Damon Hill as a child with his father, racing driver, Graham Hill.
3. A traffic jam, the drivers angry and frustrated.

p.86 VOCABULARY

Draw three columns on the board and ask the students to copy this. As a clue, tell them how many words are in each column. Students work in pairs to categorise the words, using dictionaries if necessary. Younger students may need to be given some further explanation of the terms.

ANSWERS

VERBS	PARTS OF THE CAR	TO DO WITH THE ROAD
crash	brake (noun)	lane
brake (verb)	bonnet	roundabout
swerve	gear	junction
overtake	windscreen	bend
reverse	clutch	services
indicate	steering wheel	
skid		

(**Note:** In American English *bonnet* is *hood* and *windscreen* is *windshield*.)

p.86 LISTENING

1 Get the students to read through the six descriptions before playing the tape. After listening they can confer before you play the tape again for final checking.

ANSWERS

Speaker 1 E; Speaker 2 C; Speaker 3 A;
Speaker 4 F; Speaker 5 B
D is the extra description

2 You might like to get the students started by either eliciting a summary of one of the incidents on tape or by describing an incident from your own experience.

TAPESCRIPT

SPEAKER 1: With a flick of the switch the canopy folds back and there you are with the wind in your hair and the sun in your face. This is what driving should be all about. This re-styled 900 restores some of the fun and traditional pleasures to modern-day motoring. Its sleek design and state-of-the-art sixteen-valve engine under the bonnet mean that you can effortlessly glide along the motorway although you'll have to keep an eye on the speedometer as it can go deceptively fast.

SPEAKER 2: Well, it was dreadful really, we were right near the main road and each time a lorry came by the whole building shook. I mean, it looked nothing like the brochure. We'd expected a quiet little cottage in the middle of nowhere and instead we got a massive, you know, erm dual carriageway, outside the back door. And the smell, I mean, you needed to wear a gas mask.

SPEAKER 3: Never seen anything like it, it was just like a skating rink ... cars were skidding all over the place. I'm really lucky to have that ABS thing, you know the, erm, the device that stops your car from going out of control if you brake – it's like a – a computer controls the braking on the wheels. I used it once or twice and believe me, I don't think I'd ever go for a car that didn't have it. Anyway a lot of people just gave up and erm left their cars by the side of the road. Gave three of them a lift as a matter of fact.

SPEAKER 4: Right, thought it would be you! Have you run into a bit of trouble then? Yeah that's right, junction eighteen, just after the service station, you'd better check it on the map though. So once you leave the motorway – a couple of miles past the services – erm, make sure that you, er, get into the right hand lane so that you can turn right. At the first roundabout, do a right and carry on a bit. There's a junction at the end and a petrol station, you can't miss it.

SPEAKER 5: He didn't indicate or anything. He just shot out, must have been dreaming. Anyway, the car behind was just as much to blame. He overtook on the bend and bang that was it. The second one swerved but, well, it was unavoidable by then. One of them smashed his windscreen and there was glass all over the road from the lights. I expect I'll be called as a witness, but as far as I'm concerned they're equally to blame. There was also this stupid girl, with a dog which wasn't on a lead, that can't have helped either.

p.86 READING

1 Introduce the task and remind students of examination technique – read the whole text through once for general understanding then read the extracted sentences for matching with gaps. Students work individually then compare and justify their choices in small groups.

ANSWERS

1 I; **2** D; **3** C; **4** B; **5** G; **6** H; **7** A
F is the extra sentence

2 Understanding the organisation of the text
Students can work through the questions in small groups as they involve some discussion. Monitor and check they are on the right lines. Ask groups to report back to open class when they've finished.

ANSWERS

1 It introduces/summarises the topic of the paragraph.

2a *In my opinion ...*
As far as I'm concerned ...
I am not suggesting ...
What I am saying is ...
I do believe ...
should ...

2b *The problem can be dealt with on three levels ...*
Let us now look at what can be done on a national level ...
Lastly, what can we do as individuals ...
To sum up, ...

3 *Does it mean that we will be living in a wilderness of tarmac..?*
Is it perhaps time to tackle the monster?
What can we do as individuals?
The questions are rhetorical, that, is they are answered by the writer him/herself. They are used as a way of introducing something (the answer to the question) which the writer wants us to read.

p.88 LANGUAGE STUDY

The passive

1 Get the students to complete exercise 1 before answering any questions or discussing the grammar. Check the answers are correct as students will need these as examples before answering exercise 2.

ANSWERS

1 The trees are sprayed each week.
2 More and more pollution is being produced (by that factory).
3 The company was seen dumping rubbish.
4 The oil refinery has been broken into by demonstrators.
5 All the evidence had been hidden (by the owners) by the time the police arrived.
6 The reactor was being redesigned (by a scientist).
7 A solution is needed.
8 The enquiry is going to be opened by the prime minister.
9 The police will/shall be notified about this matter.
10 The newspapers should have been written to.

2 Students can begin by identifying all the tenses/modals in the sentences in exercise 1. Check that they are familiar with the meaning of *past participle* before they work out how the passives are formed.

ANSWERS

1 **present simple**: object + *am/is/are* + past participle (see ex. 1:1 above)
past simple: object + *was/were* + past participle (see ex. 1:3 above)
2 **present continuous**: object + *am/is/are* + *being* + past participle (see ex. 1:2 above)
past continuous: object + *was/were* + *being* + past participle (see ex. 1:6 above)
3 **'going to' future**: object + *am/is/are* + *going to* + past participle (see ex. 1:8 above)
4 **present perfect**: object + *has/have* + *been* + past participle (see ex. 1:4 above)
past perfect: object + *had* + *been* + past participle (see ex. 1:5 above)
5 **modals like *shall***: object + modal + *be* + past participle (see ex. 1:9 above)
6 **modals in the past**: object + modal + *have been* + past participle (see ex. 1:10 above)

Extension
As further practice of the passive you may like to ask students to prepare a three minute programme aimed at persuading people to join an organisation opposing the spread of the motor car, or Greenpeace, to be recorded either on cassette or on video. It could draw on some of the ideas already presented in this unit. The following are examples of the type of language that might be included:
*As we all know the earth **is being slowly poisoned** ...*
*Many children **are being harmed** by ...*
*Large areas of rain forest **have been cut down**...*
*In the years to come, unless something is done, the ozone layer **will be destroyed** ...*

p.88 USE OF ENGLISH

Students should be familiar with this task type by this stage. Go through number 1 in open class then let them complete the rest individually, checking in pairs.

ANSWERS
1. need to find is
2. wasn't allowed to watch
3. has been turned into
4. last time it rained was
5. insisted on paying
6. been an increase in
7. answer must be found
8. you familiar with
9. was hardly surprised at/by
10. used to be dirty before

p.88 WRITING

The opinion question

1 Explain that there is usually one discursive composition in Part 2 of Paper 2 *(Writing)* and ask students to suggest what they think success depends upon in answering this question. Put all ideas on the board and then let them read exercise 1 in the Coursebook to compare their ideas and possibly discuss differences or additional points.

2 Vocabulary

Let students answer this in pairs and then have the answers read out to check on good pronunciation, particularly of target vocabulary. Clarify any problems with meaning which remain.

ANSWERS
1 G; 2 D; 3 I; 4 C; 5 B; 6 A; 7 E; 8 F; 9 H

3 Reading

When the students have matched the pictures to the paragraphs, tell them to look through the text again and highlight any parts that they think they might find useful to them in their composition.

ANSWERS
1. Stop using money against the poor
2. Aim for social justice
3. Give back the land
4. Control the corporations
5. Put food first

4 Discuss in open class:
- The dangers of not doing a plan, e.g. writing incoherently, going off the point, suddenly deciding you should have started in a different way.
- How long should be spent on a plan – for a 45-minute composition approximately 10 minutes.
- The different ways of making a plan, e.g. the traditional linear fashion with an idea of what will go in each paragraph, or a mind-map.
- The different things that need to go in a plan for this particular composition, e.g. introduction to problem, various solutions to the problem plus arguments for and against each one, conclusion, including writer's view of the way forward.

Pairs plan the composition which could either be written up for homework or done in class with a time limit of approximately 35 minutes. Remind students of the useful language and stylistic devices they noted in the *Curse of the Motor Car* article.

FREE TO CHOOSE

p.90 FIRST THOUGHTS

Discuss with your students what sort of changes we would see (good and bad) if cars and lorries were banned (not allowed) in city centres.

p.90 LISTENING

1 Read through the introduction with the class and elicit responses to the question and illustration. Prepare for the listening by getting students to list their ideas (positive and negative) on the impact of a by-pass. For example:
Positive: improve quality of air, reduce pollution, make streets safer for children.
Negative: difficult to get to shops, shops may lose customers and close down.

2 ANSWERS
1 B; 2 C; 3 E; 4 C; 5 E; 6 B; 7 B

3 Play the tape again. Students can tackle the question in A/B pairs. Student A listens for Bernice's opinions (questions 1 & 4), Student B listens for Charles' (questions 2 & 3).

ANSWERS

1 She thinks it will kill the centre of the village.
2 He thinks it is essential to improve the quality of life.
3 He thinks the church, the old medieval covered market and the old building will attract tourists.
4 She wants it to be a real working village with jobs and proper shops.

TAPESCRIPT

ERIC: OK, OK, now everyone has finally turned up let's get this meeting underway, shall we? Bernice, perhaps you'd like to begin.
BERNICE: Right. Thank you, Eric. Well, as I see it, if we stop traffic coming through the centre of the village, then it'll be the beginning of the end for it. I mean there are an awful lot of people who stop off in the town and use the facilities we provide. Before long we'd be a ghost town. Lots of other villages have died out because they are no longer on the road to anywhere.
ERIC: Charles. What do you think?
CHARLES: I'm afraid I just can't agree. With the by-pass we'll be able to improve the quality of life of people in the village immeasurably. We can't carry on like this, you know loads of huge lories coming through the village. After all, it's these people, the, erm, villagers, we should be worrying about rather than the needs of passing motorists.
ERIC: This is all very well in theory, and I don't think anyone would argue with you that the traffic makes the, erm, High Street unpleasant, but the thing is I'd like to bring up the effects that a by-pass could have on the village. I mean, Bernice is right ... without the passing trade then lots of small shops will go out of business. Local people use them too but without the extra business they just wouldn't be able to survive.
CHARLES: I see your point, Eric, but other businesses will grow up in their place. Just think what the centre of the village would look like without the traffic. As I see it, we'll be able to have restaurants and cafés and a lot more people would come to the village for its tourist attractions.
BERNICE: What nonsense, you're living in a dream world, Charles. What tourist attractions?
CHARLES: Well, there's the church, that's seven hundred years old ... and there's the old medieval covered market and there are lots of lovely old buildings which are really picturesque.
ERIC: And I suppose we could look into the plans we had before to open up the craft centre and the museum. Oh, and there are the ruins of the castle too. Just think of all the jobs and businesses it would create. We could have a souvenir shop and lots of things could be ...
BERNICE: Goodness me, Eric, I really don't believe it. You're as bad as he is! The place would lose its character as a real working village. I want to do my shopping not buy souvenirs. I can't eat a souvenir. A working village, with lots of people passing through, that's what I want.
ERIC: Well, that's all very well, but what's the point if the people who live here can't actually enjoy it any more. I mean, you risk your life each time you step off the pavement at the moment. It's only a matter of time before someone gets killed.
BERNICE: Well, I quite agree with Eric for once. We need to do something to make it safer but I'm sure that if it comes down to people still having shops and a job or turning into a sleepy picture postcard village, I think I know what they'll go for. Just think of the, erm, the garden centre and the garage as you come into the town. They employ loads of people ...

p.90 SPEAKING

Managing conversations

1 Let students read through the exponents and then play the tape again.

ANSWERS

The phrases used in the listening are:
I think; as I see it; I quite agree; I see your point but ...; What nonsense!

2 Put the five headings on the board and ask students to add further expressions from their own knowledge.
Giving an opinion:
If you ask me, ... ; As far as I'm concerned; I'd like to say that ...
Strongly agreeing:
You're absolutely right; I go along with that; That's true.
Partly agreeing:
I suppose so, but ...; That depends; Well ...; That's all very well, but ...
Disagreeing:
I can't go along with that; I'm not so sure about that.
Strongly disagreeing:
You must be joking!; No way!

3 Before the students begin the pairwork write an opinion on the board, e.g. *English food is the best in the world!* Elicit from students that this is an opinion and not a fact! Get them to suggest varying ways of introducing such an opinion, making sure that all the exponents in the book are included. Ask students which words would most naturally be stressed in each case. Go round the class getting students to repeat the model opinion as enthusiastically as possible using a different exponent each time. When students can do this accurately, give prompts of subjects where opinions can easily be expressed – these will vary depending on the local context and the interests of your particular students but subjects might include *smoking*, *football* and *people who drink and drive*.

After this, elicit ways of agreeing and disagreeing with the model sentence. Again, try and include all the exponents that are referred to in the book. Put them on the blackboard and make sure that students can pronounce them accurately. Then give opinions about any of the subjects that have already come up and get students to agree or disagree with you, depending on their real views. This should provide adequate practice before students work on the statements in the exercise.

One way to do this exercise would be to write the various statements on pieces of paper and put them on walls in different parts of the classroom. Half the students go and stand by a statement they agree/disagree with. The other half move around challenging their opinions.

p.91 READING

1 Ask students to look at the heading and predict the content of the article. Explain *ciggies* (a slang expression for cigarettes) and check understanding of *passive smoking* (non-smokers inadvertently inhaling cigarette smoke by being close to smokers). Students then read the article to answer the five questions. Question 5 can be discussed in groups.

> **ANSWERS**
> 1 It is a language school for foreigners and the row is about the smoking ban.
> 2 There used to be a room for smokers which has been made into a no-smoking area.
> 3 The new school director, Janine Murray, introduced the ban to protect staff and students from passive smoking.
> 4 They think it is unreasonable.
> 5 (Open question for discussion).

2 Understanding the organisation of the text.
Get the students to discuss the questions and report back with their ideas. Elicit ideas along these lines:
a headline
 – to attract attention, make the reader curious/want to read the article
b first line
 – to summarise the story, introduce what has happened
c first sentence of paragraphs
 – to introduce the topic of the paragraph or (in paragraphs 2 & 3) the person whose views are quoted
d each paragraph
 1 Introduction, summary of background events. The actions and opinions of the school's director.
 2 Mariana's point of view and her actions.
 3 The point of view of a teacher and his reasons.
e secondary headlines
 – to divide up the text into manageable chunks, to summarise the content of the paragraph which follows, to make you keep on reading.

p.91 SPEAKING

Divide the class into three large groups. Give each group one of the roles and ask them to spend a few minutes noting down their character's position on the smoking room dilemma and preparing the arguments they could use. When they are ready get them to re-divide into new groups of three, with one person from each original group in each new group. Set a time limit for their discussion. Monitor silently. When the time is up ask each group to report back with its resolution of the problem.

p.91 WRITING

A newspaper article

Put the students into groups of three or four and get them to refer back to their answers to the *Listening* exercises and the model article on smoking before beginning this task. (Play the tape again if necessary.) Start by asking them to think of a headline and first sentence. Elicit and put on the board something along these lines:
<u>Row over Marsham By-pass</u>
Councillors were unable to agree over the proposed Marsham by-pass at today's heated council meeting ...
After deciding on ages and occupations for the three councillors, students should think about their point of view (the angle), paragraphs and headings (three or four paragraphs would be most suitable). If there is time you might like groups to share their ideas with the class.
The article should be between 120 and 180 words in length and can be written as homework.

WHERE ON EARTH?

p.92 FIRST THOUGHTS

Ask students to describe their feelings about travelling to remote places. Elicit any personal experiences. Ask the students to describe the geographical position of the Galapagos islands and check the vocabulary:
iguana, tortoise, turtle.

p.92 USE OF ENGLISH

1 Students brainstorm anything they know about Darwin. Write their ideas on the board.
Background information
Charles Darwin 1809–1882, English naturalist who developed the theory of natural selection (evolution) in *On the Origin of Species by Means of Natural Selection* (1859).

2 Answers

1 They are in the Pacific Ocean, west of Ecuador, and formed from a volcano.
2 Because they were remote and uninhabited.
3 Pirates, a few hundred years ago.
4 The tortoises were unique to each island.
5 They brought rats, cats, pigs and dogs which interfered with the balance of nature on the islands. This was partly solved by hunting and killing some of these animals.
6 Tourism.

3/4 Students should tackle these individually then compare answers in small groups, explaining/justifying their choices and helping each other with any which are problematic.

3 Answers

1 C; 2 C; 3 D; 4 B; 5 B; 6 A; 7 D; 8 D; 9 A; 10 B; 11 D; 12 C; 13 C; 14 C; 15 D

4 Answers

1 few; 2 of; 3 little; 4 without; 5 once; 6 keep; 7 brought; 8 which; 9 These; 10 being; 11 taken/introduced; 12 possible; 13 In; 14 Despite; 15 which

5 Students can discuss the points in groups. If your students are all from the same country you might like to extend the activity to include making a list of the threatened places and recommendations for government action to preserve them.

6 Answers

1 although; 2 it; 3 about; 4 ✓; 5 time; 6 ✓; 7 to; 8 The; 9 very; 10 was; 11 a; 12 The; 13 ✓; 14 the; 15 much

p.93 WRITING

Compulsory letter

As the students are by now familiar with this type of task you might like them to work individually. If so, the letter can be set as homework.
If you have time to fill you could get them started by asking them to group the notes into topics (to help with paragraph organisation) or to expand the notes into sentences, for example,

Topics/paragraphs:
1 information about school facilities and children
2 questions we would like her to answer
3 arrangements to meet, etc.

Expanded notes:
children 12–17 little knowledge of the islands
The children in the science club are aged between twelve and seventeen. They don't know very much about the Galapagos islands.
Remind the students of the layout and style suitable for a semi-formal letter (see Unit 2).

8 Judging by Appearances

JUMPING TO CONCLUSIONS

p.94 FIRST THOUGHTS

Introduce the topic generally by asking the class what they think you can tell about a person's character from their face. Then put them in small groups to look at the characters in the pictures. Give them a few minutes and then get feedback from each group. Find out who is the most/least popular and get the students to explain why this is so.

p.94 READING

1 Get the students to brainstorm questions they would like answered about face analysis, e.g. *Can you tell a person's character from their face?* Write three or four of these on the board then ask the class to read the text quickly to find the answers.

2 Students should read through the multiple choice items before reading the text again. They should compare answers in pairs, justifying their answers as necessary.

ANSWERS
1 B; 2 B; 3 C; 4 B; 5 C; 6 A; 7 A

3 Read through the explanation with the class and elicit further examples. You might want to put this example on the board for further clarification:

The Dutch tend to be taller than other nationalities.
= most of the Dutch are taller.
= a minority of the Dutch are not taller.

4 Students should work in small groups. Remind them of the language of giving opinions, agreeing and disagreeing, which they studied in the last unit and which they may find useful during their discussion.

p.95 LANGUAGE STUDY

Making intelligent guesses

1 ANSWERS
1 D; 2 A; 3 C; 4 B

You could ask students to find further examples from the text:
1 *These secrets **cannot have been** that well guarded and must have got out.*
2 *... she **must** be strong-willed ...*
3 *... this time **must have been** a period of great unhappiness.*

2 Go through the pictures in open class, first eliciting descriptions of each, providing vocabulary as necessary. Then put students in pairs to make appropriate deductions.

POSSIBLE ANSWERS
1 He must have been in a fight.
2 She might have had a row with her boyfriend.
3 She must have been somewhere sunny on holiday.
4 He must have broken his leg skiing.

A further passive construction
Check that students understand the difference between tentative and definite statements. Do the first example in open class, pointing out that the subject is omitted.

ANSWERS
1 The Mona Lisa is claimed to be the world's most famous painting.
2 It is believed to have been a portrait of a noblewoman.
3 Her smile is said to hide a secret.
4 It is believed to be Leonardo's masterpiece.
5 He is known to have been a wonderful engineer too.
6 He is thought to have been unhappy in old age.

p.96 VOCABULARY

Adjectives of personality

1 Students go through the words in pairs, deciding on number of syllables and marking the stress. Go through the first two or three in open class and ensure that students say the words aloud. Get them to report back orally and check their pronunciation. Drill any which are causing problems. (Answers below, number of syllables in brackets)

2 Before students begin the gap-filling task they should try and think of a synonym or simple explanation for each one, working in small groups. Open class feedback – if one group doesn't know a word, let another group explain it. If no-one knows a word, then give a brief definition with example. Then let the students in the same group work through the exercise. This should establish whether they really have understood the meaning of the target vocabulary.

Note
Beware of the words that may act as 'false friends' to speakers of Latinate languages, e.g. *sensitive, sensible, sympathetic*.

ANSWERS FOR EXERCISES 1, 2 AND 3

	ADJECTIVES	NOUNS
1	re'liable (4)	reliability
2	sensitive (3)	sensitivity
3	mean	meanness
4	strict	strictness
5	'cheerful (2)	cheerfulness
6	'sensible (3)	sense
7	nice	niceness
8	sympa'thetic (4)	sympathy
9	tough	toughness
10	'clumsy (2)	clumsiness
11	'silly (2)	silliness
12	shy	shyness
13	'selfish (2)	selfishness
14	'trustworthy (3)	trustworthiness
15	'gentle (2)	gentleness
16	bad-'tempered (3)	bad temper
17	'loyal (2)	loyalty
18	dull	dullness
19	'stubborn (2)	stubbornness
20	'crafty (2)	craftiness

Extension

In small groups, students discuss what they think are the three characteristics they most like/dislike in other people.

3 Students should note down the nouns formed from the adjectives, using dictionaries if necessary. Answers above. Divide the class into pairs; if possible get students working with a partner they don't know very well. Each student writes a description of their new partner based on the facial characteristics only. Check that students know the vocabulary of the descriptions before starting the exercise. Ask them to report back and use this to generate a general discussion about 'judging by appearances'.

p.97 LISTENING

Note

With a particularly shy or sensitive class you might want to omit some of the discussion points suggested below and in the Coursebook. In this case simply stick to the listening exercises.

1 Before looking at the book, set the scene by discussing what lonely hearts columns are and where you might find them. Ask students if they exist in their countries and, if so, if they read them. Ask what they think of them. Then students go through the descriptions in the column in the book and try and match them up. There are no definite or 'correct' answers. You could ask students to choose the ad they would be most interested in answering! Sort out any problematic vocabulary as it comes up.

2 ANSWERS

1 C; **2** H; **3** 2; **4** 5; **5** C; **6** B; **7** C; **8** A

Extension

You could ask students to write their own advertisement for a lonely hearts column. When everyone (including you!) has done this, collect them all and read them out one by one, asking the class to guess who wrote each one. (This should be kept on a fairly light-hearted level!). Alternatively, students could write an advertisement for homework.

TAPESCRIPT

CLIVE: Hi Jenny.
JENNY: Hi.
CLIVE: How did it go then?
JENNY: Pretty mixed really.
CLIVE: Oh yeah?
JENNY: Yeah. He wasn't exactly the man of my dreams.
CLIVE: What happened then?
JENNY: It was pretty nerve-wracking, actually, waiting outside the station for him to turn up. Like being 14 all over again.
CLIVE: Yes. I know what you mean. Still, he didn't stand you up, did he?
JENNY: No, no. He turned up all right.
CLIVE: So what did he look like?
JENNY: Well, he had reddish hair, glasses – quite good-looking, I suppose – not very tall, about your height, in fact.
CLIVE: Charming!
JENNY: I didn't mean it like that but I guess I was expecting someone much sportier, someone who likes the outdoor life.
CLIVE: Well-dressed?
JENNY: Not particularly. Bit scruffy really. Wore a leather jacket and a pullover.
CLIVE: Really?
JENNY: Yeah.
CLIVE: And what was he like?
JENNY: Not that exciting I'm afraid.
CLIVE: Why not?
JENNY: Well, at first I thought he was OK but then we went off to a pub and all he could talk about was politics.
CLIVE: But you're into that, aren't you?
JENNY: Yeah, but not all the time. He went on and on. He said he had a great time but I couldn't get away fast enough.
CLIVE: Oh dear.
JENNY: He wants to see me again. Asked me if I wanted to go to a demo on Saturday.
CLIVE: You're kidding.
JENNY: No I'm not going. Anyway, how about you?
CLIVE: Well, I have to admit that I almost chickened out.
JENNY: Typical.
CLIVE: Well, I didn't and I had a great time.
JENNY: Did you? Tell us all about it then.

CLIVE: We just went out to an Italian I know and had a nice meal and chatted away merrily. You know, we found out that we'd lived in the same street as kids.
JENNY: How amazing!
CLIVE: But we couldn't remember each other.
JENNY: Was she pretty?
CLIVE: Very. She was very chic – all in black, short black hair and not much make-up.
JENNY: She sounds a bit serious to me. Not really your type.
CLIVE: No, no, not at all. She had a great sense of humour. Funny, you don't expect that from someone who's an accountant.
JENNY: Going to see her again?
CLIVE: Yeah, she said to give her a call.

p.98 VOCABULARY

Physical description

All the exercises in this section can be done in pairs or small groups.

1 Ask students to read the description and decide if the parts which are listed in the introduction (height, build, etc.) do, in fact, appear in the order suggested. What extra features are included?

2 Height and build

> **ANSWERS**
>
> frail: (old) and weak-looking.
> stocky: shortish but well-built.
> slim: attractively thin.
> plump: overweight.
> skinny: unattractively thin.

3 Age

> **ANSWERS**
>
> **A** 65 plus; **B** 13–19; **C** 17–20; **D** someone who has retired from work, 60–65 plus; **E** 40–55; **F** 1–3; **G** 31–33 *(early)*, 34–36 *(mid)*, 37–39 *(late)*

4 Face

1 Draw (or ask students to draw) the three shapes on the board. Ask students to identify classmates with these types of faces.

2 Draw the following on the board (without the labels), get students to come up and match the features with the blank labels.

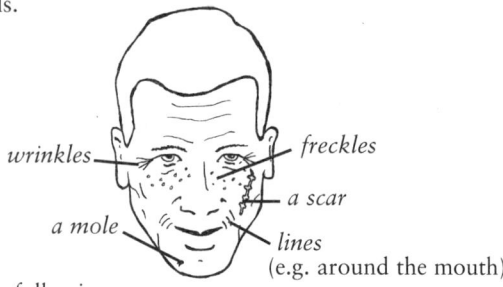

3 Elicit the following:
pale: white
tanned: brown
sallow: yellowish/unhealthy looking

5 Eyes

> **ANSWERS**
>
> Susan has got large round brown eyes.
> Klaus has got small bright blue eyes.
> Mary has large green eyes.
> Mariko has large almond-shaped dark brown eyes.

Draw a face on the board to explain eyebrows and eyelashes, or point to them on your own face.

6 Hair

> **ANSWERS**
>
> **1** A; **2** C; **3** B; **4** F; **5** D; **6** E

Draw the following on the board to explain bun and pigtails.

Bun   *Pigtails*

7 Clothes

> **ANSWERS**
>
> **1** D; **2** E; **3** A; **4** C; **5** B

p.99 READING

Students can discuss the question in pairs. They should notice the more literary style of the description, its greater detail, its use of adjectives and similes (you might want the students to list these). It is also more positive than the description of Paul and makes the reader curious to find out more.

p.99 WRITING

This can be set as homework.

COLOUR CHOICES

p.100 FIRST THOUGHTS

You could introduce this topic by asking students to describe the clothes they are wearing and their reasons for choosing them. Concentrate on colour rather than style of clothes. Elicit as many colour adjectives as possible and write these on the board. Refer to the glossary box in the Coursebook and ask students if they can apply the expressions to any of their own clothes.

p.100 READING

What really suits you?

1 Go through the expressions in the glossary on page 101 (see note above) and elicit answers to the vocabulary questions.

> **ANSWERS**
>
> 1 blusher, eyeshadow and lipstick are types of make-up. Blusher is worn on the cheeks, eyeshadow on the eyelids and lipstick on the lips.
> 2 *wardrobe* can mean:
>   – a tall piece of furniture used to store clothes
>   – the collection of clothes belonging to one person.

2 Students should read through the text quickly to answer the gist question.

> **ANSWER**
>
> Margot Henderson is a colour consultant. She helps people find the colour/s for clothes which best suit their own skin, eye and hair colour.

3 ANSWER

> (Best → worst)
> Wayne (3) – Susie (6) – Vanessa (5) – Kevin (1) – Penny (4) – Jason (2)

4 Students can complete the matching task individually then compare their choices in small groups.

> **ANSWERS**
>
> 1 H; 2 D; 3 A; 4 F; 5 C; 6 G
> The extra heading is B

5 For a change, draw the blank chart on the board. When students have completed the exercise ask individuals to come up and write in the answers, taking one section each.

> **ANSWERS**
>
> | CLOTHES | | |
> |---|---|---|
> | | ✓ | ✗ |
> | Clear | bright colours or dark/light mixtures | |
> | Light | brown/pastels/ bluey-green | black/white/dark colours |
> | Soft | blue/tones of the same colour/earthy browns | bright pink |
>
> | MAKE-UP | | |
> |---|---|---|
> | | ✓ | ✗ |
> | Clear | bronze | |
> | Light | pastels/gentle pinks or rose | red |
> | Soft | mauve/light grey | bright green |

p.101 LISTENING

Play the tape once through for general understanding and then play it again, stopping as necessary for students to complete the sentences.

> **ANSWERS**
>
> 1 were fashionable; 2 black; 3 reddish/chestnut; 4 hazel; 5 freckles; 6 warm; 7 rid of them; 8 deep; 9 turquoise; 10 pastels

TAPESCRIPT

MARGOT: Well, in the old days, I think I used to go for stuff, for colours just because they were fashionable, you know the in colours of the time.
AMBROSE: Like black these days.
MARGOT: Um, that's right. And I mean lots of people, I'd say most, look dreadful in black, it just doesn't suit them. I mean, people who are pale and blonde just look so washed-out if they wear it.
AMBROSE: But they do, 'cos of fashion.
MARGOT: Yeah that's right ...
AMBROSE: So could you tell listeners what sort of impact this has had on your life?
MARGOT: Sure, well, let me start with my details. I've got reddish, chestnut hair and hazel eyes and, like lots of red-haired people, I've got quite a few freckles.
AMBROSE: Huh huh ...
MARGOT: So all of this makes me, erm my classification, is 'warm'.

AMBROSE: 'Warm' that's interesting, so what does this mean?
MARGOT: Well, before I used to wear a lot of blues and greys but I was advised they didn't suit me and so I just, I got rid of them.
AMBROSE: Brave of you ...
MARGOT: And instead I switched to greens, golden browns and so on.
AMBROSE: That's why you're wearing these colours yourself.
MARGOT: Right.
AMBROSE: So what advice would you have for me then? Does it work for men too?
MARGOT: Yes of course! Well, you've got brown eyes and hair and black skin which makes you a 'deep' person.
AMBROSE: Deep! I like that ...
MARGOT: Hah hah, this means that you can wear black and greys, but my advice to you would be to offset them, erm contrast them with really bright, vivid colours like turquoise, red or yellow. Steer clear of pastels as they just won't suit you at all.
AMBROSE: You're right you know 'cos I remember once I bought this ...

p.101 SPEAKING

You could start this off by asking students to advise **you** on colours. Remind them that they should first decide which 'type' you are, then refer to the chart and text from the previous exercises to decide on colours. They can then work in groups to advise each other. It can be amusing to compare the theoretical choices with the clothes you/the students are actually wearing.

A summary of this advice can be written as homework.

PICTURES OF THE SOUL

p.102 FIRST THOUGHTS

Use the illustrations to elicit students' ideas on the interpretation of children's pictures. Ask them to predict/make guesses about the characters of the artists. Elicit or introduce/pre-teach the following adjectives in connection with the pictures:
energetic, neat, untidy, cautious, controlled, illegible, confused.

p.102 LISTENING

1 As a gist listening task you could ask the students to listen once and find out if their guesses about the childrens' personalities are the same as the psychologist's on the tape. Get the students to read through the questions before listening again.

ANSWERS

1 J; **2** A; **3** P; **4** J; **5** P; **6** P; **7** P

2 Managing conversations

Read through the expressions with the class. If you have time, play the tape again and ask the students to repeat the phrases, paying attention to stress and intonation.
They will have a chance to practise these in the next section.

TAPESCRIPT

JOSEPH: Yes. You're right. I can see this could be quite a useful tool for people like us, social workers and teachers. It's often difficult for us to assess the personality of some of the kids we have to deal with ...
PAUL: I'm sorry, Joseph, but I'm afraid I have less sympathy for the idea. It seems rather like, erm, black magic to me ...
JOSEPH: Well, I'm sure it isn't, Paul. Erm, do you think you could actually talk us through some examples?
ANGELA: Well, as a matter of fact I've brought some along to show you. Let's look at the first one, shall we?
FELICITY: OK.
ANGELA: Well, this looks like the work of a happy child and well-balanced individual.
JOSEPH: What makes you say that, Angela?
ANGELA: Well, there's a lot of life in it. There are people and animals.
JOSEPH: Mm, it's very energetic, there's a lot of activity in it, isn't there?
PAUL: I think you're reading too much into this one picture, Joseph.
ANGELA: Well, I take your point but let's compare it with the second one. Well, my guess is the child must be deeply unhappy.
PAUL: What do you mean? How can you be so sure?
ANGELA: It would be dishonest of me to say I was 100 per cent sure. All the same, the picture is just too neat and cautious, there are no white spaces either, there are just, erm, buildings with nothing else. There is a lot of anxiety there.
PAUL: Really? It just looks neat and pretty to me ...
JOSEPH: But that's just it. This is a picture from a kid who desperately wants to please adults, you know parents and teachers.
PAUL: So what you're saying, Joseph, is that it's too controlled, that there is no spontaneity in it.
ANGELA: Exactly. In fact, I'd say it expresses a fundamental misery.
PAUL: This is all very well but how can you really tell? How can you be that sure? You know it could be a bit irresponsible to make a very important assessment or judgement about a child on the basis of their drawings.
ANGELA: I agree. There's no point in the exercise if it's unreliable, you know, erm, hit or miss.
PAUL: Right ... So how did you actually go about working it out? Surely it's impossible to come to any conclusion without seeing a lot of drawings from the same person.
ANGELA: Oh. I see. I think I understand what you're getting at. There has been a lot of research done.

Psychologists have studied thousands of pictures by kids and matched them up .
JOSEPH: I'm sorry, but I don't quite follow you ...
ANGELA: What I mean is, is that the same kind of child tends to produce the same kind of drawing and patterns.
JOSEPH: Mmm ... I see.
PAUL: Mm, this is interesting. Let's have a look at one more, shall we?
JOSEPH: It's difficult to make out what's going on.
ANGELA: Yes, you're right. There is a lot of scribbling and quite a bit of confusion in it.
PAUL: It looks as though there is a lot of anger there.
ANGELA: There is some writing too but it's completely illegible.
PAUL: So what does it all mean, then?
ANGELA: Well, you're right about anger, Paul. We generally associate this kind of drawing with children who are disobedient, you know, who don't do as they're told. They're often incapable of concentration.
PAUL: Well, I must say, the more I hear you talking about this, the more I think there could be something in it. How could I find out a little more about the whole thing? Are there any books that you could recommend?

p.102 LANGUAGE STUDY

1/2 Point out that:
- We use an adjective after *look* when it means seem, e.g. *She looks fed up*.
- *look like* basically means *be similar to*, e.g. *She really looks like her mother*.
- *look as though/if* has a meaning similar to 1, but attention must be paid to the grammatical construction, i.e. *look as if/though* + subject + verb, e.g. *The mother looks as though she is in her late 20s*. Note that *as if* and *as though* are interchangeable.

Elicit that we use these expressions when we are making guesses and deductions based on (usually visual) evidence, or expressing our own personal opinion about something. Students analyse the sentences in pairs.

ANSWERS

1 She looks hungry/ She looks as if/though she is hungry.
2 Correct
3 Correct
4 Correct
5 The boys look as if/though they are breaking into the car.

3 In the same pairs students discuss the pictures. Monitor and check use of the conversation features and the expressions with *look*. When students have finished ask them to report back with their ideas or to compare ideas with other pairs. See if the class as a whole can agree on two or three statements about each picture (using *look*).

p.103 USE OF ENGLISH

Word building

1 ANSWERS

sympathy; anxiety; misery; anger

2 Students may find it useful to use dictionaries for exercises 2 and 3. Check that they are careful with spelling. Model each word for correct stress.

ANSWERS

POSITIVE ADJECTIVE	NEGATIVE ADJECTIVE	POSITIVE NOUN	NEGATIVE NOUN
happy	unhappy	happiness	unhappiness
responsible	irresponsible	responsibility	irresponsibility
capable	incapable	capability	—
legible	illegible	legibility	illegibility
possible	impossible	possibility	impossibility
honest	dishonest	honesty	dishonesty

3 ANSWERS

legal – **il**legal; loyal – **dis**loyal; comfortable – **un**comfortable; reliable – **un**reliable; kind – **un**kind; obedient – **dis**obedient; favourable – **un**favourable; literate – **il**literate; patient – **im**patient

When students have completed and checked their answers you can ask them to list the prefixes and suffixes as follows:
- Negative prefixes: *un-, ir-, im-, in-, il-, dis-*
- Suffixes added to an adjective to make a noun: *-ness, -y, -ity*

4 Introduce the painting and ask students to react to it. Ask them if they can apply the same analysis as was used with the children's drawings earlier in the unit.
Note: The painting is *The Scream* by the Norwegian artist Edvard Munch (1863–1944), it was painted in 1908 following a severe mental illness.
Before students complete the gap-filling ask them to decide what part of speech each gap should be and whether it has a positive or negative meaning (in brackets below). When they have agreed on this they can attempt the task.

ANSWERS

1 (*noun*) analysis; 2 (*noun*) misery; 3 (*noun – negative meaning*) unhappiness; 4 (*adjective – positive meaning*) powerful; 5 (*verb – infinitive form*) sympathise; 6 (*noun*) childhood; 7 (*noun*) loss; 8 (*noun – positive meaning*) sensitivity; 9 (*noun*) obsession; 10 (*noun*) anxiety

9 Teenage Cults

FASHION CLASH

p.104 FIRST THOUGHTS

1 For a general idea of parent-child differences, ask students to put their hands up if; a) they have ever had a real argument over their choices; b) their parents disapproved (but not strongly); c) if their parents usually accept their choices.

2 Put the students into pairs or groups. They should tell the story using narrative tenses. Then get feedback to the story.

POSSIBLE VERSION

1 One morning the Harrison family were having breakfast at the start of another typical day.
2 Liz left for school, saying goodbye to her mum.
3 Unbeknown to her parents, Liz had arranged to meet Pete, a good-looking guy she had met at a party the weekend before. She took a new outfit with her in a plastic bag. She showed it to her school friends at the bus stop.
4 Instead of going to school, Liz went into a Ladies to change and get ready for her date.
5 A little while later she made her way over to the park where she had agreed to meet Pete. He thought she looked wonderful and they walked around the park for the next couple of hours, chatting. They both liked each other a lot. Eventually, Liz said she had to go. They agreed to walk home via Pete's house which was closest.
6 As they were saying goodbye outside Pete's house, Liz's dad drove past and saw them. He was very surprised and quite angry.
7 When Liz finally got home, her dad confronted her angrily as she was going up the stairs to her room. Liz ran up to her room, crying.
8 Liz's gran, who was staying with them for a few days, saw what happened and, afterwards, went into the living room to have a word with her son. She reminded him of one or two similar episodes in his teens which made him think he had been a little hard on Liz.
9 He went upstairs and apologised for being so angry.

Now encourage the students to work out what was actually said in each of the bubbles. Accept what is best and establish a 'standard' version. You will then be able to refer back to this when you have revised reported speech.

POSSIBLE VERSION

What the people might have said/thought:
2 LIZ: Bye, Mum.
   MUM: Bye, Liz.
3 LIZ: So ... what do you think of it?
   FRIEND 1: Not bad. Where did you get it?
   FRIEND 2: I think it's great ... Just what you need!
6 DAD: I can't believe my eyes! Is that ... LIZ?!!!
7 DAD: What do you think you were doing with that boy in the middle of Park Street?
   LIZ: We weren't doing anything wrong.
8 GRAN: I remember you being a bit of a tearaway on that old Triumph motorbike.
9 DAD: I'm sorry. I shouldn't have got so angry ... it's just that I'm worried about you.
   LIZ: I know Dad – it's all right, but really, there's nothing to worry about.

p.105 VOCABULARY

Clothes

Students can work in groups in order to pool their knowledge.

ANSWERS

1 tight; 2 shrink; 3 match; 4 wardrobe; 5 suits;
6 baggy; 7 loose; 8 clash; 9 take ... in, up; 10 go

p.105 LISTENING

ANSWERS

Speaker 1 E; Speaker 2 F; Speaker 3 D;
Speaker 4 B; Speaker 5 A
C is the extra sentence

TAPESCRIPT

SPEAKER 1: Well, it was really awful, you know. It was a wedding reception, erm in the middle of town in a posh hotel. So, I was feeling really rather pleased with myself. I had on this beige Italian suit – very expensive and a beautiful tie and silk shirt. Everything went beautifully. But when I walked into the ballroom where the reception was being held I almost died. Everybody else, and I mean everyone was dressed up in evening dress. I swear everybody stopped talking when I went into the room. Well, what would you have worn at two o'clock in the afternoon? And the bride's mother – if looks could have killed! I don't think I appeared in any of the photographs.

SPEAKER 2: So anyway, I found this lovely pair of trousers, they were made of a kind of soft cotton, and I went to a changing room and tried them on. I thought they looked OK but that they were a bit loose round the waist – I wouldn't have that problem these days. Anyway, when I got out of the changing room the assistant came up to me and asked me how they felt. I said fine but asked whether they would stretch or shrink when they were washed. Quick as a flash he said to me "Well, what do you want them to do?" We both laughed and I bought them anyway.

SPEAKER 3: I was really upset ... I'd had those jeans for ages and they were really faded and looked, you know, really cool and fashionable. Anyway, I got home after school and went to change out of my uniform and I couldn't find them anywhere so I asked mum if she'd seen them. "Those scruffy old things," she said, "I threw them out," she said "They were an absolute disgrace." Scruffy old things! They were my favourite! I was really upset. If I ever have kids, I'll never do that, I thought it was really mean.

SPEAKER 4: Well, I really liked it, the colour really suited me, the only thing is that the sleeves were a bit too long. So I asked if they could take the sleeves up for me a couple of inches. The girl in the shop said it would cost me thirty pounds. I just couldn't believe it. "Thirty pounds!" I said. After all, I was ready to spend almost a hundred on a jacket. The girl said that it was because they had to send the jacket out to an, erm, outside, you know, alterations place, tailor. In the end I left it – just as well really, it would have clashed horribly with the trousers.

SPEAKER 5: It was a really beautiful day and the others suggested going for a dip. Now I hadn't brought my things with me but in the end, well, I borrowed a pair of trunks from Keith. They were a bit on the large side but I didn't think anything of it. I ran into the sea and started swimming around and we all played with a ball, you know, throwing it to each other. Then out of nowhere a huge wave came along and everybody was swept off their feet. Well, you can guess what happened. The trunks flew off and I was left stranded in the sea. The others thought it was hilarious. I had to beg them to bring the trunks back to me. Everybody on the beach was laughing too. They knew what was going on.

p.105 SPEAKING

Let students discuss the points in pairs and then get feedback in open class or join pairs together to make groups of four or six to exchange their experiences.

p.105 PRONUNCIATION

Rising intonation

1 Play the extracts on tape and ask the students to repeat. Drill until they can reproduce the rising intonation convincingly.

2 Divide the class into pairs. Go through situation A as a model:
STUDENT A: I'm going to marry my teacher.
STUDENT B: Marry your teacher!
Monitor the pairs and ask them to reverse roles when they have finished.

SUGGESTED RESPONSES

B An accident! Are you OK?

C A cyclist! Was she hurt?

D Russian!

E From my wallet! Why didn't you ask?

F The end of the month!

NEW GENERATIONS

p.106 FIRST THOUGHTS

1/2 Use the photographs and questions as a lead-in to the topic of teenage cults.
Notes on the photographs:
Hippies: Originally from California. 1960s–70s. Bright 'psychedelic' clothes and long hair. Like rock and folk music with a message. Anti-materialistic, believe in peace and (free) love. Basically optimistic. Mostly well-off, middle class kids reacting against their parents. Many university students. Usually left-wing and into peaceful demonstrations.
Teddy boys ('Teds'): 1950s. Wear long jackets, tight trousers and suede shoes. Like early rock and roll music. Working class.
Punks: 1970s. Wear black leather, cut jeans. Brightly dyed hair with spikey or Mohican haircuts. Like violent, discordant music. Anti-materialistic from necessity as they usually come from poor backgrounds. Pessimists.
Goths: 1980s–90s. Wear black clothes and silver jewellery. White faces with black make-up, black hair. Romantic, gloomy philosophy, interested in the dark side of life.
Skinheads: Wear jeans, ex-army clothing and big boots. They enjoy fighting. They like similar music to the punks. They are often poorly educated and come from working-class backgrounds. Frequently right-wing and racist.
Mods: 1960s. Very fashion conscious. Wear suits and ties and parka jackets, short hair. Ride motor scooters. Enemies of the Rockers, who ride motorbikes. Like black soul music.

ANSWERS

Photo 1 C; Photo 2 F; Photo 3 E; Photo 4 A;
Photo 5 B; Photo 6 D
The cults appeared roughly in this order: C, D, E, A, F, B

p.106–107 READING

Pre-teach *a cult, to look down on someone*. Remind students of exam technique: read through the text for general understanding first, thinking about possible headings as you read, then read the headlines and begin matching them.

ANSWERS

1 F; 2 A; 3 H; 4 C; 5 D; 6 B
E is the extra heading

Extension

After students have completed the matching task and checked their answers ask them to say which explanations they find least and most convincing and to say why.

p.107 LANGUAGE STUDY

Conjunctions

Students should refer back to the reading text if they are unsure of the meaning of any of the sentences.

ANSWERS

1 C; 2 B; 3 B; 4 C; 5 B; 6 C; 7 C; 8 A; 9 B; 10 A

p.107 LISTENING

1 Ask the students to describe the photograph in pairs. Ask them to describe (or predict from the picture) what they think the Goths' philosophy is. Elicit/pre-teach the following:
aristocratic, mystical, pessimistic, doomed, Gothic.

2 Play the tape once and give students time to make notes. Then play the tape again. Get the students to compare and expand their notes in small groups.

SUGGESTED ANSWERS

clothes/jewellery and make-up:
black, velvets and lace, soft rich fabrics, silver jewellery, white skin, based on aristocratic fashion of 200 years ago
origins/influences:
a mixture – punk, New Romantics
philosophy/interests:
mystical things, tragic/doomed/negative view of life
origin of name:
from the neo-Gothic period (of literature e.g. Frankenstein, Dracula)

TAPESCRIPT

Shall we move onto something else. Well, of course these are Goths. You can tell from the, erm the costume and make-up. They're really interesting. When they started up in the early eighties nobody thought that they would, um, you know, last.
They were a mixture of quite a lot of other fashions, you know the emphasis on black, well this was something that was very much punk. There was also another fashion at the time – I don't know whether you remember it or not – well it was called the New Romantics – people dressed up in, emm, velvets and lace and stuff like that. Soft and rich fabrics. It looked a little bit like fancy dress I guess. It took its, erm, inspiration from, what, aristocratic fashion from two hundred years ago.
Anyway, as I was saying the Goths were really a mixture of all these things. But what makes them different I suppose is their philosophy. They are into mystical things and wear silver jewellery, often with a religious significance. They can look really striking with their white skin and swept-back hair, you know they brush it right back.
Another thing is that they have a rather negative view of life. You know, you expect young people to be optimistic and full of life and enthusiasm, but, Goths aren't like that. They are quite pessimistic and interested in death. They have this attitude that everything is, erm, doomed and somehow tragic. They also have this fascination with TV programmes like *The Munsters* and *The Addams Family*. It seems to appeal to kids, and I think there are always lots in every generation, who like to look on the dark rather than the bright side of life. You can, erm, go almost anywhere in England now, even to the smallest village and find a few Goths together as a small group, very much isolated from other kids of the same age.
The name Goths, of course, comes from the neo-Gothic period, you know Dracula, Frankenstein, Mary Shelley and all that.

p.107 WRITING

Introduce the task (60 to 80 words is about 5 or 6 sentences). Students can begin by expanding their notes into full sentences, using the conjunctions to join them/give explanations, examples, contrasts, etc.
This task can be set as homework.

MODEL ANSWER

The 'Goths' cult began in England in the early nineteen-eighties and was influenced by the punks and New Romantics. Their clothes are often black and were inspired by the aristocratic fashions of the eighteenth century. They look very striking with their brushed-back hair and white make-up.

The Goths have a rather mystical and pessimistic philosophy, they tend to look on the dark side of life. Their name comes from the neo-Gothic period when novels such as *Frankenstein* and *Dracula* were written.

HANG YOUR HEAD IN SHAME!

p.108 VOCABULARY

Phrasal verbs

1 ANSWERS

1 E; 2 F; 3 H; 4 B; 5 I; 6 G; 7 C; 8 A; 9 D

2 If students find this exercise difficult it might help if they first try to fill the gaps with the definitions (A–I) from exercise 1, they can then find which phrasal verb fits that definition.

ANSWERS

1 faced up to; 2 let ... down; 3 live up to; 4 look up to; 5 put ... down; 6 look down on; 7 talking ... over; 8 go along with; 9 sort ... out

p.108–109 USE OF ENGLISH

1 Introduce the topic of magazine advice pages and ask students if they have seen/read any. Ask students to quickly read the letter and answer the gist question.

ANSWER

The writer's 12-year-old daughter was arrested for stealing some make-up from a chemist's. The girl's father doesn't seem to care very much. The girl is afraid to go out and cries all the time.

Students complete the gaps, then compare with a partner.

ANSWERS

1 when; 2 been; 3 This/It; 4 by; 5 first; 6 her; 7 so; 8 what; 9 were; 10 Since; 11 own; 12 very/that/too; 13 the; 14 over; 15 turn

2 Students discuss their advice in small groups. Before they begin briefly elicit suitable 'advice-giving' language (*If I were you ..., You should ..., You ought to ..., Why don't you ...?* etc.). Ask them to make brief notes, then to report back. Write the best suggestions on the board.

3 Firstly get students to quickly skim the text to compare Angela's advice with what they came up with. Was it the same? If different, what do they think of Angela's advice?

4 Note: In the exam this task (Paper 3 Part 4) has only 15 lines to be edited.
When students have completed the task ask them to compare in small groups, justifying their answers in the case of disagreement.

ANSWERS

1 am; 2 of; 3 ✓; 4 but; 5 ✓; 6 are; 7 an; 8 ✓; 9 a; 10 of; 11 they; 12 ago; 13 ✓; 14 ✓ 15 will; 16 a; 17 to; 18 ✓ 18 every

5 You may wish students to follow the same structured approach to this task as adopted previously. That is, to decide on the part of speech required for each gap first of all, then to decide if it has a positive or negative meaning, finally to transform the 'stem'.

ANSWERS

1 relationship; 2 expectations; 3 hopeless; 4 criticism; 5 unforgivable; 6 irresponsible; 7 disappearance; 8 helpless; 9 unreasonably; 10 misunderstanding

p.109 WRITING

Ask students to underline the expressions in the text used for giving advice, e.g. *You should ...* . Remind students of the further exponents which were elicited in the previous *Use of English* exercise 3 (p.108). Ask students to discuss their advice to Richard in small groups, making notes as they do so.
The letter can be written as homework.

p.110–111 LANGUAGE STUDY

Reported speech

1 In pairs, students correct the sentences and use the information to work out the rules A–D. Ask them to report back, and deal with any problems.
Note: This and the remaining exercises in this section can be tackled by students working in pairs or small groups.

CORRECTED SENTENCES

1 He said the problem was difficult.
or He told me the problem was difficult.
(A – *tell* is followed by a personal indirect object (*me*), *say* is not)
2 She told him to turn down the music.
(A – *tell* (not *say*) is used to report commands, instructions, orders and advice)

67

3 He asked her how much money he had taken.
4 He asked whether he could help.
(B – *no inversion of subject and verb and no question marks in reported questions. Use* **if** *or* **whether** *for yes/no questions*)
(C – *tense changes, e.g. past simple* → *past perfect, modal changes, e.g.* **can** → **could**)
5 She explained the problem to him.
(D – **explain**, *like* **suggest**, *is followed by a direct object* (**the problem**); *if there is an indirect object* (**him**) *we use a preposition* (**to**).

2 Tense changes

ANSWERS

2 Mary: I'm working.
   present continuous
3 She said she had been to Spain.
   past perfect
4 I've been living here for ages.
   present perfect continuous
5 She told me she had made a mistake.
   past perfect – no change
6 She said she had been watching TV.
   past perfect continuous

3 Changes with modals

ANSWERS

1 *may, can* and *will* usually become *might, could* and *would*.
2 Generally there is no change, but note that if we use the perfect infinitive (*have* + past participle) then we invariably change our intended meaning. For example: *I should post this letter.*
   → He said he should post the letter. (reminding himself)
   → He said he should have posted the letter. (He didn't.)
3 She told him if he did that again, she would hit him.

4 Other changes

1 ANSWERS

A 'I'm going to leave tomorrow,' she said.
B 'This is the record I bought two days ago,' he said.
C 'The parcel will arrive the day after tomorrow,' they said.
D 'Did anybody come yesterday?' he asked.
E 'Your flat will be ready next month,' we told them.
F 'I called earlier, but no one answered the door,' he said.
G 'Is today your birthday?' she asked.

2 ANSWERS

REPORTED SPEECH
A that
B the
C that day
D the day before/the previous day
E two days before/earlier
F earlier
G the following/next day
H in two days' time
I the following week/month/year

5 Reporting advice and suggestions

1/2 Study the verb forms in 1 and 2.

3 POSSIBLE ANSWERS

A She advised him to go by train.
B Arthur suggested watching TV.
C Julian suggested that she should go to the cinema.
D The doctor advised her to take more exercise.
E Fatima's grandmother advised her to wear a scarf.

6 Answers

1 Carol told Peter not to make such a noise.
2 Sue advised Richard to take the train instead of the bus.
3 The doctor told me it was/would be a good idea to take more exercise.
4 Robin suggested (that) I (should) buy shares in Sony. *(4 possible options)*
5 'I have never flown before,' he said.
6 He told them they had missed it/the train by five minutes.
7 He promised to deliver the puppy in two days' time.
8 Sharon asked her mother if/whether she had seen her tennis racquet.
9 As far as I'm concerned he should have a haircut.
10 What makes you look down on other people?

p.112 LISTENING

1 Students listen (to part A only) and complete the true/false task. Play the tape twice if necessary. Ask them to compare and check their answers in small groups and then discuss the problem and suggest suitable advice for Rachel. They report back and compare their ideas with other groups. Write on the board the main points of their advice.

Answers

1 True – *he hasn't been able to find a job since he left school.*
2 False – *a year in July*
3 True – *over the last few months he's changed quite a bit.*
4 False – *depressed and withdrawn ... moody and aggressive ...*
5 True – *... he's started mixing with some boys I don't like very much.*
6 False – *I think he's started taking drugs.*
7 False – *a cassette player*
8 True – *he's always been so keen on music.*
9 True – *some of my jewellery has gone and some money.*
10 True – *my husband spends a lot of time away.*

Tapescript

PART A
PRESENTER: Our next caller is Rachel who is from South London. Go ahead, Rachel.
RACHEL: Hello, Doctor Howard.
DR HOWARD: Hello, Rachel. How can I help you?
RACHEL: Well, you see it's about my son, Mark. He's almost 18 and he hasn't been able to find a job since he left school.
DR HOWARD: When did he leave?
RACHEL: It'll be a year in July.
DR HOWARD: And what seems to be the problem?
RACHEL: It's like this. Mark used to be such a nice, outgoing sort of boy but over the last few month he's changed quite a bit.
DR HOWARD: So, can you describe what has happened?
RACHEL: Well, after he was turned down for several jobs he got depressed and withdrawn which was bad enough, but now it's got much worse – he's become really moody and aggressive.
DR HOWARD: Moody and aggressive?
RACHEL: Yes, and he's started mixing with some boys I don't like very much. But to tell you the truth, I think he's started taking drugs.
DR HOWARD: What makes you think that?
RACHEL: Well, as I said, there are his change of moods. One minute he's very depressed and the next minute he becomes very excited – you know, he can't sit still. Another thing is stuff has disappeared from the house. Some of my jewellery has gone and some money and so has Mark's cassette player.
DR HOWARD: Does he know you know about the cassette player?
RACHEL: Yes, he does. He told me he'd let a friend borrow it. I was really surprised because he's always been so keen on music. When I asked him about it a couple of days later, he just told me to mind my own business. Another thing is that he just doesn't look after himself any more or care what he looks like. And I've noticed strange smells in the house too.
DR HOWARD: May I ask you, Rachel, are you still married?
RACHEL: Yes I am but my husband spends a lot of time away. He's in the merchant navy, you see.
DR HOWARD: From what you've said, the change in your son has been quite dramatic. What I suggest is ...

2 Students listen and compare Dr Howard's advice with their suggestions (which are on the board). Ask them to summarise the similarities and differences and then decide on which advice is best.

Answers

Dr Howard advises Rachel to:
1 try and talk things over with him as a friend.
2 ask one of his old teachers or family doctor to talk to him. Failing that, she recommends that Rachel tell the police.

Tapescript

PART B
RACHEL: Yes I am, but my husband spends a lot of time away. He's in the merchant navy, you see.
DR HOWARD: From what you've said the change in Mark has been quite dramatic. What I'd suggest is that you try and sit down with him and have a quiet chat about things. Approach him as a friend rather than

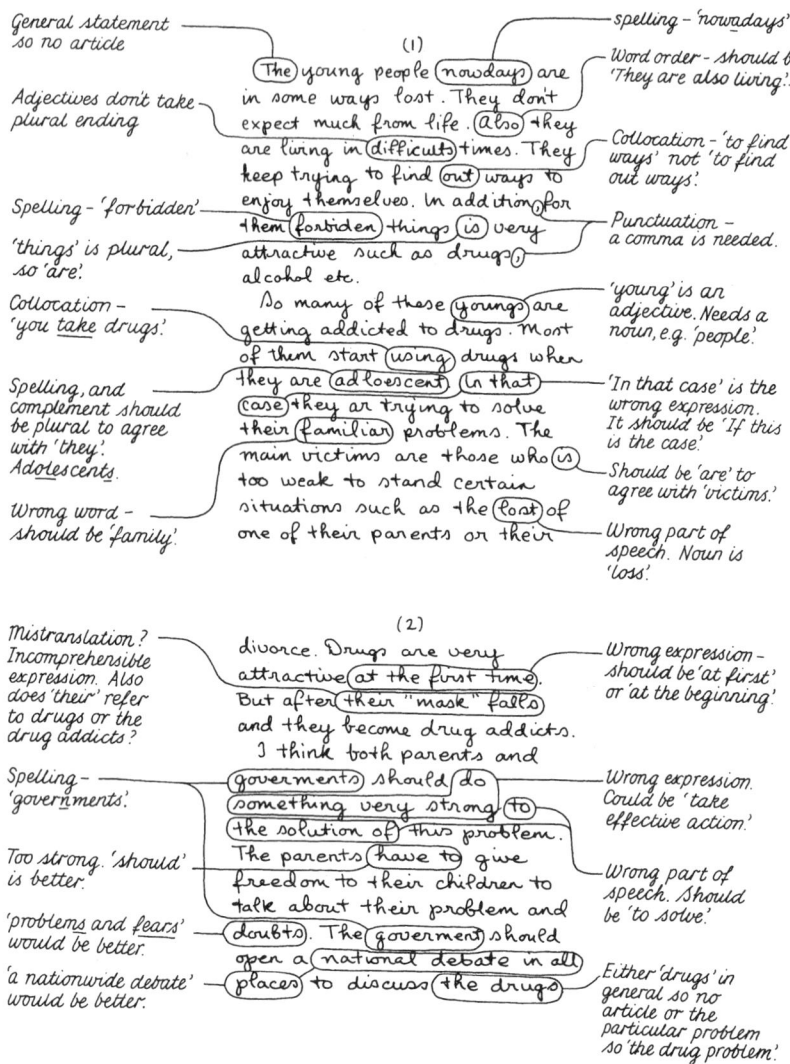

as a mother. Try to get to the bottom of things and see how he feels. Something else which I would suggest is that you get in contact with one of his old teachers or your family doctor and ask them to have a chat with Mark. Someone he respects and could have a chat with.

RACHEL: And what if that doesn't work?
DR HOWARD: Well, if you do feel he is taking drugs, then I should contact the police.
RACHEL: Turn my own son in to the police!
DR HOWARD: It may seem harsh but it's probably the best course of action in the long run.
PRESENTER: OK, thank you Rachel. I hope things sort themselves out for you and Mark. Our next caller is …

3 Note: This is designed as a short summary exercise, not as an exam-type composition.
Ask students to work individually, adding four or five sentences to the report.
(If appropriate, you might want the students to write their summaries on pieces of paper to be handed in. You can then use these later in the 'correcting' activity (number 3) as real examples of written work to be corrected. Shuffle them up and hand them out at random as this will be more effective if students correct their classmates' work rather than their own.)

p.112 WRITING

1/2 You may first want to ask students to spend a few minutes drawing up a possible plan for this question in small groups. Then they should look at the sample answer and say what they think is good about it before getting down to analysing the mistakes in detail. A suggested answer to question 2 is above.

Extension

If you collected in the students' written summaries of the listening as suggested above, now would be an appropriate time to hand them out for peer correction.

3 Try and elicit the two points from the students before turning to the book.

4 Before students begin writing their own composition remind them of the preparatory work on 'opinion' questions in Unit 7 (Coursebook page 88).
This task can be set as homework.

p.114 READING

Ask the students to describe the illustration. Read through the introduction and get students to identify the 'Socs' and 'Greasers' in the picture. Although there is some challenging vocabulary in the text it will be better exam practice for the students if you do not pre-teach any words at this stage.

1 Before students read the text in detail to answer the multiple choice questions you may wish to ask them to read the text quickly to answer the following gist question:
• What happens to Bob? (He is stabbed by Johnny)
Now ask the students to answer the multiple choice questions. They should compare answers in small groups, justifying any different choices.

ANSWERS

1 A; 2 C; 3 B; 4 C; 5 C; 6 D; 7 D

2 Deal with any vocabulary problems which students have and then ask them to predict the rest of the story, working in small groups. Get them to report back and compare their ideas across the class.

p.115 VOCABULARY

1 When the students have guessed the categories of the three verbs, demonstrate *stagger* and *gasp* and explain that *glinted* is used to describe light reflected off something, small and shiny, e.g. a ring.

2 Encourage students to use their dictionaries for this task. As a clue, tell them how many words there are in each category.
To explain the differences between the words you can use several techniques. For the first two categories physical demonstration should be both effective and amusing.
In addition, students can think of context sentences e.g. *The athlete was panting as he crossed the finishing line. The burglar crept into the hallway.* The most effective way to deal with the verbs which describe light is to ask students to list things which reflect light in that particular way (examples in brackets below).

ANSWERS
- **noise made when breathing:**
  pant, sigh, snore, choke, wheeze
- **a way of walking:**
  limp, shuffle, stroll, stumble, stride, creep
- **the way that light shines:**
  glow *(light from a window at night)*
  glitter *(points of light, usually reflecting off cut, shiny metal/gold/silver, e.g. a new, cut ring)*
  gleam *(a new car/polished brass)*
  sparkle *(points of light, e.g. usually from cut gemstones like diamonds, or from sequins)*
  Note: There is very little difference in the use of *glitter* and *sparkle*, and at this level they can be used interchangeably.

3 When you have checked the answers ask students to use some of the words as the basis for a short story. You can organise this as a competition. Set a time limit and explain that the winner is the group which manages to use most words from the list (correctly, of course) in their story.

10 Us and Animals

PROBLEMS, PROBLEMS

p.116 FIRST THOUGHTS

Students work in small groups to discuss the riddle. Elicit any more which they know and get them to try them out on the class.

> **ANSWER**
>
> A human being

p.116 SPEAKING

In the same groups students try to resolve the problem. Use the illustration to check vocabulary before they begin. At this stage it does not matter if they do not solve the problem.

p.116 LISTENING

1 Play the tape once and ask students to answer the gist questions.

> **ANSWERS**
>
> – they cannot solve the problem. They try two solutions which turn out not to work.
> – they decide to use a diagram and a button, paper clip and coin to represent the dog, farmer and goose.

2 Play the tape again, stopping as necessary for students to fill in the gaps.

> **TAPESCRIPT AND ANSWERS**
>
> MAGNUS: Well, **(1) what do you think** he should do?
> PATRICK: Well, it's tricky isn't it? He **(2) could start by taking** the cabbage across.
> MAGNUS: No, **(3) that won't work**; the goose will get eaten by the dog.
> PATRICK: Oh yeah. **(4) You've got a point**. Well how about ... first of all he takes the goose, because the dog won't eat the cabbage, will it?
> MAGNUS: **(5) That's a good idea**. But then what should he do next? I know, **(6) why doesn't he** row back to the other side and then pick up the dog.
> PATRICK: But **(7) wait a minute,** won't he still have the same problem? I mean, we can't leave the dog with the goose, can we?
> MAGNUS: Oh no, of course not. I'm not sure what to do.

> PATRICK: I know. I've got an idea. **(8) We could always** you know, work it out with a diagram. OK, this is the river and this button is the dog, the paper clip's the cabbage and erm, this coin can be the goose.
> PATRICK: Great, now **(9) let's try again, shall we?**

3 Managing conversations

Students refer back to the expressions they wrote in the gaps in the previous exercise to find examples of the 'negotiating/suggestion' language used when working together to find a solution. You might want to play the tape again and ask students to repeat the phrases, paying particular attention to their intonation.

p.117 SPEAKING

This activity provides practice of the type of task to be found in Part 3 of Paper 5 (*Speaking*). In this part of the paper the two candidates are given a sheet with a situation and options to be discussed together.

This phase of the oral exam lasts about 3 minutes but you should allow longer for the exercise in the Coursebook. Divide the class into pairs and give students a short amount of time to digest the information provided and perhaps sort out any problems with vocabulary before they begin. You should monitor carefully, particularly to make sure that individual students are not dominating and that all are participating effectively and using the 'negotiating' expressions highlighted in 3 above.

> **POSSIBLE ANSWERS**
>
> – A dog would probably be suitable for Mr Cohen. He is active, enjoys long walks and lives in the country.
> – Mr Dukes probably needs a cat. Stroking cats can help to reduce your blood pressure, so they say!
> – Emma and Gemma can't have a kitten because of their mother's allergy. They aren't old enough to look after a dog. A rabbit is possible but expensive. A hamster is the only suitable choice.
> – Elsie Grey should have a canary. Her flat is bright and sunny. The bird would sing and this would cheer the old lady up.

p.177 LISTENING

Students read through the questions before you play the tape. After the first listening they should confer with a partner; then play the tape again for final checking.

> **ANSWERS**
>
> 1 C; 2 B; 3 C; 4 B; 5 B; 6 A; 7 C; 8 B

TAPESCRIPT

1
CHILD: Oh no!
MOTHER: What's wrong, sweetheart?
CHILD: It's Teddy, he's not here. Teddy's not here?
MOTHER: What?
CHILD: I left it at grandma's.
MOTHER: What do you mean ... you left it?
CHILD: In the bedroom. I want it ...
MOTHER: But we're almost home. Are you seriously saying that you want me to drive all the way back to grandma's house ...
CHILD: Please.

2
BUTCHER: Hello, Higgins the butcher ... Yes, hello Mrs Adams ... A problem with the order? Right ... you didn't get the chops or the sausages ... what? ... and the chickens? I really don't know what could have gone wrong ... Look, if it's OK with you ... I'll check the order ... Mm ... I've got a horrible feeling it could have ... yes, that's it, gone to the wrong place. Yeah. Right you are. I'll look into it straight away and give you a ring in a couple of minutes ... bye for now ...

3
PRESENTER: So strangely, it is the male who plays an important part in the incubation and hatching process. There isn't a nest as such for very obvious reasons: the environment is unable to support vegetation. As you can imagine the eggs cannot be left for a second because of the inhospitable Arctic conditions. So what happens in this instance is the female goes off in search of food while ...

4
ADULT: And so, can you guess what happened next? Yes, Mrs Large went down to the kitchen and crept in ever so quietly, and then she stood on a stool to get the cake. See she was so hungry even though she wanted to get nice and thin ... and there inside there was only one slice left. Yes ... all her naughty children elephants had gobbled it all up. So you can imagine how she felt.

5
DOCTOR: So what happens?
PATIENT: Well, erm, I get all, you now, wheezy and things, can't breathe properly, and my eyes start to itch.
DOCTOR: I see. And it's just horses you say.
PATIENT: Yeah.
DOCTOR: Does it run in the family?
PATIENT: Sort of. My mum, she was allergic to anything, you know dogs, cats and things. That's why we never had pets, but with me it just seems to be horses.
DOCTOR: What about feathers and dust?
PATIENT: Ah well, now you come to mention it, I do sneeze a lot.

6
NEWS PRESENTER: Last night, laboratories on the Madingley road were broken into and many of the animals were released. Computers and experimental equipment were also destroyed in the raid. The Animal Liberation Front has accepted responsibility for this action. A security guard was badly injured in the attack. Members of the scientific profession and doctors investigating new drugs in possible cures for cancer have condemned the raid as totally irresponsible and say that it has put work in these vital areas back at least two years.

7
FIRST MAN: It was amazing really, there I was, just standing by the sink, you know, doing the washing up.
SECOND MAN: Oh yeah ...
FIRST MAN: When along comes this fox, I couldn't believe my eyes. It just trotted up the path as bold as brass. It finished off Toffee's food which we'd put outside, can't stand the smell.
SECOND MAN: Goodness.
FIRST MAN: And then it turned and looked at me, straight in the eye, yawned and trotted off the way it had come ...
SECOND MAN: Well I never.

8
Right, now as we approach the time of year when we are often looking for small presents, we would like to start a safety drive about these cute little things. They're called Foalings, they're little miniature horses, they're made of plastic and have manes and tails in bright fluffy material. Now these are fine, they are made to the highest standards in the States, the problem is these copies which are flooding street markets. Now they're made in the east and even though they may look the same, let's see what happens, see, the head just pops off – very dangerous for small children. Now look at how the manes catch light if they're near a flame. So they're potentially lethal toys ...

IN THE WILD

p.118 FIRST THOUGHTS

Students discuss the question in small groups, and then give feedback in open class.

p.118–p.119 READING

Jungle warfare

1 Before reading, to introduce the topic of the article, put students in small groups to come up with a list of the similarities and differences between humans and chimps. Groups then compare ideas in open class. You may also want to pre-teach the following items of vocabulary: *the wild, poke, cuddle, stepfather*.

> **ANSWER**
>
> Both chimps and humans live in families, use tools, fight wars, are self-aware, have a kind of language, and under certain circumstances adopt young.

2 Answers

1A (*In this way she hopes to observe the progress of an entire generation of chimps from birth to death.*)
2D (*chimps seem to have some kind of structured language ...*)
3D (*they were sometimes joined by a single, aggressive female ... During the war, some females left the losing side to join the aggressors.*)
4C (*... a perhaps natural hostility to aliens.*)
5A (*It has been claimed that war was a key factor in developing human social organization ...*)
6C (*older chimps may adopt younger brothers or sisters if the mother dies.*)
7C (*Such research may give us clues about human behaviour and motivation.*)

Extension

You could ask these questions: *Did anything particularly surprise you in the article? What other animals have human characteristics?*

p.119 LANGUAGE STUDY

Contrasting ideas

1 Before asking students to read the explanation in Part 1 you may decide to put on the blackboard:
She had a cold. She still played tennis.
and this list:
although but even though despite however nevertheless
Ask the students to connect the sentences with these linking words. Then look at the explanations.

2 Answers

1 correct
2 wrong – *Despite the fact that the restaurant ...*
   Although the restaurant was ...
3 wrong – *The wine was bad. However, the food was good.*
4 wrong – We can't use *although* here because there is no contrast of ideas.
5 wrong – *Even though he was rich, he was unhappy.*

3 Students should attempt this individually at first and then after a few minutes exchange their sentences with a partner to see if there are any mistakes before finally checking with you.

Possible Answers

1 Despite its age/Even though it is very old, the dog really enjoys going for walks.
2 They have got a large dog although they have a small flat.
3 They tried to housetrain the puppy but it didn't work.
4 Although pigs ... , they're actually quite clean.
5 The squirrels look tame. However, they may bite you.

One way to practise the use of the linking words is to ask each student to write a contrasting situation on a piece of paper, for example:
Elizabeth is very rich. She never turns on the heating in winter.
Collect in the pieces of paper, shuffle them and hand them back to different students. They should rewrite the situation/sentence using a suitable linking word and then pass it on.

p.120 FIRST THOUGHTS

Working in pairs, ask each student to write down the names of any three animals numbered 1, 2, 3 on a piece of paper and hand it to their partner. They should then turn to page 123. The pairs should report back to class, the results can be quite amusing!

p.120 SPEAKING

1 Animals quiz

In addition to naming the animals in the illustration you might ask students to say which animals they most like and dislike, and to explain why. The names of the animals are in the list in the Coursebook in exercise 2.

Answers

1 whale; **2** cheetah; **3** field mouse; **4** black mamba; **5** ostrich; **6** Javanese rhinoceros; **7** mosquito (because it carries malaria – some experts, however, say it is the rat, because of the bubonic plague its fleas carry.)

2 Before ordering the animals according to beauty, you may wish to ask students to order them according to size as a further comprehension check. Having ordered the animals according to beauty, put students in pairs to explain their feelings and, if possible, to try and analyse why it is exactly that they find some animals more beautiful than others.

p.120–121 LANGUAGE STUDY

The comparison of adjectives and adverbs

1 This exercise is designed to be done in pairs.

> **ANSWERS**
>
> 1 correct
> 2 wrong – James is **bigger** than Mark.
> 3 wrong – She is the **best** at English in our class.
> 4 correct
> 5 wrong – He plays tennis **well**.
> 6 wrong – His car isn't **as** good **as** mine.
> 7 wrong – She **hardly** works. Hardly means just a little.
> Compare:
> He's breathing hard.
> (because he has just run up the stairs) and
> He's hardly breathing. (Call a doctor!)
> 8 wrong – You look cold.
> 9 wrong – They play chess much **worse** than us.

2 Divide the class into groups with each group working on two or three of the questions. If they are available, distribute grammar reference books at the same time. When you have been round to check that all the groups have sorted out their questions and understood the principles involved, redivide the groups so that the students can, in each new group, between them explain the answers to all the questions to each other.

> **ANSWERS**
>
> 1 comparative – tall+er
>   superlative – tall+est
> 2 as + adj. + as
> 3 BASE   COMPARATIVE   SUPERLATIVE
>   good   better   the best
>   bad   worse   the worst
>   far   further/farther   the furthest/the farthest
> 4 A slowly; B angrily; C well; D beautifully;
>   E hard/fast;
> 5 Comparative adverbs for *good* and *bad* are *better* and *worse*.
> 6 Normally adjectives have to go before nouns and adverbs after verbs. However, with verbs of perception like *look, feel, seem, sound, smell* and *appear* we usually follow them with the adjective. But when we want to describe the way a verb is performed, i.e. its manner, we use an adverb. n*You look cold* and *He looked coldly at me*.
> 7 friendlier, cleverer

3 Use this exercise as a check that students have really understood the rules, so ask students to try it alone and then, afterwards, confer.

> **ANSWERS**
>
> 1 the youngest; 2 better; 3 as expensive; 4 the cheapest; 5 hard; 6 more slowly; 7 farther/further; 8 the worst; 9 the most boring; 10 happy; 11 more beautifully; 12 less angry; 13 good; 14 more quickly; as fast

4 Ask students individually to choose their places then put them in groups with others who chose the same place/s. Ask each group to report back to open class.

5 Sentences with *too* and *enough*

Elicit the alternative sentence with *too*:
*People had thought chimps were **too** unintelligent to use tools.*
Students re-write the sentences then compare with a partner.

> **ANSWERS**
>
> 1 Annie was too tired to take the dog for a walk.
> 2 The birdcage was too high up on the wall for the cat to reach.
> 3 The zebra was too slow/wasn't fast enough to escape the lion.
> 4 The dog is too stupid/isn't clever enough to learn that trick.
> 5 The children are too young/aren't old enough to have rabbits as pets.

p.121 USE OF ENGLISH

> **ANSWERS**
>
> 1 the fact that; 2 fast for; 3 more expensive to keep than; 4 any/another animal as cruel as; 5 sing as well as; 6 there anything cheaper than; 7 though the winter was hard; 8 dirtiest dog I have ever; 9 too expensive to; 10 as fast as

DO ANIMALS HAVE RIGHTS?

p.122 FIRST THOUGHTS

Use the photograph and questions as a lead-in to the topic.

p.122–123 WRITING

The opinion question

1 Let students brainstorm the various questions in pairs and then put all the arguments, for and against, on the board.
Pre-teach: *to breed, a trap*. Then ask students to read the composition quickly to find how many of the arguments they predicted are in the text and how many are not.

2 Understanding the organisation of the composition
Students should work on the questions individually then compare answers within small groups.

> **ANSWERS**
>
> 1 Topic vocabulary: *fur, hunters, fashion, to breed, wild, savage, cruelty, traps, artificial.*
> 2 A: *first of all, then, to begin with, next*
> B: *in addition, moreover*
> C: *on the other hand*
> D: *on balance, I believe*

p.122 LISTENING

1 Ask students to try and predict the opinions the two speakers might have before they listen. For a gist listening task the students can listen once and find out if their predictions were correct.
Then ask the students to read through the gapped notes, play the tape again and get them to fill in the gaps.

> **ANSWERS**
>
> **1** 833 3974; **2** human beings; **3** TB (tuberculosis); **4** an antidote; **5** side effects; **6** predict; **7** observation; **8** hygiene; **9** by accident **10** cruel and inhumane

TAPESCRIPT

PRESENTER: Good morning everybody. I'm Joe Templer. It's eleven o'clock, which means it's time for another edition of *Crosstalk*, the phone-in programme which looks at today's hot issues. The subject of today's discussion is whether vivisection – that's experimenting on live animals – is ever justified. Now if you want to take part in today's debate, the number to ring is 0171 – if you're outside London – 833 3974. But before that, in the studio I have two guests to open the debate. They are Professor Anna Wright from Queen Margaret Hospital and Peter Savage of the Free the Animals Movement. Good morning to the both of you.
ANNA WRIGHT: Good morning.
PETER SAVAGE: Good morning.
PRESENTER: OK then, if you'd like to put your point of view first, Professor Wright.
ANNA WRIGHT: Thank you. Now I must state categorically that for advances in medicine we count on being able to carry out experiments on animals. Without them, there would be no progress. We are unable to observe human beings in scientifically controlled conditions so, unfortunately, we have to rely on animals. Medicine's made enormous advances based on the results of vivisection. For example, our knowledge of the nervous system is largely due to vivisection. It has allowed us to find cures for many illnesses. Diphtheria, smallpox and TB used to be killers in the old days but not any more.
If you were bitten by a dog with rabies, you had very little chance of surviving. Now there is an antidote. Cancer recovery rates have greatly improved thanks to the work done on animals. And I'm afraid drugs have to be tested on animals prior to their release on the market to check for side effects. Nobody takes any pride in causing suffering and I can assure the listeners it is kept to an absolute minimum.
PRESENTER: Thank you very much, Professor Wright. Over to you, Peter.
PETER SAVAGE: Thanks. I'd like to start by saying that I'm speaking on behalf of animals. On the issue of testing drugs on animals for side effects in human beings, as we know from the thalidomide case, it's very difficult to predict what the effect of a drug will be on human beings from tests done on animals. They just don't tell us the whole story. As for understanding the nervous system, I think most experts would agree that this could have been done equally well by careful observation and nothing more. Professor Wright points to the reduction in the number of deaths from diseases like diphtheria, TB and smallpox. This is utter nonsense because these diseases were in decline already and they've been on the decline primarily because of improvements in hygiene, not animal experiments. No, the whole thing is rubbish. If we look at penicillin and aspirin, two of the most famous modern drugs, these drugs were found by accident! So much for medical research! And Professor Wright's argument completely ignores the moral dimension. The point is experiments on animals should be stopped because they are cruel and inhumane. Dogs are made to smoke cigarettes and mice have shampoo and cosmetics squirted in their eyes to see what will happen. Dogs don't smoke and rats and mice don't wash their hair. Very often these animals have suffered so much they have to be put down. Basically, we should take care of animals not take advantage of them.
PRESENTER: Thanks, Peter. OK then. So it's over to you, the listeners. Our first call …

2 Sounds in sentences
Play the extracts on tape and ask students to repeat. Write the extracts on the board and elicit/explain the features in the underlined sections. Ask students to repeat again, concentrating on correct production of the highlighted features.

TAPESCRIPT AND ANSWERS

1 It's eleven o'clock. *catenation*
   /r/ pronounced before the vowel
2 It's time for another edition /ə/ of crosstalk.
   intrusive /w/
3 I have two guests to open the debate.
4 I must state categorically. → elision of /t/ in 'must'
   /ɪ/ intrusive /j/ sound
5 In the old days elision of 'd' in 'old'
   /ə/ elision of 'd'
6 rats and mice

3 Students can tackle this task in pairs.

ANSWER

Mr West used to be crazy about photography. One day he took his car and went to a safari park. He stopped to take some pictures. Two ugly monkeys jumped on the car roof and bent the aerial. He got out of the car and tried to make them go away. Three enormous lions came and ate Mr West for lunch.

	= stress
⌢	= linking
∧	= intrusive sound /w/ or /j/
✗ ✗	= elision
/ə/	= schwa, weak form

p.123 VOCABULARY

Divide the students into small groups to work on the three vocabulary tasks so that they can pool their knowledge. Dictionaries should be used if they are available.

1 Phrasal verbs

ANSWERS

1 put down; 2 came across; 3 come up with; 4 broke out; 5 carry on; 6 back me up; 7 count on; 8 put forward; 9 turned on; 10 come about

2 Expressions with *take* + noun + preposition

ANSWERS

1 part in; 2 care of; 3 pity on; 4 pride in; 5 advantage of

3 Preposition + noun + preposition combinations

ANSWERS

1 on account of; 2 in place of; 3 on behalf of; 4 by means of; 5 In addition to; 6 in answer to

p.123 WRITING

As exam practice, you may wish to do this as a timed (45 min.) composition in class. As preparation, and if you have found that students have strong feelings on the topic, you may wish to prepare for the composition by holding a mini-debate, using the composition title as the 'motion' to be debated. Follow this procedure:

Divide the class into groups of six (two in favour, two against, two or more audience). The debaters have five minutes to prepare their arguments. The audience should prepare questions they will ask at the end. The debaters speak alternately, i.e. one for, one against, one for, one against. There should be no questions or interruptions during the speeches. At the end the audience can ask questions. Finally, the audience votes for the sides that they agree with. Having done this, to tie everything together in preparation for the composition, elicit all the different arguments that were used during the debate and put them on the board. There should also be a list of key vocabulary that students may need in writing the composition. Let students work on the plan together, putting students together who have largely similar viewpoints. You should go round helping and monitoring work on the plans.

ANIMAL FARM

p.124 FIRST THOUGHTS

Ask the students if they know of any stories where animals have human characteristics (for example children's stories and traditional fables).
Using their knowledge of these stories they should match the adjectives with the animals they are usually associated with. Elicit any further animal 'characteristics.'

> **SUGGESTED ANSWERS**
>
> pig – greedy; lion – strong; donkey – stubborn;
> fox – crafty; owl – wise; horse – brave/strong

p.124–125 READING

Animal Farm

Background note: Animal Farm was written by George Orwell (1903–50). Other famous books of his are *1984*, *Down and Out in Paris and London* and *Homage to Catalonia*. Animal Farm was written in 1945 and is an allegorical fable which satirises Communism and the Russian Revolution in particular – students will hear about this in the following listening exercise.

1 Begin by asking the students to describe the illustration. Get them to read through the summary quickly and answer the gist question.

> **ANSWERS**
>
> The pigs are greedy, but also intelligent.
> The donkey is cynical, not stubborn.
> The horse is strong and brave, but rather naïve.

2 Students should work individually then compare their matches in small groups, justifying their decisions.

> **ANSWERS**
>
> **1** G; **2** D; **3** C; **4** H; **5** E; **6** B; **7** F; **8** has no summary; **9** A

p.125 LISTENING

Begin by putting the following on the board and eliciting anything the students know about them:
Karl Marx   the Tsar of Russia   Lenin   Stalin Trotsky   communism
Let the students listen to the tape once for general understanding and to clarify the meaning of 'parallels' (what the things in the book represent in reality).
Then let them fill in the gaps as they listen again.

> **ANSWERS**
>
> **1** Imperial Russia; **2** Animal Farm; **3** the old Russian Tsar; **4** the pigs; **5** Karl Marx; **6a** the pig Napoleon; **6b** the pig Snowball; **7** the Russian working class; **8** the church

TAPESCRIPT

Of course, one of the reasons that *Animal Farm* is so interesting is that you can read it on two levels.
On one level you can read it purely and simply as a fairy tale for adults – I wouldn't recommend it to children as some pretty awful things happen to the animals, most of all Boxer.
At, perhaps, a deeper level we can read it as a criticism of what happens to revolutions in general and what happened in the Russian revolution of 1917 in particular. There are some obvious parallels and comparisons which can be drawn: Major, who talks about Animalism, is obviously Karl Marx, the creator of communism, while the pigs represent the communist intellectuals. Manor Farm is Imperial Russia and Animal Farm the new Soviet Union. The quarrel between Snowball and Napoleon reminds us of the conflict between Stalin and Trotsky. The pig Napoleon, is, of course, a kind of composite character and equals both Lenin and Stalin. Jones the farmer is the old Russian Tsar. Moses the raven – the big black bird who talks about the animal heaven of 'Sugarcandy Mountain' obviously represents the church. The other farmers who try to win the farm back are the heads of other European countries at that time, who were completely against communism. Frederick quite obviously represents Germany's Adolf Hitler. Boxer stands for the Russian working class which is worked and exploited both by the Tsar and later by his new communist masters.
I think Orwell chose to tell his story as a kind of fairy tale so that he could make his point more readily. Full histories of the period, of which there are many, run to many hundred of pages. Instead, Orwell makes his point beautifully, creates some believable and memorable characters and presents us with a poignant parable of what seems to happen with nearly all revolutions.

p.125 WRITING

1 Ask the students to read the sample composition and discuss the question. Ask them if the writer has convinced them that Boxer is 'the most interesting person'. They should be able to recognise that it is a very effective piece of writing. Some of the reasons why it is effective are analysed in **2**.

2 Students can underline/circle, etc. those parts of the text which relate to the three questions then compare their ideas in small groups.

ANSWERS

1 The writer lists Boxer's qualities using adjectives and examples:
He has qualities which are far more important (than intelligence)/loyal and hard-working/a good friend/strong and virtuous/never lets anybody down/shows tremendous courage.

2 The writer puts Boxer's negative points into perspective by comparing them with the (worse) negative points of the other animals and by explaining that intelligence is not the most important quality to have:
He is not all that intelligent but he has qualities which are far more important/so he is not that stupid! If he has a fault it is that he is too trusting.

3 The writer uses the following examples:
– the pigs, though intelligent, betray the other animals (to show that intelligence is not the most important quality)
– the battle of the cowshed (to show Boxer's courage)
– building the windmills (to show how useful Boxer is)
– questioning Squealer's judgement (to show that he is not so stupid after all)
– when he is taken away (to show Boxer is cruelly exploited)

3 This can be set as homework. Point out that the character they choose does not have to be the 'hero' (the most important person in the book) – Boxer is not the most important character in Animal Farm, for example – but should be someone they found interesting or memorable. Read through the examination question with them and highlight on the board the various parts and how they are answered:

1 *Who is the most interesting person?*
(name of person, title/author of book)
2 *An account of that person's character.*
(positive and negative qualities, give examples to show these, put them into perspective)
3 *Explanation of why you found him/her interesting.*
(explain with reasons, give examples from the book)

Remind the class that they should always read the question carefully and do what it asks, not what they would like it to ask or what they have prepared in advance!

11 Your Cultural Heritage

STONES FOR SALE!

p.126 FIRST THOUGHTS

Here are some more examples for students to identify.
Empire State Building – New York; Colosseum – Rome; Kremlin – Moscow; Forbidden City – Beijing; Acropolis – Athens; Brandenburg Gate – Berlin; Statue of Christ the Redeemer – Rio de Janeiro.
Get the students to talk about the monument which symbolises their city, and when/how/why it was built.

p.126 READING

1 Ask the class if they know what Cleopatra's Needle is and if they know anything about it. Students should then read the text quickly to check any ideas they had and to answer the questions in the book.

> **ANSWERS**
> 1 The obelisk came from Aswan in Egypt.
> 2 It was transported in a kind of cylindrical boat (a floating pontoon). During the journey six sailors drowned.
> 3 Various articles for future generations to study.

2 Discussion points

Questions 1 and 2 could be discussed in open class. But question 3 would be better done in small groups with each group suggesting five things they would choose and why. Having listened to all the arguments, the class could then vote on the best five from all those suggested.

p.127 USE OF ENGLISH

1 The photographs show
The White House (Washington);
Nelson's Column (London);
Eiffel Tower (Paris).
Ask students to guess/predict the connection between them before they read the text.
Students read the text quickly to answer the gist question.

> **ANSWER**
> They are all famous monuments which have been the subject of criminal deceptions (by Victor Lustig or Arthur Ferguson).

2/3 Can be done individually. Students should then compare answers in small groups, justifying their choices.

> **2 ANSWERS**
> 1 deceptions; 2 criminals; 3 successful; 4 persuasive; 5 unsafe; 6 suggestion; 7 favourable; 8 enthusiasm; 9 dishonest; 10 ashamed

> **3 ANSWERS**
> 1 C; 2 A; 3 C; 4 C; 5 B; 6 D; 7 B; 8 D; 9 C; 10 C; 11 B; 12 A; 13 B; 14 A; 15 B

FESTIVALS

p.128 FIRST THOUGHTS

Let students brainstorm the questions then write a list of festivals on the board. Here are some suggestions; Carnival – Rio de Janeiro; St Patrick's Day Parade – New York City; Hogmanay (New Year's Eve) – Scotland; Holy Week – Seville; Bastille Day – France.

p.128 LISTENING

You might want to pre-teach the following vocabulary: *hooligan, an admirer, procession, bloke, bull.*

> **ANSWERS**
> Speaker 1 D; Speaker 2 E; Speaker 3 A; Speaker 4 F; Speaker 5 B
> C is the extra summary.

TAPESCRIPT

SPEAKER 1: I wish they'd just ban it. I mean it's just an excuse for hooligan behaviour. There's no fun it. I don't think it's funny throwing flour and water all over people. There was also this thing of cutting off men's ties with, erm, big pairs of scissors. You know, it's a terrible thing … if you complain, then they just accuse you of being a bad sport but it was really excessive. It's just out of control. They have these big plastic club things too, which they hit you over the head with, you're supposed to laugh but well it's just not really very funny.

SPEAKER 2: You should have seen his face when he found out. I mean, we'd arranged for all the girls from the offices in Spain and Brazil to send him cards, with lots of hearts and kisses all in, ermm, lipstick. 'We love you Milton' they said. You know, 'can't wait to make you mine'. Anyway he was as proud as a peacock, inviting everyone into his office. There they were on his desk, he thought he had these admirers from all over the world. It was hilarious. We could hardly keep a straight face. When he found out he took it very well though. He was a good sport, I like someone who can laugh at himself.

SPEAKER 3: The climax of the thing was this procession through the, erm, town. It was an absolutely beautiful emotional occasion. There were these tiny children – some of them can't have been much older than six, anyway there they were on skis carrying lamps with the grown-ups not that far behind with real, erm, blazing torches – all of them were singing traditional hymns and carols. The spectators joined in too, I would have if I'd known the words and the language! We were right near the front and so we could see everything ...

SPEAKER 4: It used to be much better in the old days. It was more you know intimate when it started off. In the tent there would be the performers, the musicians and a maximum of about fifty people in the tents listening to them. There was much more of a relationship between people if you know what I mean. Nowadays it's all crowds and queues and lots of the performers use microphones and there are security guards, it's the opposite of what you'd expect a folk festival to be.

SPEAKER 5: They must have been mad to do it. I mean some of the people were no more than boys and could run pretty fast but as for the others. Well, there was a really fat English bloke and he just couldn't keep ahead. The bulls, they just ran over him. He was in a terrible state and they took him off in an ambulance. Still, by and large it was fun to watch and I guess it gave the bulls the chance for revenge. One of the worst things for the runners was the fear of tripping up and falling over. You had to be able to jump as well. Still, it must have been really exciting for them but I wouldn't have done it for love nor money. There isn't really anywhere to escape to.

p.128–129 READING

As an introduction, get the students to describe the photographs then ask the class to explain what Carnival is, where it comes from, what the origins of the word are and who took Carnival to the New World. Students should then quickly scan *Carnival Facts* for the answers. Before reading you may wish to pre-teach *cane* and *bamboo stem*.

ANSWERS

1 F; 2 C; 3 A; 4 H; 5 D; 6 E
B is the extra heading.

p.129 WRITING

Through foreign eyes

1 Ask students to describe the picture and tell you anything they know about Bonfire Night.

Background information:
Bonfire Night is a traditional English festival held on the 5th November every year. It commemorates the events of 1605 when the protestant King James I and the Members of Parliament escaped being blown up in the 'Gunpowder Plot'. Catholic plotters, led by Guy Fawkes, had filled the cellars of the parliament building with gunpowder and were planning to murder the king and all the Members of Parliament in a huge explosion. But at 11pm on the night before the king and government were due to go to parliament the gunpowder was discovered, the plotters were arrested and executed for treason. Nowadays children make models of Guy Fawkes (called guys) and go around in the first week of November collecting change to spend on fireworks. On the night of 5th November people hold or go to outdoor parties where guys are burnt on bonfires, fireworks are set off and people traditionally eat sausages, baked potatoes and drink hot soup.

2 ANSWER

Adriano didn't enjoy himself because he had to attend a Bonfire Night party at his host family's house. It was very cold and he was shocked at the food and behaviour.

Ask the students to read through the letter individually and underline anything they think is a mistake. Then put them into groups to compare their analysis and work on producing a corrected version.

CORRECTED VERSION

Dear Melissa,
Sorry for not replying to your letter but I have been in bed with a terrible cold since Guy Fawkes' night. I will never get used to the weather here. I didn't know anything about this festival before coming to England and I must say I think it is terrible.
The family I am staying with are hospitable and had a big bonfire party and invited lots of their friends. A few weeks ago the children made a model called a Guy. He was the man who tried to blow up Parliament. The children were allowed to go out into the street to ask for money from the people who were walking by. I don't understand it! Both the mother and father have good jobs but they let their children (go and) beg! In my country it would be a big scandal!
Anyway, my English family made a huge bonfire from wood and old furniture at the end of their garden. They invited lots of friends and their children. Everybody was outside even though it was freezing cold. They cooked potatoes and sausages in the fire and drank soup! It wasn't very sophisticated. In my country people would be embarrassed to give guests such food! I have never been so cold in my life; I am not used to it. The fireworks were really nice even if a bit dangerous. At the end they threw the poor Guy on the fire, everyone clapped and laughed. I was really shocked! I thought English people were civilised but now I am not sure. I thought it was barbaric!!!
Lots of love,

3 Remind students of the festivals discussed at the beginning of the unit (*First Thoughts* above) and get them to choose a suitable festival for the writing task. Put the following prompts on the board and ask them to begin by making notes under each heading:
Name of festival
Origins (historical, religious, geographical, etc.)
Preparations
What happens
How people behave
Food and drink
Your opinion
Remind them that they have to write their description as a foreigner, so they will need to explain everything clearly. The writing can then be done as homework.

p.130 LANGUAGE STUDY

Used to and would

To get the students thinking about the distinctions between the above two target structures, put the following sentences on the board for students to decide which are grammatically possible and which are not:

When I was younger	I used to go to the cinema every Friday night.
	I would to go to the cinema every Friday night. **X**
	I would go to the cinema every Friday night.
	I used to be quite fat.
	I would to be quite fat. **X**
	I would be quite fat. **X**

When they have done this and had the answers checked they should think about the rules before reading the explanation in part 1. We cannot say *His father **would work** at the car factory* because it refers to a state.

Extension

To personalise this section, ask students to describe to each other ways in which their lives have significantly changed over the years. You may like to start off by telling them how life has changed for you, as an example.

Prepositions following adjectives

Read through example and explanation with the class then let the students complete the gaps in pairs.

> **ANSWERS**
>
> **1** in; **2** at; **3** of; **4** for; **5** at; **6** by; **7** about; **8** to; **9** of; **10** for; **11** with/in; **12** from/to; **13** on; **14** for; **15** for/about
>
> **Note**: If the object is a person we say, e.g. *I'm disappointed **in** you.*

p.130–131 READING

1 Ask students to describe the cartoon and elicit the meaning of the title (European children are becoming very similar). Discuss the questions in exercise 2.

> **2 ANSWERS**
>
> **1** D; **2** G; **3** B; **4** F; **5** A; **6** C

3 Students discuss in groups. One student from each group then reports back the group's views for open class discussion.

p.131 WRITING

Before students begin planning their composition remind them of the language study points (*used to* and *would*) and the information in the text on extended families etc.
Put students into small groups to brainstorm ideas. Elicit these and put them on the board for everyone to refer to. Here are some ideas to get them started:
family relationships/marriage
technology
communications
jobs/working conditions
lifestyles
male and female roles/rights
The writing can be done as homework.

TAKING A TRIP

p.132 FIRST THOUGHTS

Divide the class into groups of three or four to discuss their tour. Get them to make notes and report back to class. The class can vote on the most interesting itinerary.
Note: If you have a mixed nationality class you can make the location of the tour the city where your class is situated.

p.132 LISTENING

A day out in Cambridge

1 Ask students to describe the photograph. It shows students punting on the river in Cambridge. Elicit anything they know about Cambridge – its university, history, monuments, etc.
Ask students to read through the gapped sentences then play the tape. Students compare their answers in pairs then listen again to check.

ANSWER

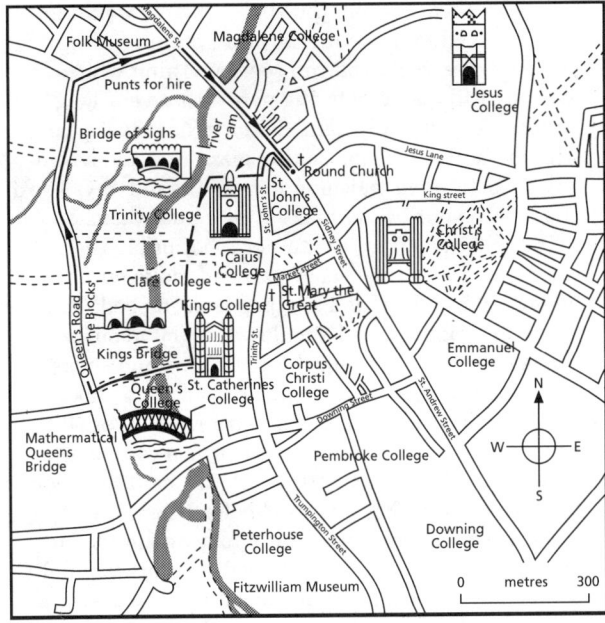

2 ANSWERS

1 Amanda; 2 Culture Tours; 3 one of the few round churches in England; 4 King's; 5 Queen's; 6 walk on the grass; 7 lectures; 8 Folk Museum; 9 boat; 10 4.30

TAPESCRIPT

Good morning, ladies and gentlemen. Please let me introduce myself. My name is Amanda Southgate and I would like to welcome you to the wonderful town of Cambridge on behalf of Culture Tours. I'm your guide today and it gives me great pleasure to introduce you to the most important sights of this town. We start our tour here at the Round Church, one of the few round churches in England. After that, we visit Trinity and Clare colleges and then walk along the backs to admire the daffodils which are now in bloom. Then we shall visit King's College and its beautiful chapel. After a brief look at Queen's college, we stop for a picnic lunch. Please may I remind you not to walk on the grass and keep to the footpath. Visitors are not allowed to enter lectures or living accommodation.

This afternoon there will be a visit to the Folk Museum which shows how people used to live in the old days. Finally, there will be an opportunity for you to experience a trip on a punt, which is a kind of boat you push along with a pole. I would not recommend you to try it yourself as it is easy to fall in the river! One last thing I would like to say before we begin the tour is if anyone should get lost, don't forget to be back here at the Round Church at 4.30 in order to catch the coach back. Many thanks for being so patient. Now let us begin the tour.

p.132 VOCABULARY

remind, *remember* and *forget*

1 ANSWERS

1 forget; 2 remind; 3 remember; 4 remember; 5 remind; 6 reminded

Extension

You may also want to bring up the difference in meaning between *He remembered to lock the door* and *He remembered locking the door*. The *-ing* form refers to things that happened **before** the remembering/forgetting, etc. took place, the infinitive refers to things happening **afterwards**.

2 This could easily and effectively be done as a role play. Explain the situation to the class and then distribute the role cards. Give students time to absorb the information and let them ask about anything they do not understand

---

ROLE CARD 1
You are a rather anxious individual, always checking that other people have understood exactly what you mean. You know that your friend is a little careless and has a tendency to forget important details but he/she is the only person you know who can help out at the moment. You must explain very carefully about how he/she must look after some exotic foreign plants which react badly to the wrong amounts of water and light. You also have some temperamental goldfish and an antique table is being delivered. You want to be sure that the table has not been damaged during transportation.

ROLE CARD 2
Your friend is very nice but worries far too much about things. He/She also tends to repeat everything three or four times quite unnecessarily which can get rather irritating. You, in fact, are very busy at the moment with work and it is not easy to find time to do all the things your friend wants you to do. You would be quite happy if someone else took care of the flat while he/she was away.

© Copyright Longman Group UK Ltd. 1989

p.132 LANGUAGE STUDY

> **ANSWERS**
> 1 Sophie invited Ann to come to the art gallery.
> 2 Leila persuaded me to go to the *son et lumière* show.
> 3 His mother encouraged him to visit the ruins that afternoon.
> 4 The guide warned us not to walk on the grass.
> 5 The curator ordered Lennie/him to stop smoking at once.

p.133 LISTENING

As an introduction, ask students what kind of museums they like, what they think are the features of a good museum, what they think about charging an entrance fee for museums.

Students study the six listening tasks before playing the tape. Play it several times if necessary and let students confer.

> **ANSWERS**
> 1
>
> | | NAME | USE |
> |---|---|---|
> | object 1 | comb | combing wool (for spinning) |
> | object 2 | warming pan | warming the bed |
> | object 3 | flail | separating the wheat from the chaff |
> | object 4 | trap | catching poachers |
>
> **2B** (*It's a shame about the weather ...*)
> **3C** (*... we can sometimes have quite a job finding out exactly what they were for.*)
> **4D** (*... looks just like a huge frying pan with a very long handle.*)
> **5A** (*... it is a couple of poles of about equal length which are held together by a strap.*)
> **6C** (*After that, it would be a short step from the courthouse onto one of those terrible prison ships bound for Australia.*)

TAPESCRIPT

CURATOR: Hello everybody. I'm glad you've been able to make it. It's a shame about the weather though, isn't it? Anyway, if you'd like to follow me into the first room, I'll tell you a little bit about some of the exhibits there.

Well, as you can see, there are a number of farming and domestic implements here which we have collected over the years. Of course, none of them are used any longer. In actual fact, we can sometimes have quite a job finding out just exactly what they were for! Now this first one I suppose you'd describe as a giant comb. And that's just what it is – not for human beings though, but for wool. Once the wool had been sheared from the sheep, then it would have to be combed to make it ready for spinning. Now if you look over here, you can see something which looks just like a huge frying pan with a very long handle. We had an Italian visitor in here last year who thought it was for baking pizza in a deep oven but it's actually a warming pan. In the old days you'd pop it into your bed to make it nice and warm. You'd take some coals from the fire or a hot brick, then you'd put it into the copper pan and make sure the lid was tight. Then, as I say, pop it in the bed. This one is an original but I should warn you about some of the ones you may come across in antique shops. They're quite often reproductions. So don't be taken in. Now, this next object is rather strange looking. It is called a flail and, as you can see, it is a couple of poles of about equal length which are held together by a strap. Now this was used before the days of modern agricultural machinery to beat the corn to separate the wheat from the chaff, the bits you didn't want. The men used to put the cut corn on the ground and then they'd swing the flail and beat it until they had separated all the wheat out.

The last thing in this room I want to draw your attention to before we move on to our Roman collection is this evil-looking contraption in the corner. Now this is in fact a man trap. It just shows how much crueller the world was in the nineteenth century. Farm workers and their families often had very little to eat, so to supplement their meagre diets they would go onto the farm owner's land to hunt for rabbits and other game, poaching in other words. And the farm owners would set these traps to stop them from doing this. Not very pleasant. And if someone did get caught in a trap, then their leg would certainly have been broken. After that, it would be a short step from the courthouse onto one of those terrible prison ships bound for Australia.

p.133 USE OF ENGLISH

> **ANSWERS**
> 1 without; 2 example; 3 until; 4 types/varieties;
> 5 an; 6 from; 7 took; 8 also; 9 which; 10 in;
> 11 shows/portrays/depicts; 12 for; 13 gives/holds/performs; 14 wait/queue; 15 all

p.133 WRITING

Ask the students to match the points in the plan with the relevant parts of the King's College model text. They should note some of the useful language used in the description:

passives
it is set in the grounds ...
it was not completed until ...
relative clauses

the painting which was given ...
concert which is broadcast ...
adjectives/comparatives and superlatives
most beautiful building in ...
beautiful stained glass windows ...
imposing painting ...

If students are from the same town, they can work in groups to plan their description. If you have a multilingual class, they will have to work individually or you might prefer to organise the task as a project. If students have access to a library, set them the task of researching a well-known building (encyclopaedias and guide books are most useful) and use this information for their written descriptions.

PRESERVING THE PAST

p.134 FIRST THOUGHTS

Students decide on the sentences individually then compare with a partner or in small groups. Ask them to report back to open class. Encourage them to give reasons for their opinions.

p.134 VOCABULARY

Encourage students to use dictionaries for these exercises. Clarify any confusion which may arise over the exact differences in meaning/collocation by asking for further context sentences for each item of vocabulary.

1 ANSWERS

1 antique; 2 old-fashioned; 3 out of date; 4 ancient; 5 a second-hand; 6 a vintage

2 If students are struggling with this exercise you might want to write the answers on the board in jumbled order as a clue.

ANSWERS

1 inherit; 2 heir; 3 heritage; 4 inheritance; 5 heirloom

p.134 LISTENING

Before you play the tape ask the students if they have any family heirlooms and how they feel about them. Pre-teach the following:
grandfather clock, pendulum, chimes, to tick, (clock)face

ANSWERS

1 T; 2 F; 3 F; 4 T; 5 F; 6 T; 7 F; 8 T

TAPESCRIPT

MATTHEW: Right, a family heirloom. Well, I suppose the most important heirloom in my family is, erm, a grandfather clock. You know, it's one of those really tall clocks with a big pendulum and chimes. It's a little like having Big Ben in your house. Anyway, it has been in my family for quite a long time from what I can gather. My father says he can remember it in his grandfather's house and I can certainly remember it in mine, my grandfather's from when I was a boy. It's got the manufacturer's name Jonathan someone, I can't remember the second name and is dated 1776. It used to sit at the bottom of the stairs in the hallway and I can remember when I was a kid I used to be scared of the loud ticking, you know tick-tock that it made. And when it struck the hour well I almost used to jump out of my skin, it used to make an incredible noise. I can remember being with my grandfather and him winding the thing up. It was a ceremony that he performed once a week and it's probably my strongest, er clearest memory of him. It is about eight feet tall I should think, it's made of dark brown oak which is shiny from being polished. At the top there's a squarish box with a round face inside. It's covered in gold leaf and is decorated with carving. It really is a lovely old object. There's a sun and a moon in it but they have never really worked from what I can gather. It really is a lovely old object with its polished wood which has been polished for years and years. Anyway, the idea is that the clock goes from generation to generation, from the eldest son to son, so one day, I might inherit it.

p.134–135 LANGUAGE STUDY

Describing objects

1 *Made of, from or with*

Read through the extract with the class and, before doing the exercise, ask students to think of further examples from their surroundings and the reasons for choosing *of*, *from* or *with*. For example:

Emiko's shirt is made of cotton. (it's recognisably cotton)
This notepad is made from recycled paper. (you wouldn't immediately realise this)
The coffee in our vending machine is made with dried milk, yuk! (dried milk is one of the ingredients used to make it)

> **ANSWERS**
>
> 1 wrong – of wool; 2 correct; 3 correct; 4 wrong – of plastic; 5 correct; 6 wrong – out of an old wooden door; 7 wrong – with beef
>
> **Note**
> If beef is the main ingredient, we can also say *made from beef*.

2 The order of adjectives
Read through the examples and explanation. Check that students are aware of the difference between a 'rule' and a 'tendency'!

3 For a change, draw the empty chart on the board. As students complete the task ask them to come up and fill in the columns (each student could complete one category, for example).

> **ANSWERS**
>
> | | |
> |---|---|
> | OPINION | rare, unique, wonderful, awful, fascinating, old-fashioned, ugly, priceless |
> | SIZE | huge, small |
> | SHAPE | square, long, oval, round |
> | AGE | old, eighteenth-century, ancient |
> | TEXTURE | shiny, smooth, rough |
> | COLOUR | silver, ivory, jade |
> | DECORATION | decorated, carved |
> | ORIGIN | French, Japanese, English |
> | MATERIAL | silver, silk, cotton, ivory, jade |

4 Ask students to make example sentences for each of the three constructions. For example:
A silver knife with intricate gold-leaf decoration.
An antique English table made of solid oak.
An elegant French clock which was made in the eighteenth century.
In pairs students then describe an object to their partner. Ask students to report back to class with a description of their partner's object.

p.135 WRITING

POSSIBLE ANSWER

Dear Inspector Jones,
Thank you for coming so quickly after the burglary. Here is a list of the stolen property:
1 An antique English writing desk made of oak with carved lions on the feet.
2 A very valuable eighteenth-century beer mug from Bavaria.
3 A delightful gold and silver Louis XV French clock. It has the intials H.P. underneath and is priceless.
4 A pair of antique duelling pistols which may be Italian.
5 A rather dirty-looking tiger skin rug which has great sentimental value as my grandfather shot it in India.
6 A tiny stone statue which is Colombian and four hundred years old.
7 Two pairs of blue and white striped silk pyjamas.
I hope you will be able find my property.
Yours sincerely ...

p.136 VOCABULARY

You might want to organise this exercise as a class competition. The first student or pair to work out all the words (correctly) is the winner. If they have a lot of difficulty you can help by giving them the first letter of each word as a clue.

> **ANSWERS**
>
> 1 exhibition; 2 gallery; 3 palette, canvas, brush; 4 abstract; 5 frame; 6 oils, watercolours; 7 portrait; 8 landscape; 9 sculptor; 10 statue

p.136 SPEAKING

Describing a painting

Note: In Part 2 of Paper 5 (*Interview*) students are shown two photographs which they may be asked to compare and contrast and then explain how they feel about the subject portrayed. It is therefore useful for them to practise describing pictures and their feelings about them, especially if they work in pairs (which they will be in the exam). As further practice of this you may want the class to compare and contrast the two paintings before they complete the writing task at the end of the unit.

1 Ask students to describe and discuss the painting in pairs or small groups themselves before reading the text.

2 Answers

1 Corrected mistakes:
*The small girl is saying something **to** the other one.*
*... it **was painted** maybe a hundred years ago.*

2 *I can see* can be replaced by *there is/are*.
Maybe can be replaced by *I think*, *probably*, *it might have* or *it looks as though*, depending on the context.

3 *in the foreground/background ...*
It might have been painted x years ago ...
It's similar in style to Van Gogh/Rembrandt.

4/5 (See the *Listening* tapescript below.)

p.137 Listening

Play the tape once for general understanding then ask the students to read through the questions. Play the tape again.

Answers

1A – *I can see* is replaced by *there are*.
– *Maybe* is replaced by *I think*, *probably*, *they look as though*, *she seems to be* and *I suppose*.

B *in the foreground* and *in the background*

2 the weather, the clothes the girls wear, when it was painted, her reaction to the painting and her own general preferences in relation to art.

3 See the last part of the tapescript.

Tapescript

WOMAN: This is a painting of a country scene. I think it was probably painted about a hundred years or so ago. Anyway, in the foreground there are two girls. They both look very poor. Their clothes are old and shabby, and there's tears and patches in them. They are sitting by the side of a field and, well, I suppose they look as though they are having a rest. The elder of the two girls has got some sort of, oh, I think it's an old-fashioned accordion. She's young, quite pretty with red hair. She's sitting with her eyes half closed, most likely because of the sun. In the background there are fields with a few animals in them and some farm buildings on the top of a hill and the most beautiful rainbow in the sky. It must have been raining but the sky is quite dark and it looks as though it might rain again. The little girl is quite enchanted by the rainbow. She seems to be telling her friend, or perhaps it's her sister, to have a look too. The other girl doesn't appear to be that interested. Oh, wait a minute. She's got something around her neck. It says 'Pity the blind'. I see. I get

it. The elder of the two girls is blind and the younger one is trying to tell her about the rainbow. Quite sad really. The colours of the painting are marvellous. Just like you get after it's been raining. There's so much beauty all around but all the blind girl can feel is the warmth of the sun on her face. She can't even appreciate the butterfly which has settled on her. I suppose she must play the accordion and hope that people give her money. Yes, it's a lovely painting. It's lovely, although in general I'm not a fan of this kind of art. I prefer Impressionist pictures, people like Monet, Cézanne. I recently went to see a big exhibition...

p.137 Writing

Begin by asking the students to describe the Breughel painting in their own words. Encourage them to put into practice the structures and vocabulary that have been discussed with reference to the Millais painting. Then ask them to study the text. Put them into small groups to analyse the particularly good aspects, encouraging them to highlight any words or phrases that they think may be useful.

The writing task can be set as homework. If possible, ask students to attach a copy or photograph of the picture to their homework as this will help you in assessing their writing.

12 Crime and Society

SCRUPLES

p.138 FIRST THOUGHTS

You may wish to pre-teach *to beat, to scratch, a tramp*. Having done this, give the class time to complete the questionnaire, adding their own fourth options. While this is going on, monitor carefully, giving assistance as necessary. Students should then pair up and compare responses and particularly any new alternatives they have created. Any really interesting ones could be read out to the whole class. Alternatively, put students into groups of three or four, purely to work on creating interesting fourth alternatives. When they have done this, they should give their questionnaire to members of another group. So, in the next stage every student is completing the questionnaire of another group. Having completed it, students should compare results within their original group. They may also, afterwards, be interested to give and receive feedback regarding the student-created fourth alternatives.

p.139 VOCABULARY

Phrasal verbs

You could focus the class's attention on the phrasal verbs in the box at the bottom before they attempt the exercise, asking them in groups to explain the meaning of any of the phrasal verbs they recognise, and, where possible, giving an example sentence. Having done this, let them try the exercise, and afterwards encourage them to learn any of the phrasal verbs which they did not previously know (at least with the particular meanings in this text). Note that these are five unconnected paragraphs.

ANSWERS

1 looking into; 2 held up; 3 got away; 4 ran over; 5 made for; 6 made up; 7 take everyone in; 8 found out; 9 gave her away; 10 up to; 11 broke down; 12 let him off; 13 went off; 14 break into

Different types of crime

1/2 Either let students read the descriptions of the crimes and match up the names given in the box at the bottom **or** write the names of the crimes on the board in random order and then read the descriptions out loud, one by one. Students in groups confer and then suggest which crime you are referring to. Having done this, you may wish to draw up a table on the blackboard for students to complete:

CRIME	CRIMINAL	ACT
1 blackmail	a blackmailer	to blackmail
2 vandalism	a vandal	to vandalise

Note: If there is no verb for the particular crime/criminal we usually say *He committed fraud/the person who committed fraud*.

ANSWERS

3 mugging	a mugger	to mug
4 shoplifting	a shoplifter	to shoplift
5 burglary	a burglar	to burgle
6 rape	a rapist	to rape
7 arson	an arsonist	to commit arson
8 forgery	a forger	to forge
9 fraud	a fraudster	to defraud
10 kidnapping	a kidnapper	to kidnap
11 drug pushing	a drug pusher	to push drugs
12 terrorism	a terrorist	to commit an act of terrorism
13 smuggling	a smuggler	to smuggle

p.139 SPEAKING

1 Give students a few minutes to rank the crimes individually then put them into pairs or groups to compare lists. If there is time, you might like them to report back so that the class can find out the overall result.

2 Students may not know the factual answer to this question but it can be used to promote discussion.

A QUESTION OF JUDGEMENT

p.140 FIRST THOUGHTS

Let students discuss the statement in groups. Get each group to report back to the class with the majority opinion.

p.140 SPEAKING

1 Divide the class into A/B pairs and explain the task. Make sure that they compare and contrast their pictures as well as describing them and their reactions to them. When they have finished talking, elicit two or three of their reactions and put on the board any useful vocabulary which emerges.

Note: The photographs show
1 the electric chair – used to administer capital punishment in some American states
2 stocks – an instrument of punishment used in the Middle Ages
3 a vandal cleaning graffiti – this can be part of the sentence imposed on vandals in Britain
4 a scene from the film 'Silence of the Lambs' – Hannibal Lector is wearing a straight-jacket, an item of clothing used to restrain mentally-ill patients.

2 Give the class time to read through the different cases and sort out any problematic vocabulary. Then divide the class into small groups to discuss who should go free. For groups that finish more quickly than others you might ask them to agree on appropriate sentences for the three who actually remain in prison. At the end each group should explain what they decided and why.

3 Read through the introduction and the first questions. Play the tape several times if necessary. (As a gist question for the first listening you can ask the class to compare Anna and Bruno's decisions with their own in the previous exercise.)

ANSWERS

1 Who do they believe should be freed?
Anna: 1 Mick Brown 2 Janet Green 3 Cynthia
Bruno: 1 Mick Brown 2 Alan Jones
What reasons do they each give?
Mick Brown: Bruno – he isn't very intelligent and needs help from a psychiatrist;
Anna – he will get worse in prison
Janet Green: Anna – prison isn't a hotel
Cynthia: Anna – her crime isn't a serious one
Alan Jones: Bruno – no reason given

2 Let students discuss this in open class.

3 ANSWERS

Why's that?
And what did you think?
So who did you choose?
... can you tell me why she chose Cynthia?
Right; that's interesting. Now, what do you think would happen in your country?
And what about you, Bruno?

4 Put the two headings on the board. When students have found the errors, ask them to correct them. Go through explaining any questions of grammar and vocabulary.

ANSWERS

MAIN MISTAKES	CORRECTIONS
we are agree for the first	we agree about the first one.
He will become worst	He will get worse
His wife is died because of him	His wife is dead because of him
a strong crime	a serious crime
stay in the prison	stay in prison

TAPESCRIPT

INTERLOCUTOR: So what have you two decided then?
ANNA: Well, we are agree for the first. We think that the first should be Mick Brown.
INTERLOCUTOR: Why's that?
BRUNO: Well, he is not very intelligent and maybe he needs help from a psychologist?
INTERLOCUTOR: Psychiatrist.
BRUNO: Psychiatrist. The prison will be a bad place for him. He will become worst.
INTERLOCUTOR: And what did you think?
ANNA: Well I am agree with him but we had a problem for to choose the other. I mean, I think Janet Green must go free. OK, she is a poor lady but the prison is not like a hotel ...
BRUNO: But I thought this was not kind, it was a cruel thing. Another thing, she has done this crime ten times. I chose Alan Jones ...
ANNA: Alan Jones! But he has killed his wife. It doesn't matter if the neighbours they say he is a nice man. His wife is died because of him. He must stay inside.
INTERLOCUTOR: So who did you choose?
ANNA: Cynthia.
INTERLOCUTOR: Bruno, can you tell me why she chose Cynthia?
BRUNO: Well, she said Cynthia hasn't done a strong crime ... I can see her point but I still think Alan must go free.
INTERLOCUTOR: Right; that's interesting. Now, what do you think would happen in your country?
ANNA: I'm not sure. Maybe, Janet, the weather is warm here so it doesn't matter if she has to sleep ermm outside ...
INTERLOCUTOR: Hah hah ... And what about you, Bruno?
BRUNO: Well, we are from the same country but I think Cynthia and Mick maybe can go free. You know murder is murder and Alan ... he would stay in the prison a long time.

4 In groups of three, students role play a discussion based on the listening, and using their thoughts from exercise 2.

p.141 USE OF ENGLISH

1 ANSWERS

1 given; 2 handing/giving/passing; 3 would; 4 because; 5 more/others; 6 wanted/intended/planned; 7 the; 8 away; 9 have; 10 rather; 11 in; 12 usually/normally; 13 obviously; 14 despite; 15 able

2 ANSWERS

1 A; 2 C; 3 B; 4 D; 5 A; 6 C; 7 C; 8 C; 9 D; 10 D; 11 C; 12 D; 13 A; 14 B; 15 C

A LIFE OF CRIME

p.142 FIRST THOUGHTS

1 Put the students into small groups to complete the idiom-matching task and the discussion questions. Ask the students if there are any situations or people in their own lives to which they could apply the four idioms.

ANSWERS

A 3; B 4; C 1; D 2

2 Discuss the phrase in open class.

p.142–143 READING

1 After students have described the photograph pre-teach *pickpocket*. Put a time limit of about two minutes on the first read-through and then, without referring back to the text, let students discuss their ideas on the questions.

ANSWERS

1 her upbringing, the death of her mother, her cruel stepmother, hunger
2 clearly subjective – should generate class discussion

2 ANSWERS

1 D; 2 E; 3 B; 4 F; 5 C; 6 A
G is the extra sentence.

p.143 LANGUAGE STUDY

Conditional sentences using *if*

1 Having conferred in groups and had the correct form of each conditional confirmed by you, students should attempt to analyse the differences in meaning resulting from the use of each conditional **before** looking at exercise 2.

ANSWERS

1 If it rains, we will not play tennis.
2 If he had a haircut, he would look nicer.
3 If she had phoned you, I would/I'd have told you.

2 Students should also try and come up with other examples of their own to demonstrate they have grasped the significance of the way the different conditionals are used.

ANSWERS

A 2; B 5; C 4; D 1; E 3

3 It is best if students attempt this on their own at first to help them see if they really have understood the grammar.

ANSWERS

1 What would you do if you were in my situation?
2 If you do that again, you'll have to go to bed.
3 If he'd been less mean, she wouldn't have left him.
4 If we leave now, we'll miss the rush hour traffic.
5 If you smoked less, you'd have much more money.
6 If we'd closed the car window, we wouldn't have given them the opportunity to break in.
7 When Alice gets here, will you show her to her room?
8 ... what would you say if I gave you a little present?
9 If you press that button, a receptionist will come to help you.
10 If you'd come with us, you would have enjoyed it too.
11 Imagine, darling. What would we do if your husband had a little accident?
12 If I were the Prime Minister, I'd bring back capital punishment.

p.143 PRONUNCIATION

1 ANSWERS

1 I'll *do* it if you *want* me to.
2 If he hadn't *come*, we'd've had a good *time*.
3 If I were *you*, I'd see a *doctor*.
4 If *only* I hadn't *said* it.

Extension

Having considered what would generally be contracted in normal speech, you may like to discuss with students when you would not make these contractions, e.g. in formal writing, when you specifically want to stress the contracted word, and so on. Equally, having elicited the appropriate sentence stress given a neutral speech situation, you may want to ask students to see how many different ways it would actually be feasible to stress these sentences for emphatic meaning.

2 When the students have listened and sorted out which conditional is being used in each case, you may want to get them to take down each sentence as dictation, in order to use the sentences as further examples of the forms.

ANSWERS

	FIRST	SECOND	THIRD	MIXED
1			✓	
2		✓		
3	✓			
4				✓
5	✓			
6				✓
7		✓		
8			✓	

TAPESCRIPT

1 I'd have come if I'd known.
2 Would you mind if he borrowed Dave's car?
3 What'll we do if the police come?
4 If we hadn't done that, we'd be all right.
5 I'll tell him if you threaten me.
6 We'd have plenty of money if we'd been insured.
7 I wouldn't do that if I were you.
8 If only you'd told me, I wouldn't have said it.

p.144 LANGUAGE STUDY

Verbs followed by prepositions

1 ANSWERS

1 of; **2** for; **3** for; **4** from; **5** for; **6** for; **7** from; **8** of; **9** on; **10** about

2 ANSWERS

1 Her employer accused her of stealing money.
2 Rose blames her parents for not bringing her up properly.
3 His mother punished him for being rude to their neighbour.
4 The lock prevented the burglar from breaking into the house.
5 The jury convicted him of murdering his wife.
6 The shopkeeper forgave the child for stealing the sweets.
7 His son was/has been arrested for selling drugs to teenagers.
8 Her nephew was discouraged from talking to the police.
9 The judge congratulated the police on catching the gang.
10 She warned the children about playing in the park after dark.

p.144 LISTENING

Let students read through the questions and sort out any vocabulary problems before listening to the tape.

ANSWERS

1 B; 2 A; 3 B; 4 A; 5 A; 6 A; 7 A; 8 A

TAPESCRIPT

1

TEACHER: I really couldn't believe it you know. When I asked her why she hadn't done her homework again she came up with this fantastic excuse which was so wild that I thought it might have been true. She said her dog had eaten it. I wish I hadn't believed her though because I noticed that there were a number of kids sniggering, you know laughing behind my back ... it was 'cos she didn't even have a dog.

2

MESSAGE: This is Connolly solicitors. I am afraid there is no one here to take your call at the moment but if you would like to leave a message or send a fax please do so after the tone ... BEEP ...

FELIX: Right, this is Felix, Felix Mortimer leaving a message for Jeremy Connolly. Jeremy, I got your message and I wish I could help you out, but the car's out of action at the moment – in the garage having the window fixed ... someone erm, smashed it to get to the radio. The times in which we live, eh? One of your clients maybe! See you soon. Once again, sorry I couldn't say 'yes'.

3

MAGISTRATE: You have been found guilty of driving while under the influence of alcohol. This is a serious offence for which the court fines you £200 and bans you from driving for one year. For failing to report a serious accident the court had contemplated a period of imprisonment. However, on taking your age into consideration, we have decided on a suspended sentence and probation. This means that every week for two years you will have to visit the probation officer and tell them what you have been up to for the past week. It's their job to supervise you and do what they can to guide you. So, you'd better watch your step young man, <u>otherwise</u> you will go to jail. Nothing is more certain.

4
LIBRARIAN: What a terrible thing to do. I mean those oaks had been there for five hundred years, that's since the time of Shakespeare. Yes, that's what I thought too, part of our heritage ... Whatever possessed the council to allow it ... If only we'd known about it earlier ... Yes that's right, a demonstration, we could have chained ourselves to the trees or something ... Vandalism. Absolutely. I'm really angry. They're just destroying the countryside.

5
MRS WILLIAMS: Forgotten your lock ...
DAMIEN: Can I just leave it outside?
MRS WILLIAMS: No, no, definitely not, of course you can't risk it. Your parents would be furious if you left it outside. Look, you'd better bring it into the hall.
DAMIEN: Are you sure?
MRS WILLIAMS: Yes, <u>provided</u> you check that there isn't any mud or anything on the tyres first.
DAMIEN: Look, I could pop back home for the lock.
MRS WILLIAMS: No, no, it'll be fine, just wheel it in. That's it. Mind those handlebars. I don't want them to damage the wallpaper.
DAMIEN: Thanks, Mrs Williams.
MRS WILLIAMS: You're welcome. I'll call Marcia ... Marcia, Damien is here, dear.

6
LANDLADY: Yes, I'd like to have a word with you, please. Now, the reason we let you have the room was <u>on condition that</u> you wouldn't cook or smoke in the room.
PETER: Yes ...
LANDLADY: Now, I've just been up and it smells smoky.
PETER: It was Mike, the boy from down the hall.
LANDLADY: I see, but it's up to you to make sure no-one smokes in your room. Another thing, I found lots of empty food cartons there.
PETER: Honestly, I wasn't cooking, it was, ermm, take-away food.
LANDLADY: Whatever, Peter, the smell's just the same.
PETER: But ...
LANDLADY: No buts, <u>unless</u> you can guarantee that this isn't going to happen again, you'll have to look for somewhere else.

7
WIFE: Can you hear it?
HUSBAND: Look just try to relax, will you?
WIFE: Honestly it's not fair. This is the third one this month ... and I've got to go to work tomorrow. I wish you'd do something ...
HUSBAND: Do something! What do you think I can do? You know what they're like. Look, just relax and you'll soon fall asleep ...
WIFE: No wonder the other people were so keen to move! They're a menace these people.
HUSBAND: I know, I know. Look, I'll give the police a ring, just so long as you accept I'm not going round there myself. I felt really humiliated last time. I wish I knew how to deal with them, but I don't.
WIFE: I wish I was a man. I'd soon show them who was boss.

8
MANAGER: Now the important thing is to look confident. If you look as though you'll take no for an answer, then they'll probably try to make a fuss. Just look at them and say 'I have reason to believe that you have attempted to remove articles from this store without paying, I'd like you to accompany me to the manager's office'. Now most of the time they come as meek as anything. You know they're scared or shocked. Now if they pull a weapon or look threatening, then just let them go and leave the rest up to the police. We're here as a deterrent as much as anything.

p.145 LANGUAGE STUDY

Ways of saying *if*

Refer students to the tapescripts on page 233 of the Coursebook and let them discuss the answers in small groups.

> **ANSWERS**
>
> **1** unless; **2** on condition that; **3** provided;
> **4** otherwise
> • *unless* has the idea of 'if not'.
> • *otherwise* is followed by a consequence.
> • *on condition that* and *provided* are followed by strong conditions.

Forms of *wish*

These exercises may be done in pairs. Combine pairs into groups of four to go through the answers.

1 ANSWERS

1a present/future – an imaginary situation.
 b He thinks it's unlikely.
2a present/future.
 b The wish is impossible.
3a He didn't wear gloves.
 b If we imagine a burglar is speaking, he is probably pretty fed up. The police probably caught him because he left his fingerprints.
4a Both.
 b No, she doesn't.
 c She finds it annoying.
 d Not really.
5a Both; b Yes; c We don't know.
6a No; b Yes.

2 Refer students to the tapescripts on pages 233-234 of the Coursebook.

ANSWERS

Part 1: *I wish I hadn't believed her* (*wish* + past perfect)
= present regret for a past action
Part 2: *I wish I could help you out* (*wish* + *could*)
= talking about ability (in this case, lack of ability)
Part 7: *I wish you'd do something* (*wish* + *would*)
= speaker is annoyed and wants her husband to do something soon
Part 7: *I wish I was a man* (*wish* + past simple)
= a desire for something in the present to be different, although this desire is impossible to achieve.

3 This can be set as homework.

ANSWERS

1 I wish I had a bigger flat.
2 I wish I could lose weight.
3 I wish I had insured my fur coat.
4 I wish he wouldn't whistle.
5 I wish I hadn't drunk so much last night.
6 I wish I could open this bottle.
7 I wish Angus would ring.

4 Get them started by making a few statements about yourself, for example:
I wish I didn't have to teach on Friday afternoons.
I wish you'd all arrive on time.
I wish I hadn't eaten that curry last night.
Note: Make sure students remember that they can't use the *I wish + would* construction to talk about themselves.

ROUGH JUSTICE

p.146 USE OF ENGLISH

1 ANSWER

Four innocent people were convicted of an IRA bombing and spent 15 years in prison before their innocence was established.

2 ANSWERS

1 adverb – unfairly
2 adjective – powerless
3 noun – weakness
4 noun – unreliability
5 noun – punishment
6 noun – admission
7 noun – innocence
8 noun – unwillingness
9 adverb – frighteningly
10 adjective – shameful

p.146 LISTENING

Get students to read through the questions before playing the tape, and explain the vocabulary. Let them confer, then play the tape again.

ANSWERS

1 C; 2 V; 3 C; 4 I; 5 V; 6 I; 7 C

TAPESCRIPT

IAN: I really do think that everyone is far too soft on crime nowadays.
VICTOR: Soft on crime, I suppose so, but what should we do then?
IAN: Well for a start I think we've got to stop rewarding the criminal.
VICTOR: What do you mean, Ian, rewarding the criminal?
CHRISTINE: Well, Victor, I suppose he means this business of sending kids off on holidays and stuff like that.
IAN: Thank you, Christine, exactly. It's a terrible business in this country I don't know where else they would do such a thing.
VICTOR: Yeah, but come on, Ian. Lots of these kids who commit crimes, they've come from really terrible upbringings and probably come from broken homes and criminal backgrounds themselves ...
CHRISTINE: And so on, we all know the excuses. But they've got to be shown the difference between right and wrong.
VICTOR: But don't you think that one way of doing this is by taking them away under supervision and

letting them sort their problems out more?
CHRISTINE: Maybe, yes. I can see the logic behind that but they've still got to pay. There should be retribution, you know, punishment as well as rehabilitation.
IAN: Right ... And so what would you do, Christine?
CHRISTINE: Use corporal punishment.
VICTOR: What you mean beat them?
CHRISTINE: Yeah. Like in the old days. A short sharp shock. Give them something to remember.
IAN: But that's erm pretty barbaric, isn't it? I'd draw the line at that. It's better to put them in jail. After all they get some, erm, guidance and help.
VICTOR: Jail just makes people worse in my opinion. Universities of crime.
CHRISTINE: They need a bit of discipline ... very often these kids have just been allowed to get away with anything, their parents have no control over them whatsoever.
IAN: So I suppose you're in favour of capital punishment too then ...
CHRISTINE: Well, as it happens I'm not.
IAN: Oh really? Well, I am ... in certain circumstances.
VICTOR: Now that's barbaric Ian.
CHRISTINE: Mm ... don't get me wrong. I'm against it not because it's cruel. Frankly, capital punishment is too good for some people.
VICTOR: So why... ?
CHRISTINE: Well, I think that ... you know I've changed my mind about this but it was the Guildford Four case.
VICTOR: Oh the, erm, IRA people.
IAN: But they weren't.
CHRISTINE: Right. Anyway. There was tremendous feeling against them at the time. I remember my dad saying – I was just a little kid – they should all be hanged. But that would have been terrible, wouldn't it? I know they spent a long time in jail but the thing is they were innocent ...
IAN: At least they're free now and have got their ordinary lives back.
VICTOR: Yeah, if they'd been hanged, that would have been the end of it, wouldn't it?
IAN: Yeah, I've lost faith in the system a bit, but all the same someone did blow up those pubs ...

p146 USE OF ENGLISH

ANSWERS

1 in taking them in
2 her responsible for
3 might have been stolen
4 found him guilty of murdering
5 accusing me of stealing
6 changed my mind about
7 in favour of
8 let him off
9 only I hadn't driven
10 had better lock

p.147 WRITING

1/2 The opinion question

After eliciting students' own responses to the question you might want to arrange them in groups which share similar points of view, as this will make the tasks and cooperation more effective.

First get students in their small groups to brainstorm any ideas they have for points they might want to include in a composition with this title. They should then try and sort them into paragraphs and decide on an appropriate framework for their composition. Having done this, tell them to read the two example compositions and hold an open-class discussion where students express their views on the relative merits of the two compositions. When their best elements have been highlighted, give students a little time to discuss how they might alter/add to their original plan. From this plan, students should write the composition at home or, to give practice in writing under exam-like pressure, immediately in class with a time limit of approximately 35 minutes, as they have already had planning time.

Comments on the two compositions

Both compositions have good ideas. However, the sentence structure and range of expression of the first essay is more sophisticated and varied. It uses ways of balancing and introducing arguments appropriate to this type of subject. In addition, the vocabulary of the first composition is much broader. Between the two essays there is a very good selection of ideas and topic vocabulary.

13 Beyond Belief

You can't take it with you

p.148 FIRST THOUGHTS

Put students in groups to discuss the questions. Check understanding of the vocabulary:
supernatural, superstition, superstitious.
Note: UFO means *Unidentified Flying Object.*
Encourage students to give examples of local superstitions. In a mixed nationality class you might want to ask them to report back to open class, as students often find other people's superstitions interesting. Write the examples on the board e.g.
It's bad luck to walk under ladders.
If you break a mirror you will have seven years' bad luck.
It's bad luck if a black cat crosses your path.

p.148 LISTENING

The Chaffin Will affair

1 Introduce the topic of wills and inheritance. Ask students to explain how wills are made. Explain that (in Britain) a will has to be signed by two witnesses (who cannot be people who benefit from it) for it to be legally binding. Set the gist question and play the tape once. See tapescript for answer.

2 Let students read through the gapped summary then play the tape again. When students have checked their answers they should discuss the final question with a partner.

> **ANSWERS**
>
> **1** 1921; **2** third son; **3** 15 years earlier; **4** to one of his other sons/four years after his death; **5** an old overcoat; **6** second; **7** the third brother/son; **8** pocket; **9** independent witnesses; **10** accepted it

TAPESCRIPT

STORYTELLER: One of the most famous and extraordinary cases of contact with the dead was the so-called Chaffin Will affair. In 1921, a certain James Chaffin died, leaving his entire fortune to his third son, Marshall, in a will which had been written a full fifteen years earlier, in 1905, and signed in front of witnesses. His wife and two other sons were virtually cut off without a penny. Marshall was not inclined to split up the inheritance he had come into any more fairly. Four years went by and then, strangely, James Chaffin's ghost started to appear before one of his other sons. The apparition had on an old overcoat which Chaffin had often worn in life. On the ghost of Chaffin's second visit to his son*, he told him that he would find a will in the overcoat pocket. The coat was actually in the possession of the third brother. Once it was found, they came across a note sewn in the lining of one of the pockets saying they should look in an old family Bible. This Bible was found in the keeping of Chaffin's widow and examined in front of independent witnesses. Sure enough, there in the Bible they discovered a later version of the will, one which divided the property and money evenly between the widow and the three sons. The will appeared to be genuine and Marshall was not prepared to challenge it in court.

(*The speaker means 'on the second visit of Chaffin's ghost to his son'.)

p.148 LANGUAGE STUDY

Relative clauses

1 Students read through the examples and explanations. They will find it useful to refer back to this (for examples of use) as they complete the other exercises in this section.

> **ANSWERS**
>
> 1 They looked in the lining of his overcoat, where they found a letter.
> 2 The will, which had been written fifteen years earlier, was not his last will.
> 3 They examined the bible, where they found another will.
> 4 That's Marshall Chaffin, whose mother and brothers weren't left anything.
> 5 Nobody understood (the reason) why Chaffin left everything to Marshall. Chaffin left everything to Marshall, which nobody understood.
> 6 Chaffin's ghost appeared to one of his sons, who will never forget the experience.

2 ANSWERS

1 where; 2 why; 3 whose; 4 that/which; 5 when; 6 who/that

3 ANSWERS

We can omit the pronoun in sentences 1, 4, 5 and 7, but not in 2, 3, 6 or 8.

4 Non-defining relative clauses

> **ANSWERS**
>
> Sentence **a** means there was only one son. The information about the son is therefore not essential (as there **is** only one). It is therefore **non-defining**.

Sentence **b** means there was more than one son and it therefore gives the essential information of **which** son was selfish. It is therefore an example of a **defining** relative clause.

1 That's the woman whose son scratched my new car.
2 This is the photograph of the ghost (that/which was) seen coming down the stairs.
3 Stonehenge, which was a miracle of engineering, was built thousands of years ago.
4 It's a hard job (which) not many people would choose.
5 This is the boy (who/m) I met on holiday last year.

5 Pronunciation of non–defining relative clauses
Read through the explanation with the class then play the tape several times. When students have checked their answers ask them to repeat the sentences after the tape. Ask one or two students to choose a sentence and read it out, the rest of the class decides whether it was defining or non-defining. Once you are sure students have the hang of it divide them into pairs to try this out on each other.

> **TAPESCRIPT AND ANSWERS**
> 1 The woman, whose husband had died, was rich.
> 2 Carol's daughter, who lives in Scotland, is a doctor.
> 3 This Bible, which was found in the keeping of Chaffin's widow, was examined in front of independent witnesses.

6 Relative clauses with prepositions
Read through the explanation and examples with the class. To check understanding elicit two or three further examples, e.g.
That's the teacher (who/that) I gave my homework to.
→ *That's the teacher to whom I gave my homework.*
This is the museum (which/that) she left all her money to.
→ *This is the museum to which she left all her money.*

7 Relative clauses with quantifiers
Note: This grammatical area is for understanding and recognition only, since students will not be asked to actively use such phrases in the FCE exam.

> **8 ANSWERS**
> 1 That's the woman to whom I spoke yesterday.
> 2 Five students, none of whom knew the answer, were asked a question.
>   OR
>   Five students were asked, none of whom knew the answer.
> 3 We got a lift to the cinema, without which we would have missed the beginning of the film.
> 4 The guests, all of whom were wearing their best clothes, arrived.
> 5 He is the friend whose car I borrowed/from whom I borrowed the car.

ANYBODY THERE?

p.150 FIRST THOUGHTS

Use the questions to introduce the idea of imaginary friends. Elicit personal experiences where possible.

p.150–151 READING

1 Read the introduction and ask students to describe the photograph. Pre-teach the following items before setting the gist questions:
a medium, psychic, pushchair, lad, to tuck someone in, commotion, stretcher.

> **ANSWERS**
> 1 She feels that imaginary friends come from the spirit world.
> 2 They helped her with her maths exams.
> 3 Her earliest experience was when she was four.

> **2 ANSWERS**
> **1** A; **2** C; **3** D; **4** B; **5** A; **6** B; **7** D; **8** A

p.151 VOCABULARY

Ways of looking

As an initial way of teaching the different ways of looking, you could mime to the students and try and elicit the appropriate word. If no one knows, you should give the word and drill the pronunciation.

> **ANSWERS**
> 1 watched; 2 glanced; 3 peered; 4 look; 5 seen;
> 6 stared; 7 gazed

In pairs, students can test each other on the vocabulary by taking it in turns to mime and then guess the word being mimed.

p.151 LANGUAGE STUDY

Abbreviating clauses

1 Write the two sentences *I'd seen Tom's spirit. It was walking beside him,* on the blackboard and see if students

can make the one sentence from them.
The difference between examples 1 and 2:
In 1 we saw part of the action; in 2 we saw the complete action from start to finish.

> ## 2 Answers
> 1 We felt the ground start to shake.
> 2 Anna noticed a strange smell coming from a cupboard.
> 3 Did you hear their dog barking all night?
> 4 The policeman caught the thief climbing through the window.

IT'S YOU AGAIN!

p.152 FIRST THOUGHTS

1/2 Start by checking understanding of *reincarnation* and eliciting students' feelings about it. Take a class vote on whether students believe in it or not. Then ask the students to describe the pictures and link them to the notes in the box.

p.152 LISTENING

Get the students to read through the sentences before they listen. You can play the tape twice (as in the exam).

> ## Answers
> 1 Y; 2 J; 3 M; 4 M; 5 Y; 6 J; 7 M

Tapescript

YOLANDA: What's that book you're reading, James? You seem very engrossed in it.
JAMES: Oh sorry, yes, it's about reincarnation. Quite riveting.
MALCOLM: Reincarnation! Ah, you surely don't believe in all that.
JAMES: That's why I'm reading this book – I'm trying to make my mind up about it.
YOLANDA: I'm absolutely positive there's something in it.
MALCOLM: But how can we know one way or the other? I mean, there's no proof, is there?
JAMES: That's what I used to think but now I'm not so sure. There are some fascinating stories in this book, you know.
MALCOLM: Oh yeah. Like what?
JAMES: Well, first of all, if we are reincarnated, this means that we must've been someone else in a previous life, right?
YOLANDA: Right. Go on.
JAMES: You see, people investigating reincarnation came up with the idea that if you hypnotised someone, they might be able to go back in time and tell you about their previous lives. And one of ...
MALCOLM: What a load of old rubbish! Do you believe this?
YOLANDA: Come on, Malcolm. Let James finish what he has to say.
JAMES: Thank you, Yolanda. Now, as I was saying, one of the people they hypnotised was someone called Jane Evans and she managed to recall something like six or seven lives. She'd been a Jewish girl who was murdered during the middle ages, a servant to one of Henry VIII's wives and a nun in a convent in the USA.
MALCOLM: Blimey! She'd been busy. I mean, come off it! She'd probably read some stories about these characters somewhere or other. I'm sure there's a logical explanation for all of this.
JAMES: Well, maybe you're right. She could have read something which entered her subconscious. That's certainly true in the case of one of her other lives. She claimed to be the servant to a French merchant. And all of the details she could remember of this past life were readily available in books. Strangely enough though, she forgot to mention the fact that the merchant was married and had five kids.
MALCOLM: There you are. What did I tell you?
JAMES: Hold on a minute! Going back to the Jewish girl, what's incredible about this past life is that she could say exactly where the girl had been killed, under a church in a, in some kind of cellar. No sooner had she told this story than some archaeologists found it. Quite by chance – they were doing some other work on the church – when they came across it and they found some skeletons down there!
MALCOLM: Skeletons! You'd surely expect to find skeletons under a church, or at least I would.
YOLANDA: I'm afraid I agree with Malcolm, James. Were there any other cases?
JAMES: Well, there's another one that's very interesting. A housewife called Dolores was hypnotised and she took on the character of someone called Gretchen Gottlieb. Now, she was murdered in Germany in a forest during the last century and what's interesting about this case is that, when she was hypnotised, Dolores spoke in German and yet she'd never learnt the language at school or anything. What's more when she came out of hypnosis, she couldn't speak any German at all.
YOLANDA: What was her German like?
JAMES: Well, not very good, I'm afraid. It was pretty incorrect and she avoided using verbs. Some of her answers didn't make sense and some of the time she hadn't understood questions she'd been asked.
MALCOLM: So did this Gretchen actually exist?
JAMES: Well, they tried to verify the story but they couldn't confirm it either way. There weren't any records or anything like that.
YOLANDA: Do you think Dolores was trying to take the researchers in?
JAMES: Well, according to the book they were sure she was acting in good faith but well, you never know.
MALCOLM: In good faith! If you believe that, you'll believe anything.

p.153 PRONUNCIATION

Rising intonation

1 Play the relevant part of the *Listening* again and see if students hear the tone of disbelief. Drill the pattern around the class.

2 Play the phrases on tape. Don't let the class shout out the answers, get them to note them down and then compare in groups. They should then listen again and repeat the phrases with correct intonation.

> **TAPESCRIPT AND ANSWERS**
>
> 1 His own daughter. *(surprise)*
> 2 His own daughter. *(disbelief)*
> 3 His own daughter. *(simple statement)*
> 4 By car. *(simple statement)*
> 5 By car. *(disbelief)*
> 6 By car. *(surprise)*

p.153 LANGUAGE STUDY

Inversion

1 Before looking at the book, you may want to isolate the target sentence on the tape and get students to take it down as dictation and then in small groups analyse the exact meaning. They can then compare their explanation with that in the book. Then read through the further examples with the class.

> **2 ANSWERS**
>
> 1 The B sentences are more emphatic and dramatic because of the use of 'negative' adverbs and inversion.
> 2 After these constructions we invert the subject and the verb/auxiliary. We need to include *than* after *Hardly* and *No sooner*.
> 3 We can use them in speaking and writing, but they are more common in writing, especially in literary English.
> 4 The 'negative' adverb is stressed.

> **3 ANSWERS**
>
> 1 No sooner had she arrived than she started to complain.
> 2 Not only does he sing but he also dances.
> 3 Never had I eaten such an awful meal.
> 4 No sooner had the match started than fighting broke out.
> 5 Hardly had I got into the bath than the telephone rang.
> 6 Never have I read such a wonderful book.

p.153 WRITING

Follow the usual procedure. Make it clear that you are expecting a humorous letter for those students who might be confused! Point out the opportunities for inversion in the notes supplied in the Coursebook and encourage students to include these in their letters. After preparation and planning in groups students can write the letter for homework.

> **MODEL ANSWER**
>
> Dear Sir,
> I am writing to complain about the night I spent at your hotel last week.
> According to your advertisement all rooms have 21st century facilities but this was certainly not the case with my room. Not only did the bathroom have no soap but there were no towels either! And the food in your restaurant was awful. Never have I eaten such a terrible meal.
> Not only was the bed uncomfortable but the room was noisy. I didn't get to sleep until 2 in the morning. No sooner had I fallen asleep than I was woken up by terrifying noises from the ghost as he shook his chains and made terrible groans. He was certainly not the friendly ghost you claimed in your advertisement.
> Considering your complete failure to fulfill the promises in your advertisement I feel justified in claiming a full refund of the cost of the room.
> Yours faithfully ...

CHILLING TALES

p.154 FIRST THOUGHTS

1/2 Use the questions as a lead-in to the topic of ghost stories. Elicit and put on the board useful vocabulary, e.g. *suspense, twist in the tail, atmosphere*

p.154 VOCABULARY

Extreme adjectives

Get the students to work through the exercises in small groups, pooling their knowledge and checking each other's work.

> **1 ANSWERS**
>
> interesting/fascinating; beautiful/gorgeous; big/huge; hungry/starving; small/tiny; sure/positive; good/wonderful; hot/boiling; frightened/terrified; bad/awful; tired/exhausted; cold/freezing

> **2 ANSWERS**
>
> 1 correct; 2 wrong; 3 correct; 4 wrong; 5 correct; 6 correct
> We modify ordinary adjectives like *cold* with modifiers like *fairly, quite, very* and *extremely*. We modify extreme adjectives like *freezing* with modifiers like *absolutely, completely, utterly* and *totally*. Note that *quite* and *really* can be used with both types of adjective.

> **3 ANSWERS**
>
> 1 starving; 2 tiny; 3 freezing; 4 awful; 5 wonderful; 6 terrified; 7 a gorgeous; 8 fascinating/interesting; 9 a huge; 10 exhausted; 11 positive; 12 hungry

4 Play the tape and ask students to copy the marked intonation of Martin's utterances. Repeat around the class until students are able to reproduce the pattern convincingly. Then divide the class into pairs to make up their own similar mini-dialogues. Monitor, checking correct use of modifiers and intonation, then ask one or two pairs to repeat their dialogue in front of the class at the end.

p.155 WRITING

The mysterious hitchhiker

1 Divide the class into A/B pairs. Ask As to read the first version and Bs to read the second. After reading their version they tell their story to their partner and note if there are any differences. Then all students look at both versions and analyse the differences.

> **ANSWERS/DIFFERENCES**
>
> The second version is incomplete and uses a greater variety of tenses, sentence length and construction than the first version. Extra details are given to make the story more interesting and the vocabulary is much richer.

2 Ask students in small groups to continue the second version, writing a short summary of their 'ending'. When they have done this they may like to read it out to the class.

Extension

As an additional fluency activity you could ask students to act out the story of the mysterious hitchhiker with their endings.

3 This could be set as homework.

p.156 USE OF ENGLISH

At this stage in the course it would be good examination practice for students to work on the two exercises individually. Go through the answers and any vocabulary points which arise at the end.

> **1 ANSWERS**
>
> 1 A; 2 B; 3 D; 4 C; 5 B; 6 A; 7 C; 8 C; 9 D; 10 B; 11 C; 12 C; 13 C; 14 A; 15 C

> **2 ANSWERS**
>
> 1 are; 2 following; 3 used; 4 own; 5 always/often; 6 few; 7 way; 8 The; 9 wave; 10 these; 11 sooner; 12 with; 13 such; 14 into; 15 away

p.157 USE OF ENGLISH

1 Use the question to introduce the topic. Ask the class to describe the illustration and elicit anything they know about the pyramids and write their ideas on the board. Check they understand the following vocabulary: *astronomy   Egyptology   Milky Way   shaft*

2 Students read the text quickly and note any differences between their ideas (which are on the board) and information in the text.

> **3 ANSWERS**
>
> 1 got; 2 of; 3 too; 4 they; 5 time; 6 did; 7 it; 8 in; 9 exact; 10 are; 11 ✓; 12 the; 13 than; 14 ✓ 15 at

Extension

Several topics have been presented in Unit 13 which lend themselves to imaginative written work or discussion, i.e. reincarnation, superstitions, astronomy, life after death, the supernatural, ghosts, etc. Choose the theme which most stimulated your class and either set a discursive type or narrative composition, or organise a class debate. For example
Debates: *Ghosts do not exist./Superstitions are sensible precautions.*
Essay titles: *The day I saw a ghost./Imaginary friends – Are they really spirits?*

p.158 READING

Creatures of the night

1 Read through the rubric with the class, explaining that it does not matter which order they give their answers in when more than one answer is required. They should read through the texts before attempting the multiple choice matching task.

> **ANSWERS**
>
> **1** F; **2** D; **3** C or F; **4** C or F; **5** A; **6** F; **7** D; **8** C;
> **9** B or E; **10** B or E; **11** B; **12** B or E; **13** B or E

2 Deal with any vocabulary problems in the text then discuss the questions in open class.

p.159 LISTENING

1 Remind students that one of the answers A–F is not required.

> **ANSWERS**
>
> Speaker 1 D; Speaker 2 A; Speaker 3 E;
> Speaker 4 C; Speaker 5 F
> B is the extra answer.

TAPESCRIPT

SPEAKER 1: Goodness me what a question. Well definitely not a housewife that's for sure. I think I must have been very bad in a previous life to have to do what I have to do every day. I don't know really, maybe something valuable, perhaps a painting or something like that. Yeah ... that way I'd really feel as though I was appreciated and people would like to look at me, you know ... I wouldn't have to worry about the shopping or cooking meals either.

SPEAKER 2: Mm, I think one of the problems affecting the world today is world peace, and I think that you know the normal solutions like wars and generals just, well, aren't the answer. I think if I came back what I'd like to be is someone like a spiritual leader who would be able to unite people and help world peace that way. I'd get people to tolerate and recognise the good in all the major religions.

SPEAKER 3: I suppose a runner or someone like that. I've competed at amateur level and won a couple of races with my club, but I guess what would give me the most satisfaction of all would be to win a gold at the Olympics. You know, the buzz must be incredible – just to know that you're the best in the world and nobody else can touch you. I can almost imagine what it must be like standing up on the podium listening to the national anthem as they put the sash around my neck.

SPEAKER 4: 'Cos it's the lifestyle that would suit me most I think. It must be incredible, going from Paris to Milan, Milan to New York and to be in demand all the time. There'd be the clothes as well. What an opportunity to wear the very latest fashions. Another thing I think is really good these days is that you can change your career, you know, once you retire at the age of thirty-something you have another career in the movies or maybe even become a pop star.

SPEAKER 5: A statesperson definitely. You know someone who was around when there were enormous changes taking place in government and things. I have strong convictions and beliefs about how the country should be run and it would be marvellous to be president or prime minister and to have a go at shaping the, erm, destiny of the country.

2 Let students discuss the question in small groups, then report back in open class. Start the feedback by saying what you would like to come back as.

14 Destination USA

Note: The Listening passages in this unit provide practice under exam conditions. The passages on cassette are in the format of the FCE exam and can be presented under exam conditions even though the tapescripts are at the back of the Student's Book.

NEW HORIZONS

p.160 FIRST THOUGHTS

The main aim of this activity is to generate interest in the topic of emigration.
The pictures:
The background has an advertisement for a passenger ship to the USA. The top left hand picture shows immigrants having their first sight of the Statue of Liberty. From their dress they look as though they have come from Eastern Europe. The picture underneath it shows three children and their belongings. The bottom pictures show a ship full of emigrants leaving home and their reception at Ellis Island where they had to undergo a medical examination.

p.160 SPEAKING

Discussion points

Put students in pairs to do this and then, after they have finished, tie the discussion together by compiling a list on the blackboard of the various reasons why people might choose to emigrate and another list of what would be difficult for someone living in a new country. In multilingual classes this needs to be done at quite a general level, but in classes where students all come from the same country the discussion can get quite specific. If you are not a native of this country, students may be interested to know what you have found difficult to adapt to, if anything. It may also be interesting to find out which is the most popular country that students would choose to emigrate to and why. If there are students with relatives who have emigrated, you may like to ask them to tell the rest of the class about the experience of their relatives.

p.160–161 VOCABULARY

Students may complete these tasks in pairs, using dictionaries if necessary.

1 ANSWERS

immigrate – immigration – immigrant: moving into a new country to settle there / **emigrate** – emigration – emigrant: moving away from your mother country

2 ANSWERS

1 exile; 2 refugees; 3 prejudice; 4 homesick;
5 hospitable; 6 fit in; 7 settle down, get used to;
8 asylum; 9 visa

p.161 USE OF ENGLISH

Note: The illustration is a scene from the film *Green Card* with Gerard Depardieu and Andie McDowell, directed by Peter Weir.

1 Students read the text quickly to answer the gist question.

ANSWER

Couple: George – a composer who wants a green card/ Bronte – a horticulturalist who needs a flatmate. They get married. There is probably a happy ending.

2 ANSWERS

1 composer; 2 Unfortunately; 3 desperation;
4 marriage; 5 immigration; 6 suspicious; 7 justified;
8 humorous; 9 investigators; 10 deepen;
11 confession; 12 suggestion

p.161 SPEAKING

Begin by reading through the instructions with the class, checking that they understand the situation. Divide the class into pairs. Half of the pairs are As, the other half Bs. Allow adequate preparation time for As to prepare their 'story' and for Bs to prepare a list of ten questions. When they are ready, ask one member of each of the A pairs to leave the classroom and wait outside. Each of the B pairs then questions the remaining member of an A pair, noting down their answers. After a few minutes stop the activity and ask all the As to leave the room. Bring in their partners from outside and ask the Bs to interview them, using the same questions. If the answers are consistent, the Bs should award the A pair a 'visa'. If the answers are not consistent, they should refuse them a 'visa'. Stop the activity as soon as most of the pairs have finished talking and bring the rest of the As in from outside the room. Ask each pair of Bs to report back to class with the results of their interviews. Ask them to explain if and how they were able to 'break' their story.
If you have time, the pairs can swap roles.

A SENSE OF LIBERTY

p.162 FIRST THOUGHTS

Do this as a group brainstorming exercise. Compile a list of national symbols on the board.

p.162 LISTENING

Before playing the tape ask students to tell you anything they know about the Statue of Liberty – its age, construction, origin, etc. They can listen and check their predictions before listening again to complete the gap-fill.

ANSWERS

1 Friendship
2 July 4th 1776
3 Bartholdi
4 copper
5 1885
6 25 tons
7 151
8 93
9 171
10 Grover Cleveland

TAPESCRIPT

OK, OK everybody, in a minute we'll be getting off the boat, but before we do, I want to tell you a little bit about the Statue. Now, although it's almost certainly the most famous symbol of America and its people, it was in fact given to us by the people of France to commemorate the friendship between the two countries. In her right hand, as you can see, is the torch of Liberty and in her left hand is a tablet which has the date July 4th 1776 on it. That's the date of American independence, of course. OK, let's give you a few facts and figures about the Statue. The idea of the Statue came from a French historian and the money for it was raised by the French people. It was designed by Frederic Bartholdi. That's B-A-R-T-H-O-L-D-I.

The Statue was made of copper sheets which were hammered together by hand. They had to be put together over a huge framework of four supports which were made by Eiffel, the guy responsible for the Eiffel Tower in Paris, France. It was finished in 1885 and then taken to pieces to be shipped from France to the USA, and it weighs 25 tons. Now the Statue itself is 151 feet high, but if you add the pedestal, that's what the Statue stands on, then it makes 305 feet, which is 93 metres. If you want to go right, if you want to go right to the top, then I'm afraid you've got to walk. There's an elevator up through the pedestal, but from then on you have to use a spiral staircase to reach the observation point in the lady's crown, and it's 171 steps. Just to finish off, before we dock, when the Statue had been reconstructed, it was dedicated by President Grover Cleveland on 28th of October 1886. OK, we're nearly there ...

p.162–163 READING

1 Ask students to read the text quickly to answer this gist question:
* *Which two specific groups of immigrants are mentioned in the text?*

ANSWER

1 Irish; 2 Russian Jews

Students then answer the four questions.

ANSWERS

1 35 million; 2 1845–48; 3 9 million; 4 4 million

2 Students complete the heading matching task.

ANSWERS

1 H; 2 G; 3 A; 4 C; 5 F; 6 D; 7 B

p.163 LANGUAGE STUDY

Numbers

ANSWERS

1 She lived for *a* hundred years.
2 The population of the USA is over two hundred *million*.
3 Five *thousand* people visit the gallery every day.
4 My telephone number is two-four-double three-eight-nine-five.
5 I would like *a dozen eggs*, please.
6 The code for London is 0 (*oh*)-one-seven-one.
7 Dozens of people walked out of the film. (*correct*)
8 The book is one hundred *and* eighty pages long. (The sentence in the Coursebook is correct in American English)
9 Altogether that's three pounds sixty-five.
10 The average family has two *point* four children.
11 The drawer is an eighth of an inch too wide. (*correct*)
12 There were thousands of people at the party. (*correct*)
13 The Battle of Waterloo was in *eighteen fifteen*.
14 My car does thirty miles *to the gallon*.

p.163 LISTENING

TAPESCRIPT AND ANSWERS

1 Phone numbers
A 01223 68991
B 00 88 1 4476 1085
2 Account numbers
A 87640328
B 925487234
3 Decimals
A 3.2
B 2.54
C 0.38
4 Fractions
A 1/4
B 2/3
C 3/8
D 5/16
5 Dates
A 11/11/1918
B 14/7/1789 (7/14/1789 in American English)
C 1/3/1963 (3/1/1963 in American English)
6 Amounts
A $6.92 cents
B £10.03p
7 Scores
A Agassi won the match 6-0, 3-6, 6-1.
B Italy beat Holland 2-0.
8 Large numbers
A 23,927,421
B 9,867,364
C 989,774

p.163 PRONUNCIATION

1 Students listen again and repeat the numbers, copying the rhythm and intonation. The numbers are broken up into their respective groups and said accordingly.

2 Students read the numbers to a partner (whose book is closed) who must copy them down. This can be extended by asking students to read out their own phone numbers, fictional bank account numbers, results of recent sports events, etc.

Extension

As further practice of saying numbers, you may like to give the class a simple arithmetic quiz, perhaps on a *first group to answer correctly gets the point* basis, e.g.

What does
1/3 – 1/4   (1/12)
2/3 x 3/4   (1/2)
10,001 – 8,764 equal?   (1,237)
91,392 ÷ 357   (256)
987 x 241   (237,867)
4.789 x 3.204   (15.343956)

p.164 LANGUAGE STUDY

The gerund and the infinitive

1 Ask students to read through part 1 and work on exercises 2 and 3 in pairs. When they have had enough time, put on the board all the additional verbs thought of for either group.

2 ANSWERS

1 emigrating; 2 to let; 3 entering; 4 to allow; 5 to deport; 6 crossing; 7 to hide; 8 showing; 9 filling in; 10 to understand; 11 to be

3 ANSWERS

+ INFINITIVE	+ GERUND
refuse	consider
agree	deny
threaten	avoid
offer	mind
pretend	finish
tend	

4 Let students work on this in small groups and then put the groups together to compare their ideas on which ones demonstrate an important change in meaning and in what way the meaning is different.

ANSWERS

1 no difference
2 big difference – in the first sentence *remembering* came before *closing the window*.
3 no big difference here, although **a** would be more common in American English.
4 big difference – the first sentence means 'I think it is a good idea to go, (but I don't necessarily go) twice a year'; the second sentence implies 'I go to the dentist **and** I enjoy it'!
5 big difference – similar to 2
6 difference – a suggests that I was going to apologise but I didn't (I had intended to) b suggests that I did something wrong and the only way I would be forgiven was if I apologised.
7 quite a subtle difference – learning Japanese was her final goal. Learning ten words a day was the method she used.

5 ANSWERS

1 to go, picking up; 2 seeing; 3 to rain*;
4 playing, to play; 5 to study/studying; 6 to tell;
7 inviting; 8 to make, to concentrate; 9 driving;
10 to wonder; 11 to do; 12 jogging; 13 to post;
14 to do; 15 lending; 16 taking off

Note:
* (We don't use the gerund after a continuous tense.)

p.165 LISTENING

ANSWERS

1 False – *Well, yes I was brought up as a Mormon, if that's what you mean, but I don't go to church as often as I should.* (She still considers herself a Mormon.)
2 True – *Is it part of the Christian Church? Oh, yes.*
3 False – *You can date it from 1827.*
4 False – *Smith was visited by Moroni …*
5 True – *This sounds a bit like Moses receiving the Ten Commandments. Exactly.*
6 False – *… it had been written in a kind of Ancient Egyptian.*
7 True – *And after that, the cult really caught on and lots of people joined it.*
8 True – *The Bible talks of the lost tribes of Israel and the idea is that one of these tribes made it to America and that's how the plates came to be buried there.*
9 True – *… you can bring your ancestors into the Church when you join.*
10 False – *… they used to but it's not allowed any longer.*

TAPESCRIPT

CHRISSY: You're a Mormon, aren't you Gina?
GINA: Well, yes, I was brought up as a Mormon, if that's what you mean, but I don't go to church as often as I should.
CHRISSY: Is it part of the Christian Church?
GINA: Oh, yes.
CHRISSY: I'm sorry to be so ignorant but when did it all start?
GINA: You can date it from 1827.
CHRISSY: What happened then?
GINA: That's when the prophet Joseph Smith was visited by an angel called Moroni.
CHRISSY: Moroni?
GINA: Yes, and he took Smith to a place where there were some gold plates buried and these plates had a holy book inscribed on them, the Book of Mormon. Mormon was Moroni's father, by the way.
CHRISSY: This sounds a bit like Moses receiving the Ten Commandments.
GINA: Exactly. The thing is, with God's help, Smith was able to read what was written on the plates, 'cos it had been written in a kind of Ancient Egyptian. And after that, the cult really caught on and lots of people joined it.
CHRISSY: And what happened to the plates?
GINA: They were destroyed.
CHRISSY: I see. And how come this happened in America?
GINA: Good question. The Bible talks of the lost tribes of Israel and the idea is that one of these tribes made it to America and that's how the plates came to be buried there.
CHRISSY: What's special about being a Mormon? I mean, in what ways is it different from other forms of Christianity?
GINA: First, baptism is very important, not just for the individual but also for the ancestors of the individual.
CHRISSY: The ancestors?
GINA: Yes, you can bring your ancestors into the Church when you join. And there are very strict rules on drinking. You can't, you can't drink any stimulants, coffee, tea, alcohol. And no cigarettes.
CHRISSY: Sounds a bit tough.
GINA: Maybe, but it's been shown that Mormons live longer than the average American because of their healthy lifestyle.
CHRISSY: And what about marriage? Is it true that the men can have more than one wife?
GINA: They used to but it's not allowed any longer.

p.166–167 FIRST THOUGHTS

Ask the students to compare and contrast the pictures in pairs. Put on the board any useful ideas/vocabulary they come up with in columns headed 'photos 1 & 2' and 'photos A & B', so they will be able to check their ideas when they read the texts in the next section.

Note: The pictures show
1 a scene from the film *Posse* – the first fully black American movie.
2 a scene from a typical traditional Hollywood cowboy movie.
A a game of baseball
B schoolchildren playing rounders

p.166 USE OF ENGLISH

1 Students read the text and compare with their ideas about photographs 1 and 2 which you have put on the board. They should explain any differences.

2 Students complete individually then compare answers in pairs.

ANSWERS

1 B; 2 B; 3 A; 4 C; 5 C; 6 D; 7 C; 8 A; 9 C; 10 B;
11 B; 12 C; 13 D; 14 B; 15 B

3 Students read the text and compare with their ideas about photographs A and B. They should then complete the gap-fill task.

> **ANSWERS**
>
> **1** take; **2** then; **3** succeeded/ended; **4** enough;
> **5** much; **6** set; **7** Not; **8** all; **9** have; **10** the;
> **11** fewer/less; **12** caught; **13** much;
> **14** biggest/greatest **15** managed
>
> **Note:**
> *So much so* is an idiom – it would be worth students remembering this one.

p.167 LISTENING

TAPESCRIPT

ANDY: Before we go to this game, can you tell me a little bit about the rules?
GUS: Sure. What do you want to know?
ANDY: Well, I know there are eleven men on the field for each team at one time, but what I really wanted to know is how you score points.
GUS: OK. First of all, you can score points in five different ways. The first is with a touchdown. When you cross your opponent's goal line, then you get six points.
ANDY: Although they don't actually touch the ball down, do they?
GUS: No, they don't.
ANDY: You have to in rugby.
GUS: Is that right? The second way is after the touchdown you can get an extra point by kicking the ball between the posts.
ANDY: That's just like rugby union except you get two points.
GUS: And the third way is a field goal – and that's worth three points – which is when you kick the ball between the posts while the ball is in play, not after a touchdown.
ANDY: I've got it. And that's it?
GUS: Well, there are two other ways but they're a little complicated and unusual so I won't go into them right now.
ANDY: OK. What about the playing of the game? You can pass the ball forward in American football, correct? You can't do that in rugby.
GUS: Yes, but only once in each play. After that, it has to be passed backwards like in rugby.
ANDY: But I've never seen it happen in the games I've watched on TV.
GUS: No, it is a little unusual.
ANDY: Now the *plays*, what are they?
GUS: A *play* is basically the bit of action between the two scrimmages. So, imagine a player gets tackled with the ball. The game stops and then restarts with a scrimmage – that's when the two teams face each other and everybody blocks and tackles. Then there's

maybe a bit of action lasting anything from two to twenty seconds until the next touchdown or tackle or the ball goes out of play.
ANDY: I see. Oh, one more thing. How does the ball change hands between the teams?
GUS: It can be intercepted when it's thrown of course, or taken off the other team but the basic idea of the game is to gain yardage and you have to gain ten yards in four plays. If you don't achieve that, then the other team is given the ball.
ANDY: It's all pretty complicated.
GUS: No, no, basically it's a very simple game, easy to understand. Now, when I went to England, someone took me to a cricket match. Now that's a complicated game.
ANDY: No, it's not. If you know baseball, then really it's quite easy …

> **ANSWERS**
>
> **1** C; **2** D; **3** C; **4** A; **5** D

FLORIDA FUN

p.168 FIRST THOUGHTS

Students discuss the questions in small groups and then report back to open class to compare their ideas.

p.168–169 READING

Introduce the text by asking if any students have been to Florida or theme parks generally. Elicit any personal opinions and experiences then pre-teach the following before students complete the multiple choice task:
(water) chute, surfing, rollercoaster, animation/animator.

> **ANSWERS**
>
> **1** C; **2** G or I; **3** G or I; **4** F; **5** D; **6** B; **7** H; **8** J; **9** I;
> **10** E; **11** F or H; **12** F or H; **13** D

p.169 LISTENING

Students answer the questions by writing: **C** for Christine, **K** for Kate or **R** for Roger.

> **ANSWERS**
>
> **1** R; **2** K; **3** C; **4** C; **5** C; **6** R; **7** K

Note: Sometimes you may get a question which can only be answered after listening to the whole script. There is one such question here.

TAPESCRIPT

INTERVIEWER: So how come you chose to go to Florida?
CHRISTINE: Well, Roger's company had had a very good year and he got a substantial bonus. And the kids were the right age.
ROGER: Kate was 13 and Nick 11 ... So we thought now or never ... and of course for once the, erm, exchange rate was quite favourable, and we had the money at that point in time, so ...
INTERVIEWER: Umm ... And er, what did you do?
CHRISTINE: Well all the usual, really ... you know, Disney – which includes the Magic Kingdom, Epcot centre, Sea World and erm, the studios.
INTERVIEWER: MGM or Universal?
CHRISTINE: MGM, although Universal are pretty near, too.
ROGER: Yeah, if you ever do it, you should remember to get erm, not a day ticket, but a, er, passport I think they call it, you know, yes, a passport which entitles you to visit the three centres ... It'll save you a fortune.
INTERVIEWER: Right, that's worth remembering ... And what did you think of it, Kate?
KATE: Just brilliant. I mean we had a great time.
INTERVIEWER: And what was the best bit for you?
KATE: The ice creams I think.
INTERVIEWER: No, I meant of the places you visited ...
KATE: Well ... they were all brilliant. Nick liked the Disney thing best, but I think for me, Sea World was the best.
INTERVIEWER: But don't we have things like that in Europe?
KATE: Yeah ... but not so big.
INTERVIEWER: Anyway. And what about the grown-ups?
CHRISTINE: Well, of course we went primarily for the kids. The Disney experience, the erm, Magic Kingdom left me a bit cold I must admit ... the rides terrified me ... it did nothing for me ... but there were lots of other things I loved like the Epcot centre, you know the erm, science and technology part.
ROGER: And of course there was the shopping ... all the goods you know like Levi's and, what's the name of the boots you got?
CHRISTINE: Timberland ...
ROGER: ... you know all the branded names, they're still expensive but nowhere near what you'd have to pay over here.
INTERVIEWER: And what about all these stories you hear about foreign visitors being targeted and robbed?
CHRISTINE: Yes, I must admit I was very scared about that and there were some really horrible people hanging around the airport, but once we, er, got away from the area and were sure that no-one was following us then it was great.
ROGER: Umm, the average American is so much warmer and more polite than over here. The way they look after you in hotels and restaurants is just so much better all round.
INTERVIEWER: Just one more thing. Didn't you ever consider going to Disney near Paris? I mean, after all it's more or less on the doorstep now, isn't it? And you've got Paris and the Louvre and everything you can also go to.
KATE: Yes, but the thing is, for the authentic American experience you've just got to go to the States.
CHRISTINE: And we'd been to Paris loads of times.
INTERVIEWER: So you are glad you did it?
ROGER: Oh yes, it was great. It cost a fortune but, after all, well, you only live once, don't you?

p.169 SPEAKING

Pyramid discussion

If you have a class of up to about 20 students follow the procedure in the Coursebook. If you have a larger class you may prefer to omit step 4. The procedure will be more effective if you set time limits on each stage and use a signal such as clapping your hands to indicate when to move on to the next step in the procedure.

p.169 WRITING

The compusory letter

Ask students what style of letter it will be. Elicit that this will be a formal letter, as it is written from a company to a client. Explain to the class that before they plan the letter they must work out a suitable itinerary. Split the class into small groups to work on this for about five minutes. Students may find it helpful to arrange the information in the notes in chart form, i.e.

	MRS GREEN	MR GREEN	SANDY	CANDY	MANDY
Universal Studios					
Sea World	X		X		
Busch Gardens	X				X
etc ...					

DAY 1 Visit Sea World
DAY 2 ....
etc.

When they have organised their itinerary they should plan the letter. It can then be written up as homework.

CULTURAL EXCHANGES

p.170 FIRST THOUGHTS

Open class discussion. Begin by asking students if there are any words they know in their language which have been 'borrowed' from English. Make a list of these on the board and ask students how they feel about them before discussing the questions in open class.

p.170 LISTENING

1 Discuss the topic of street gangs with the class and elicit their responses to the questions. Put on the board any interesting ideas and vocabulary. Make sure students include the ideas of 'territory' and 'deprived' backgrounds as these feature in the dialogue.

2 ANSWERS

1 Bloods; **2** South Central; **3** hundreds; **4** baseball cap; **5** territory; **6** a car; **7** of the jungle; **8** depressing; **9** not involved; **10** Hispanic

TAPESCRIPT

LARRY: Larry here.
TRICIA: Hi, Larry it's Tricia.
LARRY: Hi, Tricia. What can I do for you?
TRICIA: Look, I was wondering if I could pick your brains for a couple of minutes.
LARRY: Sure. What about?
TRICIA: Well, I'm doing a school project at the moment about, erm, gangs, you know, street gangs and I thought, now Larry, he's from Los Angeles and he'd be able to tell me something about the, erm, Crips and the Bloods.
LARRY: Right, right. Well I'll do my best but I'm not an expert. To tell you the truth, I wasn't actually born in LA.
TRICIA: OK then. Well, I've got a few topics written down.
LARRY: OK fire away!
TRICIA: Well the first thing I want to know is how big the gangs are and where they operate.
LARRY: Well, mm, let's start with the second one. The erm, most important area for the gangs is a bit of town called, er, South Central, which is where you'd expect, it's south of, um, downtown. Mark you, there's another area called Watts – you know there were some pretty awful riots there.
TRICIA: And what about the size?
LARRY: Well, let me put it this way ... there aren't two enormous gangs as such where everybody knows everybody else, it is like there are hundreds of gangs but they are affiliated, they have loyalty to one of the two big ones.
TRICIA: I see ... So, how do you know who belongs to which?
LARRY: Well, you either wear a red baseball cap or a blue one. I can't remember which is which. The thing is, if you're a gang member you make sure that you don't stray into another gang's territory.
TRICIA: Why, what'll happen?
LARRY: Well, you could get beaten up or even worse ...
TRICIA: What do you mean?
LARRY: Well, you could actually get murdered.
TRICIA: That's terrible!!
LARRY: Huh, huh. And there's all sorts of tit-for-tat, you know revenge killing. A favourite pastime is for these drive-by murders ...
TRICIA: What are they?
LARRY: Well, you and your buddies, you get into your car and drive into the other gang's territory and you erm, spot a rival gang member in his blue or red baseball cap and you shoot him.
TRICIA: As simple as that – for no reason.
LARRY: By and large yes. Law of the jungle ... That's how you erm, get accepted as a full member of the gang.
TRICIA: Terrible ...
LARRY: Sure is, you know, you sometimes get these programmes on TV where they look at the problem. Most of the kids who get involved are from deprived areas where the gangs dominate.
TRICIA: The gangs dominate. What do the police do about this?
LARRY: As a matter of fact, there's not much they can do. What's more, a lot of places are um, no-go areas. The police have just about given up there. Anyway, to go back to what I was saying before, TV programmes are pretty depressing. Whole classes from high school end up dead or in jail. It's just hopeless.
TRICIA: Mm ... how awful. Anyway, what's it like for, you know, ordinary folk?
LARRY: In a nutshell, not so bad as you'd think. Well, for the most part the gang members stick to their own part of town and prey on each other, you know a lot of it is drug related anyway, so unless you get caught out where you shouldn't be, you'll be OK.
TRICIA: And just one last question, Larry. Does it break down on ethnic lines at all?
LARRY: Not really, although most of the gangs are black you get some, erm, Hispanic ones too. Mind you they could be either Crips or Bloods. You can't jump to any conclusion just 'cos of the colour of their skin.
TRICIA: Right, Larry, that's really great. For someone who's not an expert you sure know an awful lot about the topic.

p.171 READING

Introduce the text by asking students about Walt Disney and the Disneyland theme parks (*Disney World* in Florida was mentioned earlier in the unit). Ask them if they know anything (or have visited) Euro Disney near Paris. Students read the text quickly to answer the gist question.

ANSWER

The writer describes Euro Disney as 'cultural colonialism'. He/she feels culture doesn't travel well. An American theme park is therefore not appropriate in Europe.

p.171 LANGUAGE STUDY

Discourse markers

Students should work on this individually and then compare their answers.

> **ANSWERS**
>
> **1/2/3** after all, mind you, the thing is; **4** there again;
> **5/6/7** nevertheless, all the same, however; **8** anyway;
> **9** incidentally; **10/11/12** all in all, in a nutshell, by and large

p.171 VOCABULARY

British and American English

1 Start off by discussing in open class what differences students are aware of between British and American English. Try to get them to be as specific as possible. Ask them if they know any words which are different in British and American English before they do the exercises.

It is important to point out to students that most native speakers of English are 'bilingual' in British and American English – they usually understand both varieties although they only use one.

> **ANSWERS**
>
> **1** H; **2** J; **3** R; **4** N; **5** O; **6** A; **7** D; **8** L; **9** F; **10** E;
> **11** C; **12** P; **13** I; **14** B; **15** G; **16** Q; **17** M; **18** K

> **2 ANSWERS**
>
> 1 Can you go to the *chemist, darling?* We need some *nappies* for the baby and a *plaster* for my finger.
> 2 Last *autumn*, I was driving along *the motorway* when I ran out of *petrol*. Luckily, a *lorry driver* stopped and gave me a *lift*.
> 3 Our *flat* is quite near the *underground* station.
> 4 It's my turn to pay the *bill*. Pass me my *handbag*; I've got a *£20 note* in it.
> 5 *Biscuits* and *sweets* are bad for our teeth.
> 6 Nothing works round here! Not only is the *lift* broken but so is the *tap* in the bathroom.

Extension

If you want to encourage students to use the new vocabulary productively, you could ask them to make up a story in groups or round the class (one sentence each) entitled *Murder In New York City* aiming to include as many of the new items of vocabulary as possible.

AMERICAN DREAMS

p.172 FIRST THOUGHTS

1 The illustrations show (A) Abraham Lincoln (president during the Civil War), (B) Martin Luther King (civil rights leader in the 1960s) and (C) John F Kennedy (president from 1961-63). They were all assassinated (possibly due to their 'liberal' attitudes in opposing racial discrimination/slavery).

2 For a change, ask a student to read the extract aloud. The extract comes from a celebrated speech made by Martin Luther King in Washington in 1963 during a civil rights march.

Discuss the questions in open class.

p.172–173 READING

1 Ask students to describe the photographs and say what they know about Schwarzenegger. Write any ideas they come up with on the board.

Background information

Born in Austria in 1947. Champion bodybuilder, became Mr Universe in 1967. Emigrated to USA in 1968. His first film was *Pumping Iron* – a documentary. Since then has starred in many action films including *Conan the Barbarian*, *The Terminator*, *Total Recall* and *True Lies*. Also in comedies *Twins*, *Kindergarten Cop* and *Junior*.

> **2 ANSWERS**
>
> Their dreams are very different.
> Martin Luther King's dream was of equal rights, freedom and justice without racial prejudice.
> Schwarzenegger's dream is one of success, of having goals and striving for them, of being better than other people.

3 Students read the text again and answer the multiple-choice questions individually. Put them into small groups to compare answers and discuss their reactions to the text.

> **ANSWERS**
>
> **1** A; **2** D; **3** C; **4** C; **5** B; **6** C; **7** D; **8** B
> **Note**: Since Schwarzenegger is not a native speaker of English, some of his phrases are not those that a native speaker would use, e.g. *I had a big need **to be** singled out,* would be correct.

Extension

Students may want to discuss the relative merits of the two 'dreams' presented in the texts. *Which do they support? Is 'equality' compatible with 'striving to be better than others'?* To develop the theme you could ask students to write about their own personal 'dream' or philosophy of life as homework.

15 Our Common Future

WHAT DOES THE FUTURE HOLD?

p.174–175 FIRST THOUGHTS/SPEAKING

Prior to discussing their answers to the questionnaire and the discussion points, you may like to help students with the range of language for expressing opinion, agreeing and disagreeing (see Unit 7).

p.175 VOCABULARY

Technology and work

1 New technology

> **ANSWERS**
>
> 1 g; 2 d; 3 h; 4 a; 5 c; 6 e; 7 b; 8 f

2 Word building

This exercise looks at how words can be built and the impact that this has on pronunciation in word stress.

> **ANSWERS**
>
> | NOUN | NOUN (PERSON) | ADJECTIVE |
> | --- | --- | --- |
> | bi'ology | bi'ologist | bio'logical |
> | 'physics | 'physicist | 'physical |
> | 'chemistry | 'chemist | 'chemical |
> | e'cology | e'cologist | eco'logical |
> | tech'nology | ——— | techno'logical |
> | tech'nique | tech'nician | 'technical |

3 Work

Students may use dictionaries for this and the next exercise.

> **ANSWERS**
>
> 1 skills; 2 strike; 3 redundant; 4 trade union; 5 dole

p.176 LISTENING

Before doing the listening exercise, ask the students to brainstorm ideas about life in the future. Write on the board interesting ideas and useful vocabulary. As a gist listening task students can find whether any of the speakers agrees with their ideas.

1 ANSWERS

1 B; 2 E; 3 C; 4 F; 5 A
D is the extra description

2 Open class discussion.

TAPESCRIPT

SPEAKER 1: Well, I think it is going to be brilliant. I mean by 2025 we'll have conquered most diseases and people will be able to live longer and more fulfilled lives. Genetic engineering will mean there will be plenty of food for everyone and that illnesses will be cured by, erm, you know, changing someone's DNA. Also robots and computers will be doing everything. All this knowledge we've got – it's going to do us so much good, you know …

SPEAKER 2: Mmm. I'm not sure, I have this fantasy, though, that it'll be very tough to tell reality from the virtual reality. I mean, technology will have become incredibly sophisticated. You won't be able to tell the difference between what is real and what is, you know, virtual. People will have virtual families and virtual relationships without all the nasty bits like rows, illness, death. You'll be able to get a new partner and start again whenever you want. Other than that, well, I think things'll be pretty much the same as they are now.

SPEAKER 3: My guess is we'll or rather our great grandchildren will be living on the moon or somewhere else like that. There'll be techniques for putting people into suspended animation and sending them off into space for maybe even hundreds of years so that when they wake up they'll be on some planet many light years away from the earth. One of the reasons for this will be pollution on earth. If we don't get away and start to colonise, then it's highly likely that human beings will just die out. It'll be like Adam and Eve all over again. I was reading this fascinating book which was going on about how they were, in fact, astronauts from another planet …

SPEAKER 4: I suppose I'm a bit of a pessimist. I mean, I think it'll be an absolute miracle if we get through the next twenty years without blowing ourselves up. There's bound to be some sort of catastrophe …
I think it is a great shame really that we have all this advanced technology but people haven't really evolved at all, have they? Just look at history from thousands of years ago. The motives and emotions people had then are exactly the same as nowadays. Technology may have improved but, well, human beings certainly haven't got any wiser, have they?

SPEAKER 5: I really can't think that far ahead I'm afraid. Things just seem to change beyond the imagination of most ordinary people. My dad told me that the first telly his family had was a big ugly box and in black and white – black and white, can you imagine? He had no idea we were going to have colour TV. You know, it won't be long before we have a screen we can hang on the wall just like picture … and now they're talking about 3-D TV, you know holograms that'll just be projected into your room, and erm, I've even heard that there won't even be TV screen or anything like that any more, they'll just project the image onto the retina of the eye.

p.176 PRONUNCIATION

Word building

Get the students to work on this in small groups. Tell them to say the words aloud to each other to practise the stress patterns. If there are any problems model the words yourself and drill them around the class.

> **ANSWERS**
>
> **1 employ**
> em'ploy *verb*
> em'ployed *past participle*
> em'ployment *noun*
> em'ployable *adjective*
> em'ployer *noun*
> emplo'yee *noun*
> employa'bility *noun*
> 'unem'ployed *adjective*
> 'unem'ployment *noun*
> 'unem'ployable *adjective*
> **2 compete**
> com'pete *verb*
> com'petitive *adjective*
> com'petitor *noun*
> compe'tition *noun*
> com'petitiveness *noun*
> uncom'petitive a*djective*
> **3 qualify**
> 'qualify *verb*
> 'qualified *adjective*
> qualifi'cations *noun*
> un'qualified *adjective*
> dis'qualify *verb*
> disqualifi'cation *noun*

p.177 LANGUAGE STUDY

More complex ways of describing the future

1 The future perfect

The explanation in part 1 can either be used as the basis for your presentation of the grammar point from the board or students could be asked to read through the section as preparatory homework.

> **ANSWERS**
>
> Will we have conquered most diseases? **Yes.**
> Will this happen before, in, or after 2025? **Before.**
> Do we know exactly when this will happen? **No.**

In going through the answers to the sentence expansion exercise, make sure that students are able to make the contractions when they give the answers orally, e.g.
I will have ➔ I'll've
I will not have ➔ I won't've.

> **ANSWERS**
>
> 1 I will have finished this exercise in five minutes' time.
> 2 By the end of the century doctors will have found a cure for AIDS.
> 3 They will have arrived by ten o'clock this evening ...
> 4 ... but they will be tired and hungry because they will not have slept or eaten.
> 5 By next April he will have been out of work for six years.
> 6 A super-intelligent computer will have been invented by the year 2020.
> 7 ... and human labour will have been replaced by robots ...
> 8 ... but they still will not have found a way to replace cleaners!

2 The future continuous

> **ANSWERS**
>
> 1 C; 2 B; 3 A

3 The future after introductory time expressions

> **ANSWERS**
>
> 2A Office workers will have jobs until new technology makes them redundant.
> B Factory workers will go on strike as soon as robots are/have been introduced.
> C Once computers are/have been programmed with all the information they will act as judges. **or** Computers will act as judges once they have ...
> D Scientists won't have discovered an alternative source of energy before oil runs/has run out. **or** Oil will have run out before scientists discover ...
> E Immediately super-intelligent computers are invented, technicians will be needed to maintain them.
> F After all these changes take/have taken place, our world will be transformed.

4 For fun, you might like to let students predict firstly for themselves in note form under given headings, e.g. family, job, achievements, and then for one or two other students. They should then get into groups with the people they have predicted for, tell them their predictions and see how much similarity they bore to the students' description of their own future. They can write the paragraph predicting their own future for homework based on their notes.

MAKING A LIVING

p.178 FIRST THOUGHTS

Students discuss the questions in small groups. Check understanding of *over-education*.

p.178 USE OF ENGLISH

ANSWERS

1 qualifications; 2 disqualified; 3 unemployment; 4 shortage; 5 enthusiasm; 6 employability; 7 increasingly; 8 irrelevant; 9 apprenticeships; 10 commitment

p.178–179 READING

Read through the introduction with the class and check understanding. Ask students if they know the book or author (they may have seen a film version).
Background information:
Aldous Huxley (1894–1963) was an English novelist, poet and intellectual. His writings criticised Western civilisation and values; *Brave New World* (1932) is his best known novel and is a critique of materialism and the effects of technology on society.

1 ANSWERS

1 C; 2 D; 3 A; 4 D; 5 B; 6 A; 7 B; 8 A

Note: If we *sigh*, we are generally unhappy/fed up **or** feel satisfied/relaxed.

2 Begin by asking students to summarize Mustapha's philosophy and write their ideas on the board. This will also give you the opportunity to deal with any vocabulary/comprehension problems with the text. Then ask students to discuss the questions in small groups. They can report back and compare ideas in open class.

p.180 LISTENING

ANSWERS

1 the eighteenth century; 2 (the time of) the ancient Egyptians; 3 are being/have been made redundant; 4 printing; 5 the cost of a local telephone call; 6 fair; 7 blacksmiths/letter writers; 8 secretarial; 9 flexible and learn new skills; 10 you were mad

TAPESCRIPT

RENATE: One thing is for sure, the, erm, rate of change isn't going to slow down, if anything it's going to increase. What we are going through is a change which is more dramatic than the first industrial revolution which took place in western Europe in the eighteenth century. Now while the industrial revolution changed things in the space of a hundred years we are going to experience far greater changes in the space of twenty or thirty.

IAN: Can you give me an example?

RENATE: Sure. I think the most obvious one is that of the postal service. You know there has been a postal service – guys delivering letters – in its various forms since the time of the ancient Egyptians. All this is changing. Right now lots of postal workers who thought they were in safe jobs have been made redundant because of all the faxes which are being sent. Not only that, you can send information down fibre optic cables that can reach its destination immediately.

IAN: Yes, it is amazing, isn't it?

RENATE: Absolutely, the erm, the invention of print more or less saw an end to the Middle Ages, the computer revolution will probably see the drawing to a close of the age we are now in.

IAN: Will books vanish?

RENATE: No, not straight away, they're convenient and portable and relatively inexpensive. What's more, this Internet, the thing they call the Information Superhighway, this means that say a professor in Japan will be able to communicate with a colleague in Bangladesh, by computer at the cost of around a local phone call. Fantastic!

IAN: But what about the erm, you know, more traditional professions?

RENATE: Ha ha. Well, there's no such thing as a safe job any more. It won't be long before we have computers programmed with say, legal or medical information which will be able to try a criminal case more efficiently, accurately and fairly than any human practitioner. The old style professions which used to look as though they were a job for life, well they're fast becoming a thing of the past. You know, you read a book about the Middle Ages and you come across blacksmiths who made horseshoes, thatchers who put straw on your roof and coopers, the erm, barrel makers. Not to mention people like the letter writers who read and wrote letters for a largely illiterate population. Anyway, the point I'm making is that these jobs disappeared. We'll lose lots of modern professions and lots of more basic clerical and secretarial jobs, although to a large extent this has already happened.

IAN: So what do you think the results of this are going to be?

RENATE: Um ... a mixture of good and bad, I think. People who are prepared to be flexible and learn new skills, and who are intelligent enough, will continue to be in demand, but for many others the challenge could be too much. My advice to people in the old-style professions would be get computer literate, after all, a few people are going to be needed to produce the programs, er, you know the software and suchlike. I think I should also say that new jobs are always going to be created by developments in technology. If you'd said to someone sixty years ago that their job was going to be either making, selling or repairing boxes which would show pictures in your living room, well they'd have said you were mad.

IAN: They'd have locked you up.

RENATE: ... and thrown away the key!

p.180-181 READING

Introduce the topic of CD-ROMs and ask students if they have seen/used them. (Some students may have used them to learn English!). Elicit any information they have about them. Ask students to read through the text for general understanding. If you want to give them a gist question, ask them which two discs they would like to have for themselves.
Ask the students to read the questions and fill in the boxes individually. Let them compare answers when they have finished.

> **ANSWERS**
>
> **1** C; **2** H; **3** D; **4** A; **5** E; **6** B; **7** F; **8** A; **9** K; **11** D; **12** J; **13** F; **14** F; **15** I

THE CURSE OF UNEMPLOYMENT

p.182 FIRST THOUGHTS

After discussing the first question get the students to brainstorm ways of helping young people to find/creating jobs and put their ideas on the board. Make sure students consider the impact of technology on jobs in their discussion.

p.182 WRITING

The opinion question – a final look

1 Divide the class into pairs and be firm about the five-minute time limit.

> **ANSWERS**
>
> Among the mistakes we could expect our students to correct within the five-minute time limit are:
> 1 ... try to **reduce** the number of employees **who are** replaced by computer* (*meaning is opposite to the intended one* – use **increase** OR **employees, and are replacing them with** ...)
> 2 industry **is trying/tries** (*concord*)
> 3 **person** should be **people**
> 4 We **use** computers, we don't **manipulate** them (*collocation*)
> 5 **company** (*should be plural*)
> 6 **look ... after** (*vocabulary* – **look for**)
> 7 we **do business**, not **make** it (*collocation*)
> 8 They don't give **university students the chance** ... (*word order*)
> 9 introduce themselves (*vocabulary* – you **join** a company)
> 10 on the other hand (*delete, unnecessary*)
> 11 take an orientation (*vocabulary* – try **have training**)
> 12 technology (*spelling*)
> 13 self-satisfied (*vocabulary* – the idea is **demotivated**)
> 14 ... don't go (*pronoun* **they** *is missing*)

2 Read through the grading system with the class. Ask students to grade the composition individually and then compare answers in groups.

> **ANSWER**
>
> Pass – reasonably correct, there are not too many basic mistakes.

3 Know yourself
While students are looking through old compositions and drawing up a 'favourite mistakes' list, you may want to go round the class and have a brief chat to each student about their particular approach to the composition paper.

4 Final advice
Ask students to read this, then have a short open-class discussion with students making comments, expressing agreement/disagreement with the advice and so on.

5 To be done under exam conditions.

p.183 LISTENING

Note: Allow at least 20 minutes to get through this section. Let students attempt this section more or less under exam conditions, i.e. a minute or so to look through the questions and then the tape played through twice with a short gap between each play through. Remind students that in the exam they will have to transfer their answers to the separate answer sheet when they have completed the exercises – time is allowed for this in the exam itself.
At the end of both the listening and answer-checking let students say what problems they had, why they got things wrong and so on. Discuss ways of avoiding or getting round these problems.

1 ANSWERS

1 B; 2 B; 3 B; 4 A; 5 C; 6 B; 7 C; 8 B

TAPESCRIPT

1
MAN: Hi ... I've been trying to send a fax but I haven't had much luck. In the end I gave up and I've, er, delivered it by hand.
WOMAN: A fax? Right, oh dear that's because the number's changed. Have you got a pen? I'll give you the new one.
MAN: Oh that's marvellous. Someone might have told me! Yeah, go ahead.

2
SHOP ASSISTANT: So what happens next? When you press the return? Well, my guess is there could well be something wrong with the disk you're using. Have you got another one handy? Yeah? Right, try putting that one in and see if it's any better ... That's right ... Sometimes they get corrupted. But you've got a back-up, you know a second copy ... Good. Listen, I've got a customer, give me, or I tell you what, I'll give you a ring when I've finished with them. OK ... yes, I promise I'll do it without fail ... Sorry to keep you waiting, now how can I help you?

3
WOMAN 3: So anyway, we got this thing for Murray. "Deviant Destroyer" it's called, and quite frankly I'm worried. It has these really graphic images of violence and, well, you know things on it. I think it's all pretty sick myself. I kind of wish we hadn't got it for him. His teacher said that these games would erm, make him comfortable with the technology, 'the nursery slopes of computing' she called them, but me I'm not so sure, after all he's only nine and he's, well, far too young for this kind of stuff.

4
DEMONSTRATOR: And the amazing thing about the Newman is that it actually recognises your handwriting. This means that things you, erm, write on the screen in your writing will actually be recognised and translated into ordinary letters. Let's have a look. There we are. Fantastic eh ! It can even read my writing. Now the Newman is even compatible with your PC so all you need to do is plug it in when you get home and you'll be able to transfer stuff as easily as anything. Let's just see how it works, shall we? Now, just for this week there is a special promotion and we're offering a ten percent discount off the list price and ...

5
MALE LINK MAN: Now here's Isabella Greenhaigh with news of next week's edition of *Pandora's Box*.
ISABELLA GREENHAIGH: And in the next *Pandora's Box*, the programme that brings you the future now, we'll be going to Tokyo where exciting new developments are taking place with so called smart buildings. There is a special feature too on genetic engineering and the strides which have been made to detect Worrell syndrome in the early stages of pregnancy. All this plus the usual round-up of science news. So tune in next Thursday at 8.15 for another fascinating edition.

6
MAN 1: Broken down? What do you mean it's broken down? Look, it's the fourth time this week I've been asked to come and sort it out.
MAN 2: But he doesn't know what to do with it.
MAN 1: Look, he knows just as much as I do. Honestly, he can't keep calling me every time there is a paper jam, you know.
MAN 2: But he says he doesn't know how it works.
MAN 1: Well, I don't believe it. It's more like he doesn't want to know. He just doesn't want to get his hands dirty, that's what it is. I'm not the engineer, I'm just another ...

7
TEACHER 1: Well it's a pretty amazing package, isn't it? I mean, I haven't come across one which would allow you to interact the way it does. You can even check your pronunciation against a native speaker.
I wonder where this is going to leave us. If things keep developing at this rate then we won't be needed in ten years' time. Nobody will want language teachers any more.
TEACHER 2: Don't worry about it, it might never happen.
TEACHER 1: You can say that, but I'm not so sure ...

8
STUDENT 1: So I've got another one.
STUDENT 2: Oh yeah ...
STUDENT 1: What do you, erm, say to someone with a degree, in erm philosophy?
STUDENT 2: A burger and fries, please ...
STUDENT 1: What, you've heard it ...
STUDENT 2: You told it to me before, not an hour ago ... Good grief, don't you remember? You and your jokes!

The joke means that the graduate is working in a MacDonalds fast food restaurant (not considered to be a good job) and the explanation is either: 1) there is so much unemployment that even graduates of a prestigious university cannot get good jobs OR 2) a degree in Ancient

History is so useless that nobody wants to employ a graduate in this subject.

p.184 USE OF ENGLISH

Here are three possible ways of treating the material from here to the end of the unit:
a) as pure exam practice to be done under exam conditions
b) as classwork where students work on an exercise, confer, are given the answers and then go over problems
c) as a mixture of classwork and homework.

1 ANSWERS

1 would; 2 had; 3 every; 4 behind; 5 been; 6 so; 7 almost/even; 8 front; 9 This/Here; 10 looked/seemed; 11 told; 12 From; 13 As; 14 came; 15 around

2 ANSWERS

1 ages since I've been/went; 2 having/getting my car serviced; 3 n't low enough for; 4 as much as; 5 (that) Ann (should) apply; 6 last time I saw him; 7 despite the fact that he; 8 I would have known; 9 not in favour of; 10 do/break it on purpose,; 11 fault according to; 12 rather we went/prefer it if we went; 13 needs to be told by; 14 such a boring; 15 can't get/hasn't got used to; 16 was never allowed (to go); 17 necessary to finish it; 18 is likely to have; 19 to take part in; 20 were you I wouldn't; 21 first time I've tasted/tried; 22 wish I hadn't broken; 23 me forget to water; 24 told the truth in my; 25 you mind not smoking; 26 large number of; 27 been so embarrassed; 28 look it/the word up in; 29 was not known by; 30 on behalf of; 31 in case it rains; 32 able to find a place/anywhere; 33 was Paul who gave us; 34 had been walking for; 35 in that case; 36 turned it/the job down as/because; 37 needn't have taken; 38 waste of time; 39 taking care of; 40 by means of; 41 is believed to have had; 42 only does he play the

Practice Exams

Think First Certificate Practice Exams has two aims:
• to provide realistic practice of the First Certificate in English examination. All of the question types are the same as those used in the actual exam.
• to provide progress tests which are based on the themes and structures covered in the coursebook. Practice Exam 1 can be used after Unit 5, Practice Exam 2 after Unit 10 and Practice Exam 3 after Unit 15. Practice Exam 4 is global and can be used as a mock exam.

Answer sheets are included at the back of *Think First Certificate Practice Exams* which may be photocopied and used with the practice exams.

PRACTICE EXAM 1

PAPER 1 READING

PART 1

1 B; 2 E; 3 I; 4 F; 5 H; 6 A; 7 D
The extra heading is C.

PART 2

8 D (*... to my surprise I saw the boat, and the men still trying to push it off.*)
9 C (*The big wave carried the boat off. I had hold of an oarlock and I went with it.*)
10 B (*... the boat was upside down – and I was under it ... whatever happened I must not breathe, for I was under water.*)
11 C (*She was a beautiful sight then.*)
12 A (*The ship was turning gradually on her nose – just like a duck that goes for a dive ... I was 150 feet away when the Titanic, on her nose, with her after-quarter sticking straight up in the air, began to settle – slowly.*)
13 B (*When at last the waves washed over her rudder there wasn't the least bit of suction I could feel. In other words he felt nothing.*)
14 D (*I was all done when a hand reached out from the boat and pulled me aboard.*)
15 C (*He was all done i.e. physically exhausted. I sat there not caring what happened. i.e. emotionally exhausted with no fight left in him.*)

PART 3

16 D; 17 F; 18 A; 19 G; 20 C; 21 E

PART 4

22 F; 23 D; 24 B; 25 C; 26 H; 27 A; 28 E;
29 F; 30/31 B, D in any order; 32/33 A,G in any order; 34/35 H,E in any order

PAPER 3 USE OF ENGLISH

PART 1

1 C forward; 2 A slang; 3 C Despite;
4 C persuade; 5 C deadly; 6 D aware; 7 D number;
8 B took; 9 D Hardly; 10 C making; 11 C possible;
12 D sleepy; 13 C out; 14 B means; 15 A filled

PART 2

16 granted; 17 look; 18 with; 19 its;
20 where; 21 well; 22 from; 23 referred;
24 quite/then; 25 one; 26 same; 27 after; 28 whose;
29 much; 30 between

PART 3

31 found it difficult to understand
32 put up with
33 in case it rains
34 taking care of
35 like pizza as much as
36 you familiar with
37 about getting rid of
38 the decision to give up
39 a great deal of
40 hardly any difference

PART 4

41 an; 42 to; 43 at; 44 and;
45 country; 46 be; 47 to; 48 ✓; 49 ourselves; 50 it;
51 the; 52 of; 53 ✓; 54 the; 55 of

PART 5

56 difference; 57 belief;
58 commitment; 59 destruction; 60 illegal;
61 performance; 62 childhood; 63 unhealthy;
64 death; 65 gracefully/graciously

PAPER 4 LISTENING

PART 1

1 C; 2 C; 3 A; 4 C; 5 A; 6 A; 7 B; 8 B

PART 2

9 Somerville; 10 cash; 11 19 Leominster Rd;
12 793 8170; 13 ring middle bell;
14 Domingo Special; 15 large;
16 Vegetarian Paradise; 17 cheese and pineapple;
18 (loaf) of garlic bread

PART 3

19 C; 20 E; 21 A; 22 F; 23 D

PART 4

24 D; 25 M; 26 F; 27 F; 28 D; 29 M; 30 D

TAPESCRIPT

Hello, I'm going to give you the instructions for this exam. I'll introduce each part of the exam and give you time to look at the questions. At the start of each piece you'll hear this sound: (tone). You'll hear each piece twice. Remember, while you're listening, write your answers on the question paper.
The tape will now be stopped. Please ask any questions now, because you must not speak during the exam. Look at Part 1.

PART 1

You'll hear people talking in eight different situations. For questions 1–8, choose the best answer, A, B or C.

1 *Listen to this woman calling a theatre. Why has she phoned?*
   A She wants to change some tickets.
   B She wants to make a complaint.
   C She wants to recover some lost property.

MAN: And whereabouts were you sitting?
WOMAN: In the erm ... upstairs.
MAN: In the circle.
WOMAN: Mm that's right. I've got the ticket here ... Row E fifteen.
MAN: Right, and it was the afternoon performance.
WOMAN: Yes ...
MAN: And you say it is a pale green mackintosh, from erm Burberry.
WOMAN: Yes ... I'm pretty sure I put it under the seat.
MAN: If you'd like to hold on I'll pop down to the box office and see if anything has been handed in.

2 *A friend is phoning to invite you to a birthday party. Where is the party going to be held?*
   A at her house
   B on the beach
   C in a hall

So it's for our eighteenth birthdays. Laura's is just a few days after mine so we thought that we'd do something together. Well, we wanted to have a barbecue down on the beach but my parents, they were dead against it. Anyway, in the end we decided that there wasn't space at either of our homes so that's why we are going to hire the memorial hall, you know up by the common, our parents have given us the money.

3 *Listen to this designer telephoning her colleague. Why is she angry?*
   A She has had a wasted journey.
   B She has got to do the drawings again.
   C She was late for her appointment.

Yeah, yeah, just like last time. I've travelled halfway across London to see this man and his secretary says he's had to go to an urgent meeting. You know, I even got here half an hour early. I worked all weekend to finish the drawings and he can't spare ten minutes to have a look at them. They must think I've got nothing better to do with my time than fight my way through traffic ... Yeah, tomorrow, that's right ...

4 *A TV presenter is introducing a guest on her chat show. What is special about the guest?*
   A She has written a story.
   B She was the pilot of a plane which crashed.
   C A television programme has been made about her adventure.

So our next guest is Angelica Price – the fifteen-year-old schoolgirl at the centre of a rescue drama in the Brazilian jungle. As you may remember, Angelica was the only survivor when the light aircraft she was a passenger in mysteriously crashed into the jungle. Her story has been made into a TV mini series. So Angelica, I'm sure viewers share my curiosity in wanting to know just what was it that kept an ordinary schoolgirl going all those days after your plane crashed. Was there ever a time when you just gave up hope?

5 *You are standing in a queue at the ticket office at the railway station when a man goes up to a woman in the queue. Why does he speak to her?*
   A He wants a favour.
   B She has dropped something.
   C He accuses her of jumping the queue.

MAN: Excuse me. Would you mind if I went first?
WOMAN: I suppose not but you should ask the other people who are waiting too.
MAN: But I am in a real hurry and my train goes in three minutes.

WOMAN: Oh, alright then, you'd better go ahead.
SECOND WOMAN: Really, what's he up to ... jumping the queue?
WOMAN: I'm sorry, he did ask.

6 *You are staying at a friend's house when she asks you a favour. What does she ask you to do?*
   A collect the children
   B answer the phone
   C take a message

Oh I hate to ask you this, but I was wondering if you could pick Rebecca and Simon up from school. You see I am waiting for an important call and I just can't risk leaving the phone unattended. I've been trying to speak to this woman in New York for days now, and you know what it's like, the moment I leave the house she's bound to ring. I'd be eternally grateful if you could fetch them.

7 *You hear someone talking about a film they have been to see. What kind of film was it?*
   A police
   B horror
   C historical

Well, it was about this erm couple. They go off to spend a weekend in an old castle and their car breaks down and so the man goes off to get some petrol. Well, basically he never comes back, he just vanishes into thin air. The rest of the film is all about what the girlfriend does, I must say it scared me to death. The last few seconds of the film where we find out what has happened to him are really chilling. I couldn't sleep for two nights. There were no special effects, just all in the mind you know.

8 *You are in a language school when you overhear the school principal talking to a large group of students and staff. What is the principal doing?*
   A announcing the results of examinations
   B saying goodbye to a teacher
   C introducing a new member of staff

We have enjoyed having her on the staff and she will be much missed in the school. Next term won't be the same without her. She has helped her students achieve wonderful examination results and perfected her Spanish too. On behalf of everyone I'd like to wish you the very best in your new career as a teacher of Spanish back home. So all that remains for me to do is to present Gemma with a small token of our appreciation and something which will remind her of her stay with us.

That's the end of Part 1.

PART 2

You'll hear someone ordering a pizza by phone. For questions 9–18, complete the order form by writing a word or short phrase in each of the boxes.

You now have forty-five seconds in which to look at Part 2.

WAITER: Domingo's pizzas. Can I help you?
FRANK: Yeah. I'd like to order a couple of pizzas please.
WAITER: Is that to collect or to be delivered, sir?
FRANK: How much is delivery? I'm local.
WAITER: It's a flat charge of one pound fifty.
FRANK: Yeah ... all right ... saves a lot of hassle.
WAITER: How are you going to pay for everything?
FRANK: Cash.
WAITER: Can I have your name, please, sir?
FRANK: It's Frank Somerville. That's capital S-o one m - e-r-v-i- double l -e.
WAITER: Address?
FRANK: 19 Leominster Road NW7.
WAITER: How do you spell that?
FRANK: It's um ... l for Leonard ... e-o-m-i-n-s-t-e-r. Er ... get the bloke to press the middle bell.
WAITER: And could I have your phone number, please?
FRANK: Yeah, 793 8170.
WAITER: Right. So that's 19 Leominster Road NW7. Middle bell. Right can I take your order?
FRANK: Yeah, I'd like one medium Domingo special. How many is that for?
WAITER: Depends how hungry you are. A medium's generally all right for two to three people.
FRANK: Oh then I'd better have a large one then and er ... the mushroom surprise, is that vegetarian?
WAITER: No it's got pepperoni on it.
FRANK: That's not green pepper then?
WAITER: No, it's a kind of sausage. We do a vegetarian pizza though, that's the vegetarian paradise.
FRANK: Yeah ... um. I'll have one of them then. Make it a small one. Could I have ... what do you want ... alright extra cheese and pineapple on it.
WAITER: What about salads, garlic bread?
FRANK: No salad ... A loaf of garlic bread though.
WAITER: So that's a large special, a small vegetarian with extra cheese and pineapple and garlic bread. Be about forty minutes.
FRANK: Fine, thanks. Bye.

You will now hear Part 2 again.

PART 3

You'll hear five people talking about sport and sporting events. For questions 19–23, choose from the list A–F the sentence which summarises what each has to say. Use the letters only once. There is an extra letter which you do not need to use.

You now have thirty seconds in which to look at Part 3.

SPEAKER 1: I used to absolutely detest it at school. We had this awful teacher who had been in the army, he was a real sadist. He was completely obsessed by sport and erm trying to build up the character of the boys. I remember we had to go on long runs, cross-country runs in the winter. It didn't matter what the weather was like, I remember once there was this one lad who cut his leg quite badly – needed stitches – from broken ice – that'll give you some idea of what it was like. The whole thing put me off rather, I thought the idea of sport was to enjoy yourselves but for old Mr Bell it seemed to be used like some kind of instrument of torture. I used to dread Wednesday and Friday afternoons.

SPEAKER 2: My erm favourite is probably tennis although I'm not all that good at it. I like the social side too. When I first came down here, well I didn't know anyone so I thought, right I'll join a club, and there was a good tennis club near where I now live. I thought that'll be a good way of meeting people. There are matches and club tournaments and I'm glad to say that I'm nowhere near the worst. Something that does annoy me though is that people assume 'cos you're a woman that you're going to be available to make teas and things like that. Anyway, I should say that a good part of my circle of friends is from the club and also from playing bridge. The people at the tennis club are early twenties you know my age whereas the ones at the bridge club, some of them are really ancient.

SPEAKER 3: By and large I find the whole thing incredibly boring ... I mean, you get all these overweight men, smoking about forty cigarettes a day, and there they are on a Saturday afternoon screaming their heads off at these athletic young players. It's all a bit pathetic really. The other thing that I don't like is that you could never take your family to a match the way they do in Italy or France. The behaviour of the fans at the average football match is absolutely disgusting. The players too, they do some really ugly and cynical fouls. They're a terrible example to young people and that's strange because there is a lot of artistry in football.

SPEAKER 4: It's got to be Maradona, hasn't it? I mean that man was an absolute genius with the ball. It's incredible really, I know he had a really unhappy time in Spain and later on he was always getting into trouble with his erm private life but on the field there has never been anyone like him. If you think what he did when he went to Naples he almost single-handedly won them the championship. The problem of course is that when he helped to knock Italy out of the World Cup, when was it in ... '92? Anyway all the fans they turned on him. Even so, the man was a genius, he has got to be the best player that's ever lived

SPEAKER 5: Yeah, well athletics, I don't know what would have happened to me if it hadn't been for boxing and that. I started when I was at an age when lots of the kids who lived around where I come from were getting in trouble with the police and school and things. I'm not thick but school was terrible. Most of the people I was at school with are either on the dole or inside. I would've gone the same way except that I started to go to a youth club, I learned to box. It helped me to get rid of a lot of my aggression and another thing it helped me to you know get a bit of respect. And now I've won a couple of championships and I am on the telly regularly and it has really changed my life. Without it I don't know where I would be now.

You will now hear Part 3 again.

PART 4

You'll hear Frank Grogan and his wife Mandy discussing their holiday plans with their son, David. Answer questions 24–30 by writing F for Frank, M for Mandy and D for David in the boxes provided.

You now have thirty seconds in which to look through Part 4.

MANDY: So Dad and I thought we'd try something a bit different this year.
DAVID: Yeah? Like what? Aren't we going to France again?
MANDY: Yes, but we thought that instead of renting a house we'd go to a camp site.
DAVID: Camping. Oh no!
FRANK: Well, it's not real camping, it's in a big caravan.
DAVID: But why can't we have a house?
MANDY: It's just like a house, it has its own bathroom and running water and things. Anyway, we thought it would be better for you, darling. You get so lonely on your own and you'll be able to make lots of friends.
FRANK: There are bound to be people of your own age there. You could have a great time.
DAVID: I suppose so ... It could be nice ... Could I bring a friend with me this year?
FRANK: Yes, provided it's not Peter Grant.
DAVID: But dad! He's my best friend.
FRANK: Sorry no. Not after the way he behaved last time.
DAVID: Can I ask John instead?
FRANK: Yes, I should think so.
MANDY: I'll have a word with his mother on Monday. Right let's fill this form in shall we?
FRANK: Do we have to? I mean it's months away ...
MANDY: These things get booked up so we'd better do it now. We could end up with nothing.
FRANK: Yes, you're right. Let's look at the brochure again.
FRANK: Right which site shall we go to?
MANDY: I don't mind provided we don't have too long a drive at the other end.
DAVID: We could always fly down to the South and maybe rent a car for a few days.
FRANK: Perhaps we'll do that one year, but it would just be too expensive.
MANDY: What about the one in Brittanny? We could get a night crossing and make it in a day?
DAVID: That sounds great, I've never slept in a cabin before.
FRANK: Actually it's not all that comfortable. Is there a short route that we can take?

MANDY: I think so ... Let's have a look in the brochure, I expect there's a possibility.

You will now hear Part 4 again.

PRACTICE EXAM 2

PAPER 1 READING

PART 1

1 G; **2** C; **3** B; **4** F; **5** E; **6** A; **7** I
The extra heading is H.

PART 2

8 B (*... the animal quietly listens for interesting sounds over a wide range.*)
9 B (*Even though a cat's ears follow its gaze it can quickly rotate one ear to the source of another sound. ... if there is a sudden noise away to the side of the animal, in which case an ear may be permitted a brief rotation in that direction without a shift of gaze.*)
10 C (*In some species of wild cats this response has been made highly conspicuous by the evolution of long ear-tufts*)
11 D (*The torn and tattered ears of battling tom-cats are a vivid testimony to the need to hide this delicate part of the anatomy as much as possible when the claws are out.*)
Choice C is wrong because *themselves* refers to the cats not the ears.
12 A (No reason is given.)
13 A (*The backs of the ears become visible from the front.*)
14 B (*the rotated ears are in a 'ready-to-be-flattened' posture should the aggressive cat's opponent dare to retaliate.*)
15 D (*The aggressive ear posture has led to some attractive ear markings in a number of wild cat species,* in other words tigers aren't unique.
All the other choices are false for the following reasons – A *Domestic cats lack these markings;* B *a number of wild cat species* have these markings so they are not rare, C tigers have *a white spot ringed with black*)

PART 3

16 A; **17** F; **18** H; **19** B; **20** G; **21** E

PART 4

22 A; **23/24** A, G in any order; **25** B; **26** E;
27 G; **28** F; **29/30** D, E in any order;
31/32 A, E in any order; **33/34/35** C, D, F in any order

PAPER 3 USE OF ENGLISH

PART 1

1 B extremely; **2** C killed; **3** D some;
4 C raised; **5** B remote; **6** A childhood; **7** B suburb;
8 C Quite; **9** A like; **10** C discovered; **11** C lively;
12 B plump; **13** C share; **14** A hard; **15** A take after

PART 2

16 piece; **17** able; **18** it's their; **19** took; **20** the;
21 accused; **22** him; **23** were; **24** away; **25** even;
26 However; **27** after; **28** what; **29** this; **30** had

PART 3

31 looks down on
32 in charge of
33 to be known
34 was opened by means of
35 under the impression (that)
36 let me pay
37 made your mind up
38 first time she had (ever)
39 cut out to be
40 advised to take

PART 4

41 ✔; **42** the; **43** However; **44** me;
45 ✔; **46** had; **47** do; **48** got; **49** ✔; **50** of; **51** it;
52 more; **53** the; **54** ✔; **55** too

PART 5

56 mysterious; **57** development;
58 anger; **59** poverty; **60** understandable;
61 powerless; **62** dangerous; **63** freedom;
64 willingness; **65** inequality

PAPER 4 LISTENING

PART 1

1 B; 2 A; 3 C; 4 C; 5 A; 6 A; 7 B; 8 B

PART 2

9 route A of the (scheduled) motorway
10 Park Street bus station
11 are not allowed
12 exactly 6:50 (6:50 on the dot)
13 waterproof covering
14 umbrellas
15 listen to speeches
16 a petition (with 60,000 signatures)
17 4:30
18 of evening traffic

PART 3

19 D; 20 A; 21 C; 22 B; 23 F

PART 4

24 J; 25 P; 26 C; 27 C; 28 P; 29 J; 30 J

TAPESCRIPT

Hello, I'm going to give you the instructions for this exam. I'll introduce each part of the exam and give you time to look at the questions. At the start of each piece you'll hear this sound: (tone). You'll hear each piece twice. Remember, while you're listening, write your answers on the question paper.
The tape will now be stopped. Please ask any questions now, because you must not speak during the exam. Look at Part 1.

PART 1

You'll hear people talking in eight different situations. For questions 1–8, choose the best answer, A, B or C.

1 You are at a friend's house when a neighbour comes to the door. Why does the neighbour call?
   A She is angry about her neighbour's dog.
   B She wants to tell her about the dog.
   C She wants to complain about some damage the dog has caused.

LISA: Hi Jenny. Sorry to trouble you, but it's about Max.
JENNY: What's he been up to this time? He hasn't damaged anything again I hope?
LISA: No, nothing like that, he's just being friendly.
JENNY: Is he getting through the hole again?
LISA: Jumping over the fence, I'm afraid.
JENNY: I'm awfully sorry, I'll get Tim to look at it when he gets back.
LISA: Don't worry, no problem. I just wanted you to know.

2 *You are in a hotel room and you can hear a TV programme from the room next door. What is the person next door watching?*
   A a quiz show
   B a soap opera
   C a documentary

PRESENTER: Welcome back to the final part of 'Dreamboat'. So now it's all, it's all up to Janine, who are you going to pick from behind the golden screen?
JANINE: Well, number one sounds gorgeous and hunky I bet he's tall. Trouble is I expect he thinks a lot of himself. But number two sounds fun with a good sense of humour. I love the voice of three, he sounds really gentle and considerate but I think I'll go for number two, a girl has got to have fun.
PRESENTER: Right. So it's number two. But first let's see just what you'll be missing. Let's lift the screen on number one ...

3 *You are waiting in a shop when someone approaches the person standing next to you. What is the relationship between the two women?*
   A business colleagues
   B close friends
   C old acquaintances

JULIA: I don't suppose you remember me, do you?
JUDITH: Wait a minute. It's er ... Julia Mason.
JULIA: As was, I'm married now. Well, I recognised you immediately.
JUDITH: You look exactly the same. A bit older ...
JULIA: And a bit more weight ...
JUDITH: Didn't like to say, ha, ha, ha ...

4 *You are listening to a radio programme which talks about the latest fashion craze with young people. What is it?*
   A dying hair
   B body piercing
   C decorating the body

PRESENTER: So I know lots of mums and dads are really afraid of all the erm dangers of body piercing, nose and eyebrow rings and things but I don't think they can object to this too much. They're these really great temporary tattoos, nothing you'll be landed with for life and they can last up to a week if you take care of them. You can put them on your arm or chest or somewhere really private! They won't come off with soap but when you're tired of them you can get rid of them just like this with a bit of baby oil.

5 You are at an auction of furniture. What happens to lot 54, the wardrobe?
   A It isn't sold.
   B Nobody is interested in it at all.
   C It gets a very good price.

AUCTIONEER: So, any advance on three hundred pounds, three hundred and twenty, from the back, three hundred and fifty ... Come on this is a wonderful example of marquetry work ... three fifty ... any advance on three hundred and fifty ... no well, I'm afraid we have instructions, the owner won't let it go for that. Pity let's move on.
Right now lot 55, an enamel Edwardian bath with claw feet and the original taps ... shall we start at one hundred pounds?

6 You are waiting to use a public telephone when you hear a man having a conversation. Who is he calling?
   A a decorator
   B a tailor
   C a garage

MAN: But they've had the stuff all week ... Been ill? Oh, I'm sorry to hear that, but, look can you get someone else to finish it off? But the wedding is in four days time and I want the paint to be dry ... Huh, huh ... OK ... Huh, huh ... Alright, so you'll work tomorrow and the day after and hang the paper on Friday ... Right, I'm really banking on you now. This is my daughter's wedding we're talking about ...

7 You are in a shopping mall with a group of friends when a man approaches you with a petition. Why does he want your signatures?
   A He wants to ban smoking in the mall.
   B He wants things to stay as they are.
   C He wants the council to take action.

MAN: Do you think I could have a couple seconds of your time, you see I'm collecting signatures against this new regulation the council wants to bring in ... you know to ban smoking anywhere in the mall. Now I, or rather my organisation thinks it should be up to individuals whether they smoke or not and it is the decision of individual cafés and restaurants to decide what they want to happen. We don't know why they are trying to introduce this. Things seem to be alright as they are.

8 Listen to this woman talking to a friend. Why can't she go to the party?
   A She has to look after a relative.
   B She has a previous engagement.
   C There's someone she doesn't want to see at the party.

MARY: Oh, hi, Candy ... I tried ringing you earlier, but you were out, I'm glad I've bumped into you. Thanks for the invite.
CANDY: But you can't come ...
MARY: Sorry, no. It clashes with an end of term dinner I have to go to. My students would be really disappointed if I didn't turn up.
CANDY: Oh well. Come along later if you're not too late back.
MARY: I will. I'd love to see everyone.

PART 2

You'll hear a recorded message about a demonstration which has been organised against the building of a new motorway. For questions 9–18 complete the notes which summarise what the speaker says. You will need to write a word or short phrase in each box.

You now have forty-five seconds in which to look at Part 2.

This is a recorded message for everybody wishing to take part in the demonstration against route A of the scheduled motorway. Arrive at the coaches at Park Street bus station; remember that's Park Street not Jubilee Crescent, no later than 6.30 and report to a steward and pay your eight pounds thirty for the coach. Children under fourteen will not be allowed on the coach. I'm sorry about that but no kids under fourteen. Coaches leave at 6.50 on the dot; we can't hang about for any late arrivals. Bring sandwiches, hot soup and some kind of waterproof covering as the weather forecast for tomorrow predicts rain. Don't bring umbrellas as the police may consider them as offensive weapons. Repeat, no umbrellas. We should arrive in London at Hyde Park at around 9.30. There will be speeches from Alison Green of Spearhead and Ken Stanley, the Shadow Environment Minister. We shall then proceed to the Prime Minister's house in Downing Street to hand in our petition. That's the petition with 60,000 signatures we've collected; the television cameras should be there. Anyway remember to rejoin the coaches no later than 4.30. Evening traffic will mean we won't be back before nine o'clock.

You will now hear Part 2 again.

PART 3

You'll hear five people talking about how they think the towns or cities where they live could be improved. For questions 19–23, choose from the list A–F the key suggestion which each one makes. Use the letters only once. There is an extra letter which you do not need to use.

You now have thirty seconds in which to look at Part 3.

SPEAKER 1: I suppose the thing that gets me is how dirty the whole place has become. I think it is because of all the fast food places which have opened up recently, it means that by Saturday afternoon the whole of the High Street is full of wrappers and boxes and stuff like that. Nowadays there is so much wrapping on everything, isn't there? I think that one

121

of the things the council could do is make the fast food restaurants responsible for the rubbish that piles up outside their premises, fining people who drop stuff on the street doesn't seem to work. Catching them in the first place is a big enough problem, isn't it?

SPEAKER 2: One of the things that has always struck me about going to the continent is the life you find out on the streets, erm particularly in squares. I have many memories of evenings over a cup of coffee or an ice-cream at one of those cafés you seem to find everywhere in the rest of Europe. I think that if we could borrow that kind of culture ... what I would like to see are more places, cafés and restaurants, where you can sit out and watch people go by and generally feel relaxed. I know that the weather isn't always with us but at least in the summer months it is something that we could consider.

SPEAKER 3: I think the most important thing would be to do something about motor vehicles and all the difficulties which are associated with them. I know some people want to ban them from the centre altogether but I think that is just madness, that is completely unrealistic, we live in the age of the motor car. What we want is for people to come in and do their shopping. I think what is needed is more car parks within walking distance of the centre so that half the people you see driving round and round looking for somewhere to put their car would be able to park without too much fuss.

SPEAKER 4: It's just so dead here at night. There's virtually nothing to do, there are only two clubs, one of those is quite posh you know for people who have got lots of money and the other one, well, it's just trouble. I've never felt safe going there. There just isn't enough choice for young people. Yeah, so the thing that would make the biggest difference for me would be to have some kind of community centre where we could get together where the idea wasn't just to get money off people but to get them together to have some fun and things.

SPEAKER 5: Well, I know that we depend a lot on foreign guests but I really do think that it is time to cut down on the number of people who come here each year. I mean they just clog the streets and force you off the pavements, there is never any room on the buses in the summer and I just don't know whether it does anyone any good. They can't enjoy it all that much because there just aren't the facilities, you know the services. In the pubs you can never get a seat because of all the students you know at language schools who treat the place as though it was some kind of youth club ... Perhaps it should be like lots of museums nowadays, you know you buy a timed ticket which entitles you to stay for an hour or two and then you have to make your way.

You will now hear Part 3 again.

PART 4

You'll hear three people, Cathy, John and Paul talking about growing up and their early childhood experiences.
Answer questions 24–30 by writing C for Cathy, J for John and P for Paul in the boxes provided.

You now have thirty seconds in which to look through Part 4.

CATHY: I really loved that article, didn't you? Um, the one by Maeve Binchy when she talks about her early life and how, er, what happened when her dad tried to tell her about the facts of life.

PAUL: Yeah ... it was a real laugh. Sounds as though she had a really good childhood though and no real upsets. What about you, John: Did you have any early memories like that at all?

JOHN: Of course ... They're pretty mixed in a sense. I suppose my earliest memory is when I was, ooh, I must have been about three I suppose. I had this accident you see.

PAUL: Really! What happened, John?

JOHN: I fell down the stairs. From top to bottom. I'd been given this little, tiny wheelbarrow as a birthday present I think and anyway I decided to put all my stuffed animals and teddy and things into it and take them to play in the garden. Anyway, you can guess what happened, I tripped and fell.

CATHY: Gosh. Were you hurt?

JOHN: No not really. A bit shaken up, but you know how resilient kids are to that type of thing.

PAUL: Yeah ... they can survive things like that really easily, can't they? I'm not so sure myself though about emotional upsets people can have.

CATHY: Like finding out there isn't a Santa Claus you mean.

PAUL: No come on, Cathy. I'm being serious. When I was little my parents were pretty young and they were always hard up and I always remember the rows I heard when I was in bed and I was supposed to be asleep. They'd be quarrelling for hours about this and that.

JOHN: Oh God! What sort of thing did you hear?

PAUL: I couldn't actually hear anything ... any words like but I knew they were arguing. They'd really raise their voices and then my dad would lose his temper and it would end up with lots of crying.

CATHY: So what sort of effect do you think it's had on you, then, all this?

PAUL: Well, it has made me hate rows. I just can't stand getting involved in anything like that ... I'll do anything to avoid getting into an argument. I suppose it has made me pessimistic about relationships as well ... you know, whether two people can actually live together for a long period.

CATHY: It must have been awful for you ... I suppose I had a lovely childhood. Most of all I remember the summer holidays. They were great. You know my dad's Irish. Well, we'd all go over to my grandparents' house in Ireland, right in the south in the Republic where granddad had a farm. Well, anyway we kids had a fantastic time. There would be all of my cousins, about seven of us in all. We had all kinds of games. I learnt how to ride a bike and because I was the oldest I was always the leader and said what was what. I was awful then ... Do you know, I once tied up William and made him eat a worm sandwich!

JOHN: Yuk.

PAUL: I can just see you doing that. I wonder if he's still got any hang-ups. This explains a lot. Why you're super confident these days, Cathy ... it was because you had a happy childhood.

CATHY: Yes, but it wasn't all like that ... it all ended when I was eleven and my grandparents died quite suddenly within a year of each other and the farm was sold off and that was the end of it. What about you, John ... was your childhood happy ... accidents aside and things?

JOHN: Oh yes, it was great but being an only child my parents really mollycoddled me you know. I was treated like a prince until I was twelve but then my brother was born. I was really surprised and really hated him at first ... my parents, poor things just didn't know what to do.

PAUL: My elder brother says he was like that when I came along.

JOHN: Anyway ... I eventually got over that and that was fine. The worst thing that happened to me though was when I went to school. You see my dad got a job in the Middle East for a couple of years and there was no choice but to send me off to boarding school. The first term was absolute hell ... Not only was I homesick and missing my family and everything, but a couple of the bigger boys picked on me and made my life a misery.

CATHY: How awful, John. So what happened?

JOHN: Well, my teacher found out what was going on and got hold of the two boys and really gave them a telling off. He reduced them to tears and asked them what it felt like to be bullied. In the end they were really sorry and apologised to me for what they had done. I even made friends with one of them and for the rest of my time at school we did everything together.

PAUL: So it all ended happily? Thank goodness for that! And John, did you forgive your parents for sending you off?

JOHN: Yes, I suppose so.

You will now hear Part 4 again.

PRACTICE EXAM 3

PAPER 1 READING

PART 1

1 C; **2** I; **3** G; **4** A; **5** F; **6** E; **7** B
The extra heading is D.

PART 2

8 D (*he decided to take a year off.*)
9 A (*Dominic wandered into 'Archer and Son' ... and asked if there were any positions available.*)
10 D (*Mr Pinkerton, the manager, prided himself on his ability to assess character*)
11 A (*Mr Pinkerton ... felt that the money had been taken by a lurking customer*)
12 C (*he worked out a rota so that only one person ... would be responsible for opening the till and ringing up any sales*)
13 B (*At times he felt the tension so hard to cope with that he was tempted to admit to the crime himself.*)
14 C (*the relationship between the team of assistants had been poisoned for good*)
15 C (*when ... the thief was unmasked it took everyone by surprise.*)

PART 3

16 D; **17** E; **18** B; **19** C; **20** A; **21** G

PART 4

22 C; **23** D; **24** A; **25** B; **26** D; **27** A; **28** D;
29/30 B, D in any order; **31/32** B, C in any order;
33/34/35 B, C, D in any order

Paper 3 Use of English

PART 1

1 B such; **2** B let; **3** A persuaded;
4 D rival; **5** A rather; **6** C chance; **7** D seeking;
8 C came across; **9** D ingredients; **10** A apart;
11 C delightful; **12** D virtual; **13** C trustworthy;
14 D took; **15** A until

PART 2

16 called; **17** kept; **18** its; **19** Although;
20 between; **21** for; **22** avoided; **23** all; **24** been;
25 bought; **26** have; **27** generous; **28** some;
29 be; **30** doing

Part 3

31 taking part in
32 spent three months getting
33 come up with
34 was found guilty
35 let me forget
36 off on account of
37 so/as long as you look
38 it so difficult to
39 sooner had he seen
40 should be banned in my

Part 4

41 a; 42 become; 43 ✔; 44 she;
45 ✔; 46 ✔; 47 in; 48 time; 49 ✔; 50 of; 51 to;
52 yourself; 53 otherwise; 54 for; 55 a

Part 5

56 actress; 57 tragic; 58 imaginary; 59 loneliness;
60 historical; 61 punishments; 62 judgement;
63 variety; 64 ability; 65 disagreements

PAPER 4 LISTENING

Part 1

1 B; 2 C; 3 A; 4 B; 5 A; 6 B; 7 A; 8 C

Part 2

9 where you hear it/which region you are in;
10 unlucky;
11 28th April;
12 before April 16th;
13 should have already left/migrated;
14 how long they have to live;
15 how long they will have to wait for a husband;
16 a hair (the colour of the hair of his wife to be);
17 up to no good;
18 busy giving human beings important messages

Part 3

19 F; 20 E; 21 B; 22 C; 23 A

Part 4

24 C; 25 A; 26 B; 27 A; 28 B; 29 C; 30 A

TAPESCRIPT

Hello, I'm going to give you the instructions for this exam. I'll introduce each part of the exam and give you time to look at the questions. At the start of each piece you'll hear this sound: (tone). You'll hear each piece twice. Remember, while you're listening, write your answers on the question paper.
The tape will now be stopped. Please ask any questions now, because you must not speak during the exam. Look at Part 1.

Part 1

You'll hear people talking in eight different situations. For questions 1–8, choose the best answer, A, B or C

1 *Listen to this woman talking to two teenage boys. How does she feel towards them at the end of the passage.*
   A suspicious
   B friendly
   C nervous

WOMAN: Hey, what are you two up to?
BOY 1: Nothing, we were just having a look, honest.
BOY 2: It's an E type isn't it? How old? 1970?
WOMAN: 65, actually.
BOY 1: It's lovely inside … Leather seats?
WOMAN: Well, I've got a few minutes, would you like to have a quick ride?

2 *Listen to this presenter talking about a book. Who is Jane Ray?*
   A a novelist
   B a publisher
   C an illustrator

So, my very favourite is this erm *Noah's Ark* with pictures by Jane Ray. It really is absolutely gorgeous. It is a treat for children and adults alike. Her use of colour and gold and the way the animals are done is absolutely fabulous. Her publishers certainly haven't stinted on anything. A classic, something to be passed down the generations.

3 *Listen to this man talking about a night in a hotel with a difference. How did he find his stay there?*
   A uneventful
   B comfortable
   C restful

So anyway, we went to this Hall which is supposed to be haunted. The idea is that you don't sleep at all you just wander round and drink in the spooky atmosphere. We wandered round trying our best to scare each other but there was nothing remotely supernatural about it at all. I don't know where the ghosts were, probably on their holidays!

4 *Listen to this man. What is he talking about?*
  A *a kind of handicraft*
  B *a dance*
  C *a traditional game*

Well, what we do is we erm wear white and have bells around our legs and handkerchiefs which we wave. Then of course there's the sequence we do with sticks, we clash the sticks together. I think in the old days it must have been done with swords. It is done in formation and you have to keep going sometimes for ten minutes or so. There are fixed patterns and routines and it's erm quite hard to remember all the steps although the music helps. It has certainly helped me to keep fit.

5 *Listen to these two friends talking. What happened after they had arranged to meet?*
  A *There was a misunderstanding.*
  B *They had to make another appointment.*
  C *One of them was late.*

RAY: So what happened to you?
STEVE: I could ask you the same thing. I was up at the Flask as we'd arranged, you know, in Highgate.
RAY: You're kidding ... Guess where I was?
STEVE: Not the one in Hampstead?
RAY: Oh no, we didn't say which one, did we? I immediately assumed it would be the one near me.
STEVE: Ah well ... And how long did you wait?
RAY: Only about two hours.
STEVE: Me too!

6 *Listen to these colleagues discussing the response they had to a job advertisement. What are they going to do?*
  A *read a selection*
  B *choose a few people to interview*
  C *re-advertise*

MIKE: Good grief, I never imagined we'd get so many applications for a simple clerical job. There must be eight, nine hundred.
PAUL: What are we going to do? Start again, put another ad in?
MIKE: No we can't do that. I suppose we could just open the first fifty.
PAUL: But what about the others? I guess we'll just have to read all of them and choose five or six to call in.
MIKE: There goes the weekend.

7 *You will hear someone calling a school about a training course. What does she want to do?*
  A *start the course*
  B *receive more information*
  C *postpone the course to a later date*

Yes ... I see ... so there will be other people like me then ... right, so a mixture of people with a bit of experience and beginners ... um ... OK ... so there aren't two separate groups then? ... Because of the numbers, I see. Well that'll be fine, no no, I think I've got everything I need and I've already got your brochure, you've answered my questions. So I'll be starting on the 18th as agreed. Thanks. Bye.

8 *Listen to this police officer taking part in a TV programme. What is she talking about?*
  A *crime prevention*
  B *the prison service*
  C *the results of a court case*

Well, that was not the point of view of the inquiry or of the jury. The officers concerned were cleared of the charges. They used force, which was regrettable but only an appropriate level of force for the circumstances. The death of Mr Abbott is tragic but the officers concerned were only doing their duty. There was no whitewash. There was a trial and justice was seen to be done.

PART 2

You'll hear part of a talk about the folklore surrounding the bird the cuckoo. For questions 9–18, complete the notes which summarise what the speaker says. You'll need to write a word or short phrase in each box.

You now have forty-five seconds in which to look at Part 2.

What I would like to do this evening is discuss how important superstition can be in the folklore of our country and about the rich seam of belief surrounding simple household objects, creatures and birds. I would like to tell you something to begin with about the cuckoo, just to illustrate this particular point. We are all familiar with its famous 'cuckoo cuckoo' call in the springtime but what we are probably not altogether familiar with are all its various different meanings which, as you might expect, vary considerably from region to region in the British Isles. In England, for example, it's extremely unlucky to hear the call if you are still in bed but will bring you good fortune if you're dressed and up and about, roaming the countryside. So all you lazy bones beware! In Wales you're in for a good year if you hear the call for the first time on the twenty-eighth of April but you're in for bad luck if you hear it before April the sixteenth. It is really bad news to hear it after August; by then, of course the bird should have headed off to warmer climes. Anyway, if you hear it then, your days are supposed to be numbered and they say you haven't more than a year left to live. Good luck will also depend on the direction that the call comes from, it's supposed to be bad luck if it comes from the left, you know. Up in Scotland they say that the number of calls the bird makes will actually tell an old person how long they have left to live. As you can imagine there are more romantic connotations too. A single girl can find out how long it will take her to find a husband by the number of times the bird calls. My apologies to the ladies in the audience, as this kind of thing seems terribly out of date and sexist in this day and age, doesn't it? Still I didn't make it up you know. Still the men get some advice too. So you men, when you're out walking and you hear the first cuckoo, then take off your right shoe. If you find a hair in it, it'll be the same as your wife to be's! You kind of wonder who must dream these things up don't you! It can also tell married men that their wives are up to no good while they're out in the fields hunting. Yes, the cuckoo is a pretty important bird in terms of the things it is supposed to be able to tell you. This is why, apparently, the bird dumps its young in other nests. It is so busy giving us human beings important messages that it doesn't have time to look after its own young. Now I've bombarded you with quite a few superstitious beliefs about the cuckoo, what I'd like to do is try to establish whether or not these beliefs have any basis in fact. Right then ...

You will now hear Part 2 again.

PART 3

You'll hear five women talking about their experiences with animals and their attitudes towards them. For questions 19–23, choose from the list A–F the sentence which matches what each one has to say. Use the letters only once. There is an extra letter which you do not need to use.

You now have thirty seconds in which to look at Part 3.

SPEAKER 1: Well, when I was at college, I had this professor of zoology and sometimes she'd invite her students round. It was always an experience, 'cos she'd have all sorts of weird and wonderful animals in her house. In fact you could hardly call them pets because they were wild really. Anyway, I'll never forget one day going to the bathroom and, you know locking the door, I heard a frantic scratching from the bath and when I lifted the shower curtain there was this metre long alligator trying to get out! I almost fainted.

SPEAKER 2: I suppose I have very mixed feelings about them, I'd really love a dog, but they're so anti-social aren't they? I mean the mess they make. It would be different if I lived in the countryside, then it could run around, but I think it's unfair on everyone to have a dog in built up areas unless it's one of those funny little ones. I have a neighbour who has a German shepherd and she goes out to work and the poor thing stays nine, ten hours at a stretch tied up in a tiny garden.

SPEAKER 3: We got Tonta and Lola from some friends. They knew I was lonely in London and so they turned up with these two tiny kittens in a shoe box. They're not special, you know pedigree or anything but when we had to come back to the States I couldn't bear to leave them so they came with us. It cost an absolute fortune and my family thought I was mad, but I went ahead anyway. Do you think they purr with an English accent?

SPEAKER 4: It's a shame really, 'cos she's at that stage lots of little girls seem to go through, you know, crazy about ponies and she'd like to take up riding. I feel mean saying no but I just can't be near horses or anyone who's got horse hair on their clothes. My eyes start itching and streaming and I can't breath properly, I'll have to see if there's some way of getting this fixed. In the meantime there's just no way we can let her go riding.

SPEAKER 5: Well, it was awful, we foolishly volunteered to erm look after the school guinea pigs – you know those furry little creatures – during the school holidays but after a few days one of them, a beautiful brown and white one with a bit of black just died. We were horrified about what the kids would think so Bill and I spent the next two days visiting every pet shop in a twenty mile radius looking for another one. In the end we got one that looked the same and nobody seemed to notice.

You will now hear Part 3 again.

PART 4

You'll hear a conversation between a gentleman called Mr Boyle and a police officer. Mr Boyle is being interviewed by the officer about an incident which took place in his home. For questions 24–30, decide which of the choices A, B or C is the correct answer.

You now have 30 seconds in which to look at Part 4.

POLICEWOMAN: Right then, Mr Boyle, can you tell me exactly what happened?

MR BOYLE: Well, yes. There were two of them ... two women you know ... they rang the front doorbell and asked if they could come in. They said they were from ... now what was it?

POLICEWOMAN: Sometimes these people say they're from the electricity company ...

MR BOYLE: No it wasn't that. Yes, they said they were from the social services department.

POLICEWOMAN: And did you let them in straightaway?

MR BOYLE: No not really ... you know, you hear these stories about old folk on their own ... so I asked for some identification. The elder woman waved this card at me and, I did have a look. As a matter of fact I took it off her and had a good look. It looked like the real thing to me but I'm no expert – I didn't have my glasses on of course. Anyway I let them in.

POLICEWOMAN: And what happened next, sir?

MR BOYLE: Well they said they were from the social services department and that they were checking up on me and wanting to find out if I was actually claiming all the benefits which I was entitled to. Er, we sat down and she started talking about the various benefits and forms and things and this went on for about half an hour. And then the younger one, she suggested that we have a cup of tea. I thought it was a bit cheeky really ... you know coming into someone's house like that and asking for some tea. Anyway I said yes and before I could get up she'd already gone into the kitchen.

POLICEWOMAN: And how long was she away?

MR BOYLE: Just a couple of minutes. She came back with the tea and we sat down again. After about ten minutes I don't know what happened. I think I just nodded off you know. When I woke up it was dark and I had a terrible headache.

POLICEWOMAN: That'll be the stuff they put in your tea.

MR BOYLE: The stuff in the tea? I thought as much. Yes they must have put something in it to send me to sleep. I was frozen stiff too.

POLICEWOMAN: I'm afraid they've played the same trick on some other elderly people too, sir. They've no conscience, it's terrible it really is. And when did you realise something was up?

MR BOYLE: Almost immediately ... I guessed at once what must have happened. I went upstairs as quickly as I could ... they'd turned my mattress over you know ... anyway I looked at the bottom of the wardrobe for the money I keep hidden there for emergencies and luckily it hadn't been touched. I'll be sure that I keep it in the bank from now on ... What had gone though was some jewellery which had belonged to my dear wife. They took a heavy gold bracelet and other stuff. Quite valuable, I think. It was Victorian, the bracelet you know. It had belonged to her grandmother. Oh dear ... it's funny though. They didn't take my medals which were in the same box.

POLICEWOMAN: Anything else?

MR BOYLE: Yes they pinched this lovely Japanese radio I had in the bedroom, which was a present from my grandson last Christmas. Do you think there's any chance ...

You will now hear Part 4 again.

PRACTICE EXAM 4

PAPER 1 READING

PART 1

0 D; **1** F; **2** B; **3** E; **4** I; **5** G; **6** H; **7** C
The extra heading is A.

PART 2

8 D (*mothering was thought to be an uncomplicated business.*)
9 A (*Mothers convinced themselves that nanny would do a better job.*)
10 C (*she was ... amazed that her mother could hold her head without appearing to be disgusted.*)
11 B (*The best nannies compensated for a mother's shortcomings.*)
12 D (*as they grew older they became closer.*)
13 A (*The other choices are wrong as she clearly remained bitter towards her mother and did not worship her as Mary did hers.*)
14 C (*The entire text has many instances of how middle and upper-class mothers were remote.*)
15 D (*Children were left to their own devices.*)

PART 3

16 B; **17** H; **18** F; **19** G; **20** D; **21** E

PART 4

22 C; **23** E; **24** D; **25** A; **26** E; **27** B; **28** E; **29** D;
30/31 B, E in any order; **32/33** A, E in any order;
34/35 A, C in any order

PAPER 3 USE OF ENGLISH

PART 1

1 B challenges; **2** A possibility; **3** D ask;
4 B After all; **5** B granted; **6** D total; **7** B imagine;
8 A theory; **9** B killed; **10** D Despite; **11** D allow;
12 D remain; **13** C yet; **14** A raised; **15** D having

PART 2

16 woken; **17** that; **18** being; **19** even;
20 himself; **21** as; **22** there; **23** meantime;
24 by; **25** out; **26** them; **27** while; **28** In; **29** only;
30 around/up

Part 3

31 would rather you didn't
32 doesn't get on with
33 make up my mind
34 with reference to
35 as I am concerned
36 'll miss the train unless
37 this the best one
38 you fancy going
39 didn't mean to break
40 only does she speak

Part 4

41 ✓; 42 there; 43 ✓; 44 be; 45 he;
46 ✓; 47 of; 48 such; 49 on; 50 ✓; 50 itself; 52 At;
53 up; 54 about; 55 ✓

Part 5

56 technological; 57 qualifications;
58 immediately; 59 disability; 60 unthinkable;
61 managerial; 62 responsibilities; 63 depressing;
64 unemployment; 65 expectations

PAPER 4 LISTENING

Part 1

1 C; 2 C; 3 B; 4 C; 5 B; 6 A; 7 B; 8 A

Part 2

9 his thesis ready
10 on 877439 (before lunchtime)
11 advertising agency
12 the weekend
13 about five hours
14 a new clutch
15 about £200
16 you want to go ahead
17 LH 427 from Frankfurt
18 terminal 2 at 7:15 p.m.

Part 3

19 E; 20 D; 21 B; 22 A; 23 F

Part 4

24 C; 25 C; 26 A; 27 B; 28 A; 29 A; 30 B

TAPESCRIPT

Hello, I'm going to give you the instructions for this exam. I'll introduce each part of the exam and give you time to look at the questions. At the start of each piece you'll hear this sound: (tone). You'll hear each piece twice. Remember, while you're listening, write your answers on the question paper.
The tape will now be stopped. Please ask any questions now, because you must not speak during the exam. Look at Part 1.

PART 1

You'll hear people talking in eight different situations. For questions 1–8, choose the best answer, A, B or C.

1 *You are having breakfast when you hear this news item about an accident. Where did it occur?*
A on the road
B in the air
C at sea

News has just come in of an oil spill off the coast of North Devon. A tanker which collided with a fishing boat in last night's storms has shed half its load. The crews of both vessels have been evacuated by helicopter. Local people are hoping that the oil will be broken up before it hits the shore. The army is on stand-by to implement any possible clean up operation. More of this later when we ...

2 *You overhear a woman talking about a trip she made. What did she think about the place she visited.*
A It was amateurish.
B It was hard to imagine how the people lived.
C It was expertly done.

Well it was really interesting, you could see how they must have lived, there were these communal huts for nearly everyone although the chief had his own of course. There was this gruesome snake pit, apparently the Iceni used to throw wrong-doers into it. It made my flesh creep rather. It was very well done, the whole reconstruction was based on research and erm, archaeology ... and there were all these people running around in erm woad, you know that blue dye.

3 *You hear someone talking about a newspaper article. What kind of article is it?*
A current affairs
B tourism
C finance

Despite everything that has happened there, the article says it is still superb and that the erm trouble is well and truly over. People are supposed to be hospitable and ready to welcome foreigners again. It sounds as though the big tour operators are offering good packages, you know, all-in deals. There are some great places to visit too and the exchange rate is brilliant, we could give it a try. What do you think?

4 *You are listening to an expert discussing a painting. What kind of picture is it?*
  A a battle scene
  B a portrait
  C a landscape

Well now this is fascinating, because Constable, who is famous for his natural looking country scenes has actually played around with nature. You couldn't get the rainbow and the sun in these positions, he has defied basic law of optics. Yet they suit the composition as a whole. The river and trees and pastures are all brilliantly executed.

5 *Listen to this businessperson leaving a message on a colleague's answering machine. Why has he called?*
  A to arrange a meeting
  B to describe his plans
  C to apologise

Hi Micky ... Listen, that flight we were going to take together to LA. I'm going to have to change it. I've just had a fax from Head Office and I'm going to have to go to New York first. I might see you next Thursday in LA. OK?

6 *Listen to this short extract from a book which is being read on the radio. What kind of book is it?*
  A a fairy story or legend
  B a factual history book
  C a spy thriller

So the goblin sat on a rock by the pool as the white haired wizard told the tale of how a knight had slain a dragon using a magic sword from metal from one of the god of war's meteorites. What the brave knight had not reckoned with was the dark power of the sword or the lengths that people would go to to take it from him.

7 *You overhear two young women in a café talking about someone they both know. Who is he going to marry?*
  A someone he was at university with
  B someone he knew from elsewhere
  C a neighbour

ANTHEA: Do you remember Raymond?
KIRSTY: Is he the one who lives near you? The good-looking boy?
ANTHEA: Yeah, that's the one, well, he's just asked Janine at work to marry him.
KIRSTY: Really! That's fast work. I thought she'd only been in the area a couple of months.
ANTHEA: That's right but apparently he used to go to university with her brother so that's how they first met.
KIRSTY: Mm small world!

8 *You are at a friend's house when a man comes to the door. What does he want?*
  A to offer to buy something
  B to sell something
  C to ask for directions

MAN: Oh, hello, I am sorry to bother you but I am an antique dealer ready to pay cash for antique furniture, paintings, coins and so on.
WOMAN: Well, I'm not sure, I don't think we have got anything we want to part with.
MAN: Of course, you'll want to think about it. I'll leave my card just in case. I'm in the area for the next couple of days, I'm supposed to be staying at The Bull. It's in the village, isn't it?
WOMAN: That's right, opposite the church.

PART 2

Julia Amis runs a secretarial agency. You will hear four messages which have been left on her telephone answering machine. For questions 9–18, complete the notes which summarise what each of the speakers says. You will need to write a word or a short phrase in each box.

You now have forty-five seconds in which to look at Part 2.

Hello ... um this is Pete Marsh. Can you phone me as soon as you get in ... I want to know how you're getting on with my thesis. Like, is it ready yet? I'm on 877439 until lunchtime.

Hello Julia ... this is Anthea Merry from the advertising agency. Look Julia love we've got this rushed job on. We need to get some reports typed up by the weekend and one of our girls is down with 'flu. It's about five hours work ... I'm counting on you to do it, so I'll be sending someone over to drop the manuscript off this afternoon at about two-thirty.

Wright's garage here. Can you give us a ring? It's about your car. Worse than we thought, I'm afraid. You need a new clutch. It's going to cost you about two hundred pounds. Er ... I won't be able to fix it until next week. Give me a ring if you want me to go ahead with the work.

Hello Julia. This is your brother Larry here. I'll be coming on Thursday 19th on flight LH 427 from Frankfurt. It gets in about 7:15 in the evening. Terminal two. I'll have quite a bit of stuff so it will be great if you can pick me up.

You will now hear Part 2 again.

PART 3

You'll hear five people talking about different items of electrical equipment. For questions 19–23, choose from the list A to F which item is being described or discussed. Use the letters only once. There is one extra letter which you do not need to use.

You now have thirty seconds in which to look at Part 3.

SPEAKER 1: Anyway, so there I was and then suddenly the screen went blank, I was in a terrible panic and I just didn't know what to do. I tried moving the mouse around and I looked in the manual but I just couldn't work out what the problem was. I thought maybe it was a problem with the software or even the hard disk. In the end I rang this help line and they talked me though what had happened and they got everything working again. It was amazing really – like one of those films where the pilot dies and ground control helps a passenger land the aircraft. I don't know what I would have done without them.

SPEAKER 2: Well, if anyone asked me what the greatest invention of the twentieth century was I'd say it was this, not space travel or the computer or anything like that. All you've got to do is load it up and put the powder in this erm place here and away you go. Even if it's not being used, you know actually op-operating, it's a much better place to hide your dirty plates than piling them up in the sink.

SPEAKER 3: Right, now what you do is you put these headphones on, are they nice and comfortable? Let, me adjust them for you, and then you take the handle like this … you're right-handed, aren't you? Steady it with the other hand. Now, hold the button down, this is so you don't waste any of the battery. What you do then is you hold it about four or five centimetres off the ground. No don't ever drag it along the dirt. That's it. So what happens is if it picks something up it starts to go 'beep beep beep', then you dig down and hope for the best. Most of the time it's just a rusty old nail or tin can, I'm afraid. Just walk over here and try it out.

SPEAKER 4: So anyway, the second time I took it back I showed it to the manager again and I said look this is the second cassette it's eaten, it's just like spaghetti here and what she said was well you should use you know just C60s or C90s and that the machine couldn't cope with long playing ones and I said there must be something wrong with the machine. After all it was from a reputable manufacturer and it is still under guarantee. In the end she changed it for another one but it's the last time I buy anything from Nixon's I tell you.

SPEAKER 5: It's brilliant really, I still haven't worked out half the things you can do with it. This is clever. You can store up to ten numbers and dial them just by pressing this memory button and a number one to erm ten. So it's great if I'm calling Jeff in the States or Keith and Kay in Saudi … The thing I really like though is that with this you can erm find out who was the last person to have rung you up. I sometimes get these scary calls you know when someone doesn't say anything at the other end, now I'll be able to catch them out, won't I?

You will now hear Part 3 again.

PART 4

You'll hear a conversation which takes place in a radio studio between Melissa Grey, a recruitment consultant who helps companies find the right employees and an interviewer. For questions 24–30, decide which of the choices A, B or C is the correct answer.

You now have 30 seconds in which to look at Part 4.

INTERVIEWER: It must be incredibly difficult, Melissa, I mean, knowing just the sort of person you need, or one of your clients is going to need for an important job.

MELISSA: Well, it's not always easy so we certainly try to discuss with the client the kind of person that they are looking for, and help them with the job description and drawing up a realistic specification for applicants.

INTERVIEWER: You say realistic.

MELISSA: Yes, that's right. We often find that companies want the best educated and qualified kind of person while only being able to pay small change. You know what they say, if you pay peanuts you get monkeys. Anyway, the main problem with this is that it often cuts really good people out of the application stage. For example, a lot of companies expect employees to have a degree, come what may, but this means that they are discounting lots of really good applicants.

INTERVIEWER: Are you saying that paper qualifications are unimportant?

MELISSA: No, I'm not saying that. Obviously, in technical and scientific fields qualifications are the only sure way we have of establishing if a candidate has the basic knowledge, but what I'm saying is that companies should also put a value on experience. Also things like commitment, um you know, motivation, and personality are absolutely crucial. You just know with some people that even though on paper they'd be great for a job, they just wouldn't fit in when it comes down to it … you know the atmosphere and cultures within companies can vary enormously.

INTERVIEWER: And how do you go about assessing someone's personality? You know as well as I do that some really good people come across as being hopeless in an interview situation. I remember when I was being interviewed for a job and there was this row of faces in front of me … it was terrible.

MELISSA: Um, I know. That's why as far as possible we've done away with this big panel interview. We'd much rather a person was interviewed on a one to one basis over the space of say a day than by a big group all at the same time.

INTERVIEWER: Um, I see. And what do you think about these psychological tests some companies insist on. You know the type of thing where they say for instance … er 'I'd rather work outside than in an office' and so on, and you have to say whether you agree with the statement or not.

MELISSA: Well, being a professional recruiter, it's quite tempting to use them because it makes what you're doing look so much more scientific and um less subjective. But er I don't really believe in them all that much.

INTERVIEWER: Really? Why's that?

MELISSA: Well. Two main reasons I suppose. The first one is that I think anyone with half a brain can see through them and can fool the test. Also I believe that people are more complicated than that and that there are many factors which make up a personality.

INTERVIEWER: Well, that's quite damning. So do you feel the same way about people's handwriting? Lots of companies use graphology, don't they?

MELISSA: um … I suppose I've got quite a bit of time for it really, there's definitely something in it. It can really help you to screen out people … I know that this isn't really graphology but if someone has filled in an application form badly or scruffily written an accompanying letter then I feel that they're not really taking things all that seriously. Um, if they can't treat their application with seriousness and respect then what are they going to do in a job? But that's not really graphology as such … probably more of a personal prejudice.

INTERVIEWER: One I share … Anyway, what about graphology then?

MELISSA: Right … well, I'm not an expert but there are certain tell-tale signs I look out for which show whether someone is really honest or not …

INTERVIEWER: You can do that?

MELISSA: Oh yes. There're some well established and recognised indicators. For instance, if someone can't write on the line. A real giveaway is when the 'a's and 'o's are open at the bottom … that's a sure fire indicator of dishonesty. People who don't cross their 't's strongly tend to have weak personalities and are susceptible to being led and manipulated.

INTERVIEWER: Wow! Are there any other signs?

MELISSA: Well, I don't know if they show dishonesty or not, but when people go over the same letter a couple of times or mess about with the letters too much, then that can be a sign of a neurotic personality. I suppose something I always have a good look at is someone's signature. If it's too ornate or fussy then it tends to put me on my guard. I think it shows that someone has got an exaggerated ego … a bit of a big-head who thinks he is more important than he really is.

INTERVIEWER: Well, I'd better not let you see my handwriting! Just one more thing. How do you feel about telling people the truth about their prospects?

You will now hear Part 4 again.